The English Middle Classes

Are Alive and Kicking

The English Middle Classes

Are Alive and Kicking

IAN BRADLEY

COLLINS
St James's Place, London
1982

William Collins Sons and Co Ltd
London · Glasgow · Sydney · Auckland
Toronto · Johannesburg

Bradley, Ian, 1950-

The English Middle Classes Are Alive and Kicking
1. Middle classes - England - History
I. Title
305.5'5   HT690.G7

ISBN 0 00 216276 8

First printed 1982

Photoset in Times Roman
Made and Printed in Great Britain by
William Collins Sons & Co Ltd, Glasgow

Contents

PREFACE

Writing about social class in England is rather like talking about food in France or discussing industrial efficiency with the Japanese. Because it touches on a major national obsession, it is a risky and even a presumptuous enterprise which is beset with pitfalls and dangers.

If I have avoided some of these, it is because of the help that I have received during the writing of this book from family and friends. My parents read the entire manuscript in draft form and made many useful corrections. David Kynaston helped me over the sections on sport and John Winckler steered me in the direction of some useful sociological and literary sources. I have also benefited from the comments of my editor at Collins, Robin Baird-Smith, and my agent, Giles Gordon.

I have relied heavily on many other published works, most of which I hope that I have acknowledged in the text or footnotes. My debt to Angus Maude and Roy Lewis will be obvious to all those who have read their splendid pioneering study on the English Middle Classes. I have also made much use of the work of Dr John Goldthorpe of Nuffield College, Oxford, with whom I have discussed the fascinating subject of social mobility.

I am grateful to Messrs Weidenfeld and Nicolson and Penguin Books for permission to quote from *The Ice Age* by Margaret Drabble, and to the Controller, Her Majesty's Stationery Office, the Director, the National Foundation for Educational Research, Professor Ivor Crewe of the University of Essex, and Professor G. S. Bain of the University of Warwick for permission to quote copyright material in the statistical tables.

I have made considerable use of that unique sounding board

for English middle-class opinion, the letters page of *The Times*. For permission to quote from it, and from *The Times* leaders, I am grateful to the editor and to the correspondents, including Mrs C. Fothergill, Mr A. R. Munday, Mr Tom Benyon and Mr M. D. Preston, Mrs Joyce Sibly, Mr David Green, Mr F. E. Rogers, Sir Reginald Murley and Mr Martin Birstingl. To any others that I have omitted I offer my sincere apologies. While I was writing this book the future of *The Times*, letters column and all, hung precariously in the balance. Let us rejoice for the sake of authors of future books on this subject, as well as for the sanity of the middle classes themselves, that it survives.

I.C.B.
New Year's Day, 1981.

INTRODUCTION

For more than a hundred years the middle classes all over the world have lived under a death sentence pronounced by Karl Marx. In fact, in every country, including those behind the Iron Curtain, they have survived to confound Marx's prediction that they would be crushed from above and below and eventually absorbed into the proletariat.[1] This book is about the survival of the middle classes in one particular country, England.*

Friedrich Engels, whose own activities as a middle-class entrepreneur subsidized Karl Marx's sustained attack on the species, once described England as 'the most bourgeois of all nations'. It would not be difficult for a visitor to gain the same impression today. The nation's favourite radio serial, *The Archers*, regularly listened to by three million people every week, is not so much an 'everyday story of country folk' as a chronicle of the quintessentially middle-class lives of the church-going, horse-riding, grammar-school-educated family in the title. One of the most popular television comedy series, *Yes Minister*, is set in the higher corridors of Whitehall and explores the relationship between a minister and his senior civil servants. The Poet Laureate, Sir John Betjeman, has gained a special place in the affections of his countrymen for his celebration of life in commuter land and suburbia. The English may love a lord, but they also have a soft spot for the bourgeoisie.

It would not take a visitor long to discover either that some

---

* I should make it clear that in this book I will be writing primarily about the English, and not about the less class-conscious and class-divided Scottish, Welsh and Irish, although perforce many of the statistics quoted will refer to Great Britain as a whole.

are more bourgeois than others. England, as George Orwell observed, is 'the most class-ridden country under the sun'.[2] No other people in the world have the same fascination with the small subtleties of accent and education which define a man's precise social position, nor draw such momentous conclusions from the fact that he has dinner rather than lunch or goes to the toilet rather than the lavatory.

It is extraordinary how many basic aspects of life in England are still organized on class lines. While the inhabitants of most other countries describe their earnings in terms of so much a month, we divide our working population into weekly wage earners and those with annual salaries. The Englishman's most popular place of recreation outside his home, the local public house, is still often divided into a public and a saloon bar, with different prices and styles of furnishing, so that even drinking becomes a socially segregated activity in a way which it is not in the cafés and bars on the Continent.

Above all, of course, the strength of the English class system shows itself in the nation's political life. In few other countries are politics organized so clearly along class lines with one major party openly representing organized labour and the other representing the interests of managers, entrepreneurs and members of the professions. Where else would the chairman of the main left-wing party say of his wife, as Mr Frank Allaun did at the 1979 Labour Party Conference, 'Thanks to her life-long experience in the working class, she's the best political adviser I could have had'? Where else could the leader of the main right-wing party build a successful election campaign, as Mrs Margaret Thatcher did in May 1979, around a direct and deliberate appeal to 'middle-class values'?

This obsession with identifying and maintaining class distinctions is regarded by many foreigners as the root cause of Britain's chronic industrial unrest and poor economic performance. Chancellor Schmidt of West Germany recently told a group of British journalists, 'As long as you maintain that damned class-ridden society of yours, you will never get out of your mess.'[3] The first action of the Japanese Sony Company when it took over a factory in South Wales was to tear down the partitions which divided managerial staff from manual workers in the canteen. It then went on to persuade managers, technicians and labourers to wear the same uniform.

There is, indeed, virtually no ill in contemporary British life for which someone does not lay the blame on the class system. A recent report in the *Guardian* newspaper cited it as a contributory factor in the collapse of the British motor cycle industry because of the class status conferred by car ownership. Writing in the *Observer*, Mr Anthony Sampson blamed the poor quality of restaurants in Britain on the 'puritanical emphasis on high thinking and plain living which cast its blight on the British professional classes' and on the fact that British workers kept their plain eating habits as they became more affluent and moved up the social ladder. He concluded, 'We are back once again with the British class system.'[4]

There is as yet little sign that we have heeded these criticisms. The national sport of identifying precise social origins shows no sign of losing its popularity. Politicians, trade union leaders and senior industralists seem as keen as the rest of us to maintain class distinctions and to make the most of them. Predictions in the 1950s that a new classless age was dawning have signally failed to come true. The results of the last general election seemed to show the country more sharply polarized than ever between the predominantly working-class Labour north and the middle-class Conservative south.

The persistent fascination with the class system in England, and the persistence of the system itself, have produced a large number of books on the working classes but comparatively few on the middle classes. Somehow bank managers and school teachers do not have the same romantic appeal to historians and sociologists as miners and railwaymen. It is difficult to imagine someone doing for the bourgeoisie what E. P. Thompson did for the proletariat in his monumental work, *The Making of the English Working Classes*, just as it is hard to conceive of a study of the culture of suburbia on the scale of Richard Hoggart's classic study of working-class culture, *The Uses of Literacy*.

The fact is that the middle classes are rather reserved and embarrassed about their history and culture just as they are about everything to do with themselves. Only one thing has brought them out of their reticence and that has been their recurrent feeling that they are in imminent danger of extinction. It is a feeling that goes back a long way. The earliest recorded use of the term 'middle class' in the *Oxford English Dictionary* comes from a report in the *Examiner* for 1812 about 'such of the middle class of society who have fallen upon evil days'.

Several of the best books on the English middle classes have been written during subsequent periods of gloom about the future of the species. Angus Maude and Roy Lewis wrote their extremely valuable study, *The English Middle Classes* (1949) in the aftermath of the Second World War when austerity and socialism seemed to threaten the material and moral strength of the bourgeoisie. In the preface they wrote that they had originally thought of entitling the book *The Decline and Fall of the English Middle Class*, but had decided not to 'because it became clear that the middle classes were kicking so hard that they must still be alive'.[5]

In fact, that title was adopted by the late Patrick Hutber for a book first published in 1976 and subsequently reissued in paperback. Writing during a period of high inflation and with a Labour Government apparently committed to bringing about an irreversible shift in the balance of wealth and power towards the working classes, Hutber argued that 'this is a time of crisis for the middle classes, who are subjected to unprecedented pressures and, at the same time, to unprecedented denigration'.[6]

The crisis of the mid-1970s, in which the middle classes found themselves having recourse to the new weapon of militant trade unionism as well as to their more usual technique of setting up defence organizations, has also produced a number of more academic studies. Foremost among them is the collection of essays edited by Roger King and Neil Nugent and entitled *Respectable Rebels: Middle Class Campaigns in Britain in the 1970s* (1979). Particular aspects of the response to this crisis have been dealt with in *White Collar Unionism: The Rebellious Salariat* (1979) by Clive Jenkins and Barrie Sherman, and *White-Collar Proletariat: The Industrial Behaviour of British Civil Servants* (1980) by Michael P. Kelly.

The present book was first conceived in those same years of crisis which provoked Patrick Hutber's gloomy predictions that the middle classes were about to sink into oblivion. It is now clear that they have successfully weathered that particular storm, as they have every other difficult period in their history, and that they are in remarkably good shape. For their ability to survive, if for nothing else, the middle classes deserve investigation.

There are other reasons for trying to answer anew the four questions which Angus Maude and Roy Lewis first posed more than thirty years ago: Who are the English middle classes? How have they developed? What is happening to them? Do they still have a distinct role and value in modern society? The middle classes have undergone considerable changes in that time. So have some of their values. However, their basic principles of disinterested public service and open-minded liberalism have survived. It is those principles, rather than the possession of a particular amount of wealth or political power, which have traditionally lain at the heart of English middle classness. This book is written in the conviction that their continued existence is vital to our survival as a civilized society, and on the understanding that they are by no means the sole prerogative of those who would be defined, or who would define themselves, as middle class according to the socio-economic classifications of social scientists and market researchers.

1

The Ladies and Gentlemen
on the 8.23
An Introduction to the Middle Classes

It always surprises me how few sociologists travel by British Rail, or at least, if they do, how little use they make of the experience. Train journeys provide one of the best opportunities for gaining a detailed insight into the contemporary lifestyle of *Homo Britannicus*, his dress, his way of speech, his diet, his reading habits, and his attitude to his wife and children. Even a cursory glance over the variety of litter that is left on the seats and floors of Inter-City and suburban carriages when they reach their destinations indicates far more about the persistence of social and regional differences in modern Britain than some academic theses and opinion polls.

Railway carriages are particularly good places for observing the middle classes. The upper class tend to travel mostly by car. So do many of the working classes, who anyway travel less since they tend to live close to their work, their friends and relations, their shops and their entertainments. It is those in between who are the most avid users of Awayday tickets, Big City Savers, senior citizens' and students' railcards and all the other cut-price schemes devised by the marketing men in British Rail. It is no coincidence that the posters extolling the benefits of taking the train feature such archetypal middle-class figures as the harrassed businessman, the avid theatre goer, the bewildered prep school boy and the respectable maiden aunt in slightly straitened circumstances.

Many of the most important milestones in middle-class life involve railway travel: the journeys off to boarding school which start with tearful farewells from mother at Waterloo after tuck-box, cricket bat and navy blue raincoat have been carefully stowed on the luggage rack, and end in chaos with the frantic swopping of Matchbox toys, autographs and gossip as the train nears some quiet South coast town; the boat train from Victoria which begins the first holiday abroad without the parents, either ski-ing in the Alps with the prospect of sexual adventure in the chalets, or the school-organized visit to the major classical sites in Greece, with its promise of Retsina and cheap cigarettes; the journeys up to university with their sense of escape and freedom as the suburban semis recede and the dreaming spires approach; the trip to the first job interview with neatly pressed suit and equally neatly folded copy of *The Times*; the first and last experience of commuting, the daily battle that lasts for forty years to secure a seat, finish the crossword and keep calm in the face of signal failure, frozen points and staff shortages.

If it is on the Clapham Omnibus that the common man most clearly shows himself, then it is on the Southern Region commuter lines from Surrey, Kent and Sussex that the middle classes are to be found in greatest proliferation. There is, perhaps, no better way to observe the species than to travel with them into Charing Cross, Waterloo, London Bridge or Victoria.

Poundford, a mythical but typical commuter town twenty miles or so from London, is as good a place as any to start a journey of exploration into English middle-classness. Like other predominantly middle-class towns in the South East of England, it has a higher proportion of owner-occupiers than the country as a whole, more than its fair share of doctors and a better than average pupil-to-teacher ratio in its schools. These include a public (i.e. private) boarding school for boys, a private school for girls and two independent boys' preparatory schools. Thanks to the determined resistance of the Conservative controlled county council to comprehensive reorganization, there are still also a boys' and a girls' grammar school which maintain high academic standards. Poundford has a substantial population of civil servants, professional people, white-collar workers and small businessmen who, with their wives, are the mainstays of its thriving civic society, philharmonic choir and orchestra, and numerous voluntary organizations. It returns a Conservative Member of Parliament and often puts a Liberal in second place.

To see all the varieties of middle-class life that inhabit

Poundford it would be necessary to take at least four different London bound trains. A trip on the earliest train on which cheap day return tickets can be used would reveal the females of the species on their way to town to shop, to see friends or to get some culture. Many combine all three, spending the morning in Oxford Street, meeting an old friend for lunch in Selfridges, and then going on to a matinée performance at the Aldwych or an exhibition at the Royal Academy. During school holidays, this train is also likely to be crowded with middle-class children, with or without their parents, bent on a similar pursuit of culture and conspicuous consumption.

A journey on a late afternoon train towards the end of the week would reveal the middle classes at play, with public schoolmasters travelling to wine tastings and old boys' dinners, well-groomed ladies going up to join their husbands for receptions at the Law Society or evening performances at the National Theatre, and smartly dressed young wives bound for a show or dinner in the West End. A Sunday evening journey would provide the best opportunity for observing the young of the species as they returned to their flats and student digs in town after a weekend with their parents, their carrier bags stuffed with home-made marmalade, Athena Society prints and textbooks on tort.

The biggest concentration of middle-class Poundford is to be found on a train that gets its passengers to London just before nine in the morning, say the 8.23. The predominant type on this train is, of course, the commuter, clad in his distinctive plumage of dark suit and bound for his desk in one of the office buildings in Central London. There are others whose purposes in travelling are less immediately obvious: the retired schoolmistress bound for a committee meeting of the Friends of the Educational Voucher; the opthalmic surgeon going to the bi-weekly surgery in Harley Street that is his one indulgence in private medical practice; the housewife going for her quarterly check-up with the dentist just off Harley Street that is hers; the architect on his way to a seminar on concrete; the local secretary of the Cancer Research Campaign going to a regional meeting on fund-raising; the gentleman's outfitter travelling to see his wholesaler; the small builder attending the conference of the National Federation of the Self-Employed – all of them bound for the appointments, the professional engagements, and the meetings of voluntary bodies which make up the daily round of active middle-class life.

Perhaps the strongest sensation that comes from travelling on the 8.23 is of the self-contained privateness and calm of the other passengers. Hardly any of them talk to each other, and if they do it is normally to exchange rather unexciting information about the children, the garden or the weather. There is nothing to suggest that the middle classes of Poundford are in a state of collective gloom or feel that they are facing extinction, as some of the media would have them believe. It is quite clear that their own immediate individual thoughts, about how they can go on paying the mortgage and the school fees, whether they remembered to lock the door, or whether they should treat themselves to a taxi, are infinitely more important to them than any collective middle-class consciousness which they share with the other occupants of their carriage. It is only in rare moments of provocation, when the train has been standing outside London Bridge for twenty minutes or a lout has switched on a transistor radio, that a sense of collective outrage wells up strongly enough to over-rule their basic diffidence and individualism.

A glance around any carriage on the 8.23 is also enough to indicate another important sociological fact about the passengers: that there are at least as many varieties of middle classness as there are different newspapers hiding their faces. Indeed, at the risk of some rather crude generalization, it is possible to deduce from the different newspapers they read what are the main groups making up the English middle classes.

Those who read *The Times* are perhaps the easiest to categorize. They are most likely to be civil servants, lawyers or other professional people, almost certainly university graduates, a fairly high proportion of them having been educated at public schools and Oxford or Cambridge. They tend to live in the substantial but rather draughty houses built at the beginning of this century in North Poundford near the prep schools and the public school, to which they probably send their sons.

The *Financial Times* readers differ primarily in their jobs from those who take *The Times*. They are more likely to work in the City or in large companies. In other respects they are very similar, although because they are often better off, they probably tend to live in less draughty, more secluded houses in the north of the town or in one of the surrounding villages from which they drive in to the station.

Between them, *The Times* and *Financial Times* readers represent the upper middle-class 'establishment'. Several of them are active in the affairs of the civic society and the philharmonic society and are regular church-goers. They are also quite likely to buy and read books, to go to plays and concerts and to maintain some links with cultural and intellectual life in London. Their wives tend to be active in voluntary work and to be members of a distinct North Poundford set which revolves partly around the school, and partly around cocktail parties, dinner parties and wine tastings at each others' homes. Although a majority of this group votes Conservative, a substantial minority supports the Liberals.

The *Daily Telegraph* readers are a much larger and more heterogeneous group. They include a large number of retired professional, business and military men and a sizeable proportion of wives of *Times* and *Financial Times* readers. But the biggest group of *Telegraph* readers on the 8.23 consists of smartly dressed men, aged between eighteen and forty-five, who are in junior managerial or senior clerical positions in insurance, banking or other commercial or industrial businesses. Comparatively few of them are graduates, although a fair proportion went to public schools and they are nearly all determined to send their sons there. They mostly live in the modern 'executive type' detached and semi-detached houses on the private estates that have been built on to the north end of Poundford since the war.

This group of *Daily Telegraph* readers represents the up-and-coming new middle class. They are quite likely to be involved in Poundford's Round Table, Lions Club, camera club and in local sports clubs. Their wives tend to form their own 'north' North Poundford set and to meet each other at dinner dances, Conservative Party socials and regional sales conferences and management training courses put on by their husbands' firms. They are mostly Conservative in politics and have a strong admiration for Mrs Thatcher.

The *Daily Mail* and the *Daily Express* are read on the 8.23 by two distinct groups. The first is made up of clerks and secretaries who work in offices either locally or in London, and among whom there is a high proportion of women who particularly favour the *Mail*. The second is made up of shopkeepers and owners of small businesses, most of them locally based, among whom the *Express* is probably marginally more popular.

Together the *Daily Mail* and *Daily Express* readers make up the lower middle classes. They are very unlikely to have gone either to public schools or university and several of them live in the south (i.e. less desirable) end of Poundford, although they own their own homes and are very conscious of their social superiority over council house tenants. The shopkeepers and small businessmen in particular take an active part in the life of the town and form a majority of the members of the local chamber of trade, the Rotary Club, the St John's Ambulance Brigade, and of the Nonconformist churches. Although there is a Conservative majority in this group, there is also a fair sprinkling of Liberals and several have also retained the Labour allegiance of their working-class upbringings.

Perhaps the most puzzling passengers on the 8.23 are the readers of the *Guardian*. In social background and education, they most closely resemble *The Times* readers. Yet many of them choose to live at the wrong end of Poundford, albeit in streets which are rapidly becoming 'gentrified'. They are typically teachers, journalists and social workers with a fair sprinkling of tender-hearted and socially concerned civil servants and members of other professions. They may well have sent their children to state schools out of deliberate choice, although they are probably secretly rather thankful that the obduracy of the local authority, which they attack violently at Labour Party meetings, has meant that they have not had to face the agonizing choice between comprehensive and private education which has confronted many of their friends in other parts of the country.

The *Guardian* readers represent the radical, anti-establishment middle class. They overlap to a considerable extent in interests and social activities with *The Times* and *Financial Times* 'establishment' but, despite their greater poverty, they are even more avid book buyers and theatre goers. They are also more likely to be sympathetic towards, if not actually 'into' alternative lifestyles, whole foods, feminism and the problems of the Third World. They generally vote Labour or, in some cases, Liberal.

Anyone who has spent the last thirty years commuting to work on the 8.23 will have seen surprisingly little change in the appearance of his fellow-passengers, just as he will have seen no change in the rolling stock, which, like some of its occupants, seems to have been neglected, under-rated and progressively down-graded over the years. There are more women than there used to be on the train and fewer bowler hats and pin-striped suits, but the expressions and the newspapers are the same. The four groups into which we divided the middle classes have been around for a long time.

They even existed a hundred years ago, although they could not then have been observed together on a commuter train and their relative size and composition were different. The members of the upper middle-class establishment would have been most immediately recognizable: they read *The Times* and were in the same professional and business occupations as they are today. The up-and-coming element were then as likely to read the *Manchester Guardian* as the equally Liberal *Daily Telegraph*. They included a high proportion of manufacturers, mill owners and merchants from the North and Midlands of England. The lower middle classes included a rather larger number of shopkeepers and small businessmen and rather fewer white-collar office workers and they did not yet have tabloid newspapers to brighten their lives. The radical, anti-establishment middle class was a smaller group than it is now, but scarcely less prestigious, counting among its members such eminently middle-class critics of middle classness as Matthew Arnold, Thomas Carlyle and William Morris.

The subtle distinctions and snobberies which might be observed among the different groups on the 8.23 have also existed for a long time. The professional upper middle classes have always prided themselves on their culture, their liberal values and their tolerance. The up-and-coming middle classes have always made virtues of ambition and competition. The lower middle classes have always been preoccupied with propriety and decency, with doing the right thing and keeping their distance from the working classes. The anti-establishment rebels have always attacked the rest of the middle classes for their snobbery, their materialism, their puritanism and their philistinism.

That brief introduction to the ladies and gentlemen on the 8.23 has at least revealed one very important fact. There is no single homogeneous English middle class. There never has been. There are rather a number of different groups who lack a strong sense of collective class consciousness. Nor do they even find themselves in the same relative position to one another. Indeed, the middle classes have always resembled travellers on a department store escalator, with some moving down towards the bargain basement and others ascending towards the top floor.

But it is time to turn from metaphors of transport and subjective generalizations to some more rigorous and precise definitions of who the middle classes are.

2

Who are the Middle Classes?
Some Definitions

In the old days it was a simple enough matter to determine who belonged to the middle classes. Angus Maude and Roy Lewis remark at the beginning of their book:

> Before the war, when textile supplies and laundry facilities were more ample, it might perhaps have been held that the middle classes were composed of all those who used napkin rings (on the grounds that the working class did not use table napkins at all, while members of the upper class used a clean napkin at each meal), and that the dividing line between the upper-middle and lower-middle classes was the point at which a napkin became a serviette.[1]

Things are no longer so simple. The mass of data regularly collected by Government departments, market researchers and sociologists has greatly widened the range of possible criteria for establishing who are the middle classes. We know, for example, that they are twice as likely as the working classes to use contraceptives and retain all their own teeth, and less likely to be members of trade unions, watch football, die of lung cancer, become teenage brides or commit crimes (except shop-lifting). They have smaller families, longer holidays, thinner figures and higher incomes than the national average.

People's perceptions of the size and composition of the middle classes vary considerably. Some see them at the top of the class pyramid, some as the broad middle of a diamond, and others as a narrow compressed stratum squeezed from above and below. One school of sociologists emphasizes the extent of social mobility in Britain, and the ease of moving into the middle classes from lower down the social scale, another emphasizes their closed and caste-like nature. In attempting to answer the question 'Who are the middle class?' a leading article in *The Times* in 1975 pointed out: 'They can be defined in relatively restricted terms so that they appear to be a small minority of senior professional men, or they can be defined to include everyone who owns his own house, or works in a white collar job. In that case the middle class is at least half our society.'[2]

On one important point, however, there seems to be general agreement. Opinion polls taken over the last twenty-five years show that the great majority of the population continue to recognize the existence of different social classes in Britain. The classless society that was heralded by some sociologists in the 1940s and 1950s has not arrived, at least in the eyes of the general public.

The polls also show that most people see only two basic classes, middle and working. In a survey undertaken in 1970, for example, in which people were asked what class they put themselves in, 77 per cent spontaneously described themselves as 'middle class' or 'working class', 5 per cent gave more precise answers such as 'upper middle', 'lower middle' or 'upper working', and 1 per cent described themselves as 'upper class'. When the remaining 17 per cent were prompted, all but 1 per cent were willing to assign themselves a middle or working class label.[3]

Despite the continued existence of a hereditary peerage, a landed aristocracy and a House of Lords, there is apparently no longer a strong concept of a separate upper class in Britain. The middle classes, it would seem, now reach up to embrace the aristocracy. They are no longer seen, as they were in the nineteenth century, and as they still are in the United States, as an industrious middle mass sandwiched between the rich and the poor.

Evidence from opinion polls and statistical surveys also shows a remarkable measure of agreement about who the middle classes are, how they should be defined, and what proportion of the population they represent. Polls in which people are invited to assess their own social class position, the social classifications derived from the national census, and the investigations of market researchers, all give remarkably similar results. They agree that the middle classes are to be defined principally by their occupations, that they are made up broadly of those who do non-manual jobs and their families, and that they form 40 per cent or more of the population.

Not surprisingly, since it is still generally considered a desirable thing to be middle-class, the polls in which people are invited to assess their own position generally produce the highest figure for the size of the middle classes. A 1980 survey by the Gallup organization, for example, showed that, when asked which social class they belonged to, 46·5 per cent of respondents described themselves as middle-class, and 48 per cent as working-class. The exact breakdown was as follows:

	%
Upper or upper middle	2·5
Middle	31·5
Lower middle	12·5
Working	48·0
None; don't know	5·5

The national census, which is carried out every ten years by the Government's Office of Population Censuses and Surveys under the direction of the Registrar General, provides the most authoritative and comprehensive picture of the size and composition of the different social classes in Britain. The 1971 census, the most recent from which data is available, produced a figure for the size of the middle classes only slightly smaller than that produced by self-assessment.

It is a sign of the national obsession with class that Britain should have been the first country in the world to introduce social classification as one of the main forms in which the information derived from its census was presented. Social classes were first defined in 1911 for use in analysing statistics on fertility and infant mortality. Since 1921 the Registrar General has recognized five basic classes based entirely on the occupation of heads of households. Class I comprises those in professional occupations which normally require a high level of training; Class II managers, administrators, those in less highly trained professional occupations, and those in certain intermediate occupations like farmers; Class III those in skilled occupations; Class IV those in partly skilled manual occupations; and Class V those in unskilled occupations.

An important new feature was introduced into this five-point scale in the 1971 census when Class III was divided into III NM, covering skilled non-manual occupations, and III M, covering skilled manual occupations. Taking the non-manual/manual distinction as dividing the middle classes from the working classes, the 1971 census showed 43 per cent of the population of the United Kingdom to be middle-class and 57 per cent to be working-class. The full breakdown was as follows:

	%
Class I	4
Class II	18
Class III NM	21
Class III M	28
Class IV	21
Class V	8

Market research organizations use a similar class scale based primarily on occupation to present the results of their surveys of public opinion. Their scale, developed in the 1950s, also has five basic classes with the third sub-divided to distinguish non-manual and manual workers. Its detailed composition is different from that of the Registrar General, however, largely because it takes more account of income and spending power.

The market researchers' Class A includes those in higher managerial, executive and professional occupations, also farmers with over five hundred acres and senior officers in the Armed Forces (who are, along with all other members of the Services, unclassified in the Registrar General's scale). Class B covers those in middle-range managerial, executive and professional occupations, including teachers, general medical practitioners and farmers with between a hundred and five hundred acres. Class C1 comprises junior managers and executive officers, small businessmen and shopkeepers, clerks and salesmen. Class C2 includes all skilled manual occupations and some lower-grade white-collar jobs like typists and shop assistants. Class D covers all in unskilled manual occupations, and Class E those with no earning capacity, including old age pensioners, invalids and the unemployed.

Because it classifies as manual certain occupations (like typists and shop assistants) that the Registrar General classifies as non-manual, and because it includes all pensioners and invalids in its bottom class, the market researchers' scale tends, when applied to the population as a whole, to produce a rather smaller middle class. If the C1/C2 division is taken as marking the dividing line between the classes, an analysis by the Institute of Practitioners in Advertising of the United Kingdom population in 1980 put 38 per cent in the middle classes and 62 per cent in the working classes. The full breakdown was as follows:

	%
Class A	3
Class B	13
Class C1	22
Class C2	32
Class D	21
Class E	9

There are several advantages in taking occupation as the main criterion for establishing social class. As well as being the method used by Government, market researchers and most sociologists, it is also probably the most common single factor on which most ordinary people base judgements of class. When a survey in 1963 asked people to name the main criterion which they would use for determining whether someone belonged to the middle classes, 61 per cent gave occupation, 21 per cent income and only 18 per cent other factors such as education, attitudes or politics.[4]

The non-manual/manual distinction in particular has often been used as a simple way of establishing the dividing line between the middle and working classes. In 1948 the Labour politician, Herbert Morrison, rhetorically asked: 'What is the middle class? Perhaps the best generalization is that it is that varied section of the community that works with its brain rather than with its hands.' A correspondent to *The Times* in 1975 defined the middle classes as those 'having to do with people rather than with things'.[5]

The distinction is also useful in that it still represents a real division in terms of pay and conditions of work. In general non-manual workers earn more than manual workers (an average of £141·30 a week compared to £111·70 for full-time men in 1980), work shorter hours, have longer holidays, are more likely to receive full pay when they are sick and to enjoy occupational pensions when they retire. Even if they lose their jobs they are treated differently by the authorities. The middle classes could be defined as those who, if unemployed, would be put on the Professional and Executive Register and have a regular list of job opportunities sent to them at home, and the working classes as those who have to make do with the vacancy cards on the notice boards in their local job centres.

Occupation is also a useful criterion for establishing membership of the broad groupings within the middle classes. Certain middle-class occupations have always had clear hierarchical divisions establishing upper-middle, middle-middle, and lower-middle class status. This is true, for example, of the Civil Service with its traditional division into administrative, executive and clerical grades, and of the teaching profession where there is a generally accepted social distinction between those who teach in universities, those in secondary schools, and those in primary schools. These distinctions are recognized by the Registrar General who puts civil servants of assistant secretary level and above with university teachers in Class I, civil servants between the level of higher executive officer and senior principal with other teachers in Class II and all other civil servants in Class III NM.

It is possible to distinguish four main occupational groups within the middle classes. Three of them – the professions, managers and administrators, and non-manual or 'white-collar' workers – are broadly recognized as distinct classes by the Registrar General and most people would probably agree with his hierarchical ranking of them. The fourth group, comprising entrepreneurs and proprietors, is rather more difficult to categorize.

For many people the professions are synonymous with the middle classes. *The Times* library has no specific classification for the middle classes. Instead it files cuttings on the subject under the heading 'the professional classes'. In 1948 the *Economist* described the independent professional man, as distinct from the profit maker or wage earner, as 'the essential core of the middle class'.[6] In terms of their status, although not necessarily of their income, it is perhaps more accurate to say that the professions represent the upper middle class. Opinion polls consistently rank lawyers, clergymen and doctors higher than most other occupations in general public esteem. George Orwell observed nearly forty years ago, 'Middle-class people are really graded according to their degree of resemblance to the aristocracy: professional men, senior officials, officers in the fighting services, university lecturers, clergymen, even the literary and scientific intelligentsia, rank higher than business-men, though on the whole they earn less.'[7] It remains true today that the Church of England vicar with an annual stipend of around £5000 still often has a higher social standing than the marketing manager with a salary three times bigger.

The Registrar General broadly agrees with Orwell. He unhesitatingly puts all those in the old-established learned and chartered professions into his top class, above managers and administrators. However, he relegates to Class II other groups who often claim professional status, including actors, journalists, teachers, social workers and librarians.

The distinction is one that most people would almost certainly accept. Practitioners in the old learned professions of the law, medicine and the Church, and in the chartered professions like accountancy, architecture and engineering, form a tight-knit group at the top of the middle classes. They are highly educated, having generally been to university and also undergone a lengthy period of training in some specialized body of knowledge. They tend to be members of professional associations which regulate their conduct with regard both to their clients and to other members of the profession. They also share with others in Class I, like senior civil servants and most university academics, a strong commitment to professional ethics of confidentiality and integrity and a high sense of public responsibility. This combination of characteristics is not universally found among the professions put into the Registrar General's Class II, although many of them do share the ethical commitment and sense of responsibility.

Managers and administrators form a second group which most people would unhesitatingly classify as middle-class. Whether working in private industry, public corporations or for local or central government, they fulfil the German sociologist Max Weber's classic definition of a bureaucrat. They are salaried, they are appointed to a position in an organization on the basis of technical qualifications and are given clearly defined areas of competence and accountability, their work is predominantly done on the basis of written documents, they enjoy pension rights and are only liable to dismissal in special circumstances. Clearly not all managers are of equal status. The chairman of a large company educated at university and with professional qualifications can hardly be regarded as the social equal of the manager of a supermarket who started his working life as a shelf filler (Class IV). But there are obvious reasons for regarding them, as the Registrar General does, as a single occupational group.

Those in routine non-manual 'white-collar' jobs form the largest of the occupational groups which are normally regarded as middle-class. They are predominantly made up of the shop assistants, clerks and secretaries who, since the days of Uriah Heep and Mr Pooter, have traditionally been the most poorly paid, deferential and yet fiercely class-conscious of all the middle classes. Nowadays they include a very substantial proportion of women.

The members of this group are often referred to as lower middle class. It is a reasonably accurate description of what is the most marginal of the four main middle-class occupational groupings. However, it conceals the fact that the group contains people from manual working-class backgrounds who are working their way up the class ladder and others from professional and managerial families who are merely serving their time in a relatively lowly station before taking their place in a higher group.

Many of those in the lower reaches of the Registrar General's social class III NM are hovering uncomfortably close to the working classes. It is, indeed, arguable that several of the occupations in that class should not be regarded as middle-class at all. It includes shorthand typists, retail shop cashiers, check-out and cash and wrap operators who are put by the market researchers with manual workers into Class C2. Policemen and firemen are classified as non-manual workers by the Registrar General, but ambulancemen are relegated to

Class III M and prison officers to Class IV. It is difficult to know exactly where to draw the line.

Entrepreneurs and proprietors are perhaps the most heterogeneous of the main occupational groups within the middle classes. They range from the owners of landed estates and giant businesses, who would qualify for inclusion in the upper class, to self-employed window cleaners and chimney sweeps, who are both ranked by the Registrar General in Class V. Clearly, there are proprietors distributed throughout all levels of the middle classes. Perhaps the largest and most significant group, however, is made up of the small business-men and independent shopkeepers, the classic *petits bourgeois*, who since the days of John Gilpin have been 'citizens of renown' playing an important role in the civic and economic life of England. This group has traditionally been seen as contributing scarcely less, and some would say considerably more, than the professions to the unique strength and genius of the English middle classes.

Some small businessmen and shopkeepers, of course, have professional qualifications. The Registrar General includes pharmacists, ophthalmic and dispensing opticians and char-tered engineers running their own small businesses in his top social class. The majority, however, lack higher education and specialist training but, as independent traders on their own account, faced with having to grapple with the mysteries of value added tax and to balance their books, and with personal relations with their customers which can sometimes approach a professional practitioner's relations with his client, they clearly warrant inclusion within the middle classes.

There is one major objection to using occupation as the main index of social class. While it may be accurate enough in the case of those who are or have been in formal occupations, it offers no necessary insight into the social class of others like children or housewives who are not. The statistics about the class distribution of the population derived from both the census and the market researchers' polls strictly speaking apply only to heads of household or to economically active or retired people. Projections from them to cover the whole population must rest on the assumption that wives and children automatically belong to the same social class as their husbands or fathers. That may give a slightly inaccurate picture.

Another criterion by which social class is commonly judged, that of income, is also open to the same objection. Wealth has long been regarded as an accurate pointer to middle class status. R. H. Gretton, one of the first writers to explore the phenomenon of English middle classness in the twentieth century, observed in 1911 that 'wealth, money, possession are the distinguishing marks of the middle class'. Subsequent opinion polls have shown that many people share that view that the middle classes consist of the wealthier members of the community.[8]

For a long time, indeed, the middle classes could be defined as those who paid income tax. Probably no single action did more to arouse a middle-class consciousness in Britain than William Pitt's decision in 1792 to levy a tax on incomes to help pay for the war against the French. Since the First World War, however, the starting point of income tax has been lowered and it is now paid by many people who would not be regarded, and who would not regard themselves, as middle-class. There has also been a narrowing of differentials between the earnings of non-manual and manual workers which has put the incomes of some in traditionally middle-class occupations below those of others in the working classes.

As Table 1 shows, on the whole middle-class jobs are better paid than working-class jobs, although lower middle-class groups like shop assistants and clerical workers have lower earnings than miners, electricians, lorry drivers and some factory workers. A more detailed examination of the level of earnings in individual occupations would reveal further anomalies, with some of those in the Registrar General's Classes I and II earning less than those in the lower classes. A survey in 1979 found that 40 per cent of barristers earned less than £5000 a year, and 20 per cent less than £1500. In 1980 Church of England curates, with annual stipends of between £3100 and £3700, and nurses and midwives, with an average salary of £5085, were earning less than many manual workers. Compositors on Fleet Street newspapers, by contrast, with basic salaries of over £12,000, were earning more than many in professional and managerial occupations.

But if income is no longer the infallible guide to social class

TABLE 1

Average gross weekly earnings for full-time men,
aged twenty-one and over
(SOURCE: Department of Employment New Earnings Survey, 1980)

Non-manual occupations		*Manual occupations*
Professional and related supporting management	£167·7	
Literary, artistic and sport	£148·6	
Professional and related in science, engineering and technology	£147·5	
Managerial (excluding general management)	£145·6	
Professional and related in education, health and welfare	£139·6	
Security and protective service	£135·8	
	£119·7	Processing, making and repairing (metal and electrical)
	£113·4	Construction, mining and related
Selling	£113·1	
	£111·8	Materials processing (excluding metals)
	£110·9	Transport operating, materials moving and storing
	£110·2	Making and repairing (excluding metal and electrical)
	£107·7	Painting, repetitive assembling, product inspecting, packaging
Clerical and related	£103·5	
	£93·8	Catering, cleaning, hairdressing and other personal services
	£87·6	Farming, fishing and related

that it once was, it remains a useful pointer. It is not just the amount that a man earns which indicates his social class. Equally important is how it is paid to him. Middle-class employees are likely to be on an annual salary paid monthly, those in the working classes to have a weekly wage. Manual workers obtain a much higher proportion of their total earnings from overtime, bonuses and shift payments (29·3 per cent) than non-manual workers (9·5 per cent).

There is another important difference between the earnings of the middle and the working classes. The former can expect to become progressively better-off as they advance in their careers, while the latter remain in a relatively static economic position throughout their working lives. A Government survey in 1973 showed that over 90 per cent of non-manual workers were paid on incremental scales, compared with only 3 per cent of manual workers. Lorry drivers and dockers in their late twenties may well be earning more than doctors and lawyers of the same age, but by their forties they will probably be earning half as much. Most male manual workers reach the peak of their earnings between thirty and thirty-nine, when they are at their healthiest and family commitments are at their greatest. Non-manual workers, by contrast, reach their peak earning power in their forties and fifties.

There remains a strong conviction among certain sections of the middle classes that there should be a clear differential between their earnings and those of the working classes. A recent newspaper allegation that a lavatory attendant and park keeper employed by the London Borough of Hammersmith and Fulham were each earning more than £10,000 a year produced a swift response from the Conservative chairman of the finance committee: 'As soon as we realized this was happening we put a stop to it. We were pretty horrified, especially when we found there was a possibility there would be more blue collar than white collar workers getting over £10,000 a year.'[9]

Similar sentiments were nicely expressed, along with a characteristically middle-class concern for propriety and keeping up appearances, by a higher executive officer in the Civil Service, earning £5718 'and no perks at all', who found himself on picket duty outside the Ministry of Defence

during a one-day strike by the Civil Service unions in February
1979:

> I don't like doing this sort of thing and I rather hope that my
> neighbours in Orpington just think I have gone to work. But what
> I do know is that when I started eighteen years ago this was a job
> with a respectable, average middle-class salary. Now bus drivers
> do better than I do.[10]

That mention of Orpington provides a convenient introduction to a third test which is commonly applied to determine
whether someone is middle-class, namely where he or she lives.
Orpington, like scores of other commuter towns in the South
East of England, is unmistakably middle-class territory. Most
of its inhabitants are engaged in white-collar jobs and own
their homes. A high proportion are 'settlers' who have come to
the town from outside rather than 'natives' born and bred
locally. They predominantly vote Conservative but returned a
Liberal MP from 1962 to 1970.

The English middle classes are not distributed evenly across
the country. They are disproportionately concentrated in what
are known as the 'Home Counties' around London. The South
East has 32 per cent of the United Kingdom's total population,
but 42·6 per cent of all those in the Registrar General's top
social class, and 37·6 per cent of those in Class II. The Surrey
commuter towns of Esher and Croydon have respectively the
highest proportion of managerial and professional workers
and the lowest proportion of semi-skilled manual workers in
the country. It will come as no surprise to readers of *The Times*
to learn that, after London, Oxford and Cambridge, the most
frequently occurring addresses on the paper's letters page are in
the counties of Sussex and Surrey.

Certain towns, and certain parts of cities, are considerably
more middle-class than others. Central London has two and a
half times more of its inhabitants in the professional and
managerial classes than the textile towns of Lancashire and
West Yorkshire, and five times more than the Clydeside area of
Scotland. Esher has more than fifteen times the proportion
of those in social Classes I and II among its inhabitants than
does central Glasgow, while Solihull, an exclusive residential
suburb of Birmingham, has twenty times smaller a proportion

of those in Class V than the Scotland Exchange area of Liverpool.[11]

It is not surprising that both geographical origin and present place of residence are commonly used criteria for assessing social class. Moving into the right town or district is one of the main ways of establishing middle classness for those who have come up the social ladder. Significantly, one of the main characteristics of predominantly middle-class towns and districts is that a high proportion of their inhabitants were born elsewhere. Although the working classes are becoming more mobile, they remain less likely to leave the area where they grew up. A study of the working-class London district of Bethnal Green in the mid-1960s found that over 90 per cent of the inhabitants had been born there and had other members of their family living near. A study of Woodford, a middle-class commuter town in Essex, found, by contrast, that 74 per cent of the inhabitants had been born outside the area and did not have relatives living near.[12]

Having a middle-class address is not just a matter of living in the right town or city but also of living in the right part of it. In London there is a considerable social difference between adjoining districts like Stockwell and Brixton, Kensington and Earls Court, and Putney and Fulham. Many towns have their 'desirable' (middle-class) and not so desirable ends. For some reason, perhaps to do with prevailing winds, the former seems more often than not to be the north, as in Poundford. Within this favoured area, there are further clear geographical and social divisions between the new estates which house the up-and-coming and the lower middle classes and the roads of older, more substantial houses where the more established middle classes live.

Perhaps even more than living in the right place, owning your own home is a sure sign of middle classness. Indeed, if the middle classes can no longer be defined as those who pay income tax, they can perhaps be defined as those who have mortgages. Home ownership is a peculiarly English mark of social status. On the Continent, many middle-class families live in rented flats and apartments. In the United Kingdom, however, four-fifths of those in professional and managerial occupations own their homes. Almost exactly the same proportion of manual workers do not. There are few more certain indicators of working-class status than living in a council house. In the same way buying a house on a private estate is one of the clearest signs that a young couple have made it into the middle classes. Whether the drive by the present Government to sell council houses to their occupants will invalidate this particular social indicator remains to be seen.

The desire to keep council houses well away from their own territory has long been a strong middle-class instinct. In the 1930s it led the owners of a private estate in North Oxford to erect seven-foot-high brick walls across two roads to cut off their houses from those on an adjacent municipal estate. Despite efforts by the Communist Party and the City Council to have them removed, the Cutteslowe walls, as they became known, remained in place until 1959.

Less dramatic protests still occur when, by some accident or because of some idealistic planner's quest to create a mixed community, the middle classes find that they have council houses at the bottom of their gardens. In 1977 people who had bought new houses in what had been described as a 'select development' near Bristol were shocked to discover that they would be sharing the estate with council tenants. Owners of private houses who were making mortgage repayments of £100 and more a month protested that they would have neighbours who were paying weekly rents to the council of between £5·50 and £9·50 for identical homes. They complained that the mixed character of the estate would reduce the value of their houses by at least 15 per cent. A residents' association was hastily formed and abandoned polite middle-class methods of protest by staging a sit-in at the development company's offices, jamming its switchboard by telephoning on a rota, and occupying its show houses.

Nor is it only the middle classes who object to the arrival of immigrants from another social class on their traditional territory. In the mid-1970s the working-class residents of Islington, one of London's poorer boroughs with a high proportion of council houses and cheap rented accommodation, made a well-publicized protest at the 'gentrification' of the area by young middle-class couples who were buying up houses and converting them. They complained that as a result the price of property was soaring and the composition of the local population being changed.

Like place and type of residence, education has traditionally been seen as an important indicator of social class. A poll in 1975 found that it was placed overwhelmingly first by people asked what factor most clearly determined class differences. The middle classes are often referred to as the educated classes. Most of the intellectual debate and much of the cultural life of the nation takes place within their ranks.

Certainly education is a subject on which the various voices of English middle classness ring out clearly and characteristically, whether it is in the common room chat of cricket and Christianity in public schools, the last-ditch defence of selective schooling by small businessmen in provincial towns, or the attempts by guilt-ridden old Etonians to conceal their privileged upbringing by saying that they were educated at a comprehensive school near Slough and lending their support to the Campaign for the Advancement of State Education.

Having been to a grammar school has long been taken by many as a sign of middle-class status. Passing the old Eleven-plus examination was seen as one of the most effective escape routes from the working classes. In fact, recent research suggests that it was overwhelmingly those who came from middle-class backgrounds already who went to grammar schools. Whatever the position, it would seem reasonable to count as members of the middle classes the 25 per cent of the population who went to grammar schools before the wide-spread reintroduction of comprehensive schools in the late 1960s.

Since comprehensive re-organization it has not been so easy to define the middle classes in terms of their education. Perhaps one of the best indicators is the fact of having stayed on at school after the minimum leaving age. A Government survey in 1977 found wide discrepancies in the proportion of children born into the Registrar General's different social classes who continued in full-time or part-time education beyond the age of sixteen:

	%
Class I	78
Class II	54
Class III NM	51
Class III M	37
Class IV	28
Class V	26

Having been to university is another fairly sure indication of middle-class status. In the contest for the Labour Party leadership that followed the death of Hugh Gaitskell in 1963, James Callaghan contemplated standing as the only 'working-class' candidate. When he was asked to define the term, he said that he regarded himself as working-class because he had not been to university. Graduates sometimes try to deny that they have cut themselves off from the proletariat, but, as a polytechnic principal recently commented, 'the fact is that higher education is a middle class activity and anyone who goes through it is marked for life. There should be a special ceremony upon graduation, like a nun taking off the veil, when the graduands formally give up their membership of the working or any other class and accept the uniform of their new community.'[13]

In the popular mind there are few more certain indicators of membership of the middle classes than education at a public (i.e. private) school. In fact public schooling is a distinctly upper middle class experience, enjoyed by only a relatively small minority. Government figures show that only 30 per cent of parents in the Registrar General's top social class, 15 per cent of those in Class II and 4 per cent of those in Class III NM send their children to independent schools.

For those who go to them, however, the public schools certainly constitute a middle-class world which is even more self-contained and all-embracing than that of the professions. It is a world with its own language and rules, of stigs, and novi, and fagging, of no hands in pockets and only prefects with top jacket button undone, of house matches in everything from rugger to debating and junior house colours if you win, of compulsory chapel and the Combined Cadet Force. For mothers it means endlessly sewing on Cash's woven name tapes, watching performances of operettas written for unbroken boys' voices with titles like *The Batsman's Bride*, of choosing a dress to wear for Founders' Day which will withstand the rigours of the English July and will not be the same as anyone else's mother is wearing. For fathers it is a matter of finding the money for boarding fees and violin lessons, of proudly watching sons come third in the 220 yards or score twelve runs as number six, of applauding the chairman of the governors as he repeats his annual incitement to the boys to pursue the three Is, industry, integrity and independence, and of reliving their own memories, triggered off by the strains of 'Lord, Dismiss Us With Thy Blessing' coming from the chapel on the last day of term.

The public school world has its own complex class distinctions just as much as the Civil Service and the Poundford commuter train. There are major schools and minor ones and many in between. To its critics, of course, the whole system is one gigantic piece of snobbery designed to enable those with money to purchase upper class status for their children and so perpetuate and exacerbate social division and inequality. To their defenders, on the other hand, the public schools exist not to maintain class distinction but to preserve and foster certain values – academic excellence, team spirit, Christian upbringing and responsible behaviour. With those values we have moved beyond simple definitions of the middle classes and begun to penetrate the subtler mysteries of middle classness.

3

What is Middle Classness?
Some more Subtle Definitions

Occupation, income, place and type of residence, and education are all useful criteria for establishing who the middle classes are. However, they do not tell us very much about middle classness, that distinctive combination of habits, prejudices, lifestyle and values which cannot be measured by statistical tables. When seeking to define that quality the English tend to forsake the findings of sociologists and to rely instead on more instinctive and intangible factors. For some, like the lady who wrote to *The Times* in 1980 it is a simple matter:

> Sir,
> There have been a series of rather complicated formulae put forward recently to define 'class'.
>
> But surely 'class' in human beings derives from the same factor that determines 'class' in race horses and pedigree dogs, namely good breeding over two or three generations.

Good (or bad) breeding is something that most people recognize almost immediately. There have always been far quicker ways of telling someone's class than questioning him about his job or education. George Orwell noted in 1944:

> Thirty years ago the social status of nearly everyone in England could be determined from his appearance, even at 200 yards distance . . . The great majority of the people can still be 'placed' in an instant by their manners, clothes and general appearance. Even the physical type differs considerably, the upper classes being on average several inches taller than the working class.[1]

Forty years of the Welfare State and of economic advance have diminished the validity of that last test, although there remain some physical differences between the classes.

According to figures produced by the British Nutrition Foundation, for example, working class women between the ages of twenty and thirty-nine are nearly twice as likely as middle-class women in the same age range to be overweight. Most people, however, are still able to make accurate judgements of social class on the basis of a very short acquaintance. Accent, vocabulary, dress, diet, drinking habits, manners, and taste convey a host of subtle messages about social origins and social pretensions.

Orwell also observed that 'The most striking difference between the classes is in language and accent. The English working class . . . is branded on the tongue.' Certainly in no other country does accent convey so much about social as well as geographical origins. Where but in England would it have been possible to set the play, *Pygmalion*, later turned into a successful musical *My Fair Lady*, about the social transform- ation of a flower girl taught to speak 'proper' by a professor obsessed with phonetics? The English middle classes can be defined as those who talk 'posh'. They pronounce their 'h's' and enunciate their vowels properly. If they live in the south, they speak what is known as received standard English without any trace of a regional accent. If they are upper middle class, or lower middle class with pretensions, they pronounce often to rhyme with orphan and cross to rhyme with horse.

There is still much truth in Bernard Shaw's remark that 'an Englishman's way of speaking absolutely classifies him. The moment he talks he makes another Englishman despise him.' Despite the pervasive influence of television with its classless, mid-Atlantic accents, there are still profound differences between the way the middle classes and the working classes speak and the one still jars on the other. It is not just a matter of accent but also of the pitch and tone of voice. Many of the middle classes, and particularly of the upper middle classes, tend to talk in rather loud voices and often in a way which suggests a sense of superiority and condescension. Professor Richard Hoggart, the distinguished academic and literary critic, who celebrated the cultural values of his working-class childhood in his book, *The Uses of Literacy*, recently admitted, 'I still find the tone of voice of certain middle-class professional people who went to public school and Oxbridge as deeply offensive as I did when I left school at fourteen.'[2]

What people say is almost as important in indicating their social class as the way they say it. Once again it is a peculiarly English characteristic. In what other country would a professor of linguistics spend much of his time, as Professor Alan Ross did, drawing up a list of U (upper class) and non-U words, or would one of the most popular poems of the Poet Laureate, *How To Get On In Society*, be entirely composed of a series of social solecisms like saying sweet instead of pudding and serviette instead of napkin?

Using non-U words may not be quite as terrible an offence in polite society as it was thirty years ago when Angela Thirkell recorded the following exchange in her novel *Love Among the Ruins*: '"You mean like saying couch for sofa and lounge for sitting-room?" said Mrs Belton. "And worse," said Mr Carton, "scholars are coming up to St Paul's, young men of considerable ability, who whenever they cough say 'Pardon'."' But it is still an unmistakable sign of a working class or lower middle-class upbringing to talk about going to the toilet.

Dress, for both work and play, is a much less certain indicator of social class than it was in the days before St Michael became the patron saint of fashion for both high and low born in England. The working man may still be distinguished by his overalls and cap and the white-collar worker by his suit, but subtler distinctions between different groups in the middle classes are more difficult to make. Senior civil servants and professional men, who used to insist on stiff detachable collars, are now indistinguishable from junior colleagues in their apparel. That supreme symbol of upper middle-class respectability, the bowler hat, which was still a comparatively common sight on commuter trains in the 1950s, has virtually disappeared. Sir Ian Bancroft, the head of the Civil Service, told a meeting at the Royal Institute of Public Affairs in December 1980 that he only knew of one civil servant who still wore one to work. There are those who maintain that you can tell a man's class by the distance between the stripes on his shirt and the width of his lapels (the broader, the lower) but it hardly seems an infallible guide.

Preference for natural rather than synthetic fibres is a middle-class trait and there is still an instantly recognizable type of upper middle-class woman who goes around in tweed skirt and sensible shoes. Her daughters often sport the headscarf and quilted anorak that are the badges of the 'Sloane Ranger'. Upper middle-class men eschew cardigans, shoes with built-up soles, and fleecy-lined car-coats.

Diet is still partly a matter of class, although there are significant regional variations as well. Certainly it is a clear social indicator in the eyes of many members of the middle classes, one of whom told a journalist in search of the characteristics that distinguish the classes in Britain:

> I'd look at diet . . . A lot of what the working class buys tends to be convenience foods and rather starchy. Filling. Yes, agreed his wife, sweet and sticky stuff, cakes which tend to be gooey. The working class also buy tinned peaches rather than fresh fruit. They eat a lot of sandwiches and cake, whereas we eat a lot of yoghourt, fresh fruit and cheese.[3]

The Government's annual household survey confirms that families in Classes C2, D and E eat more carbohydrates, snack foods and sweets and less fresh fruit and vegetables than those in Classes A, B and C1. The working classes tend to prefer white to brown bread and not to share the enthusiasm of a growing section of the middle classes for whole foods and polyunsaturated margarine. They do not necessarily prefer cheaper foods, however. Surveys show that many working-class families spend proportionately more on food than middle-class families and often actually buy dearer items. This is another point that is often seized on by the middle classes:

> I don't like to talk about the working classes because it sounds very snobby, but take your C/D people: when I see them in front of me at Sainsburys or the freezer centre, you notice their trolleys are overloaded with rubbish. You'll see the middle class people filling up with stewing steak and fresh veg. We spend time looking for inexpensive but wholesome food, while the others will have a load of rum babas, all that absolute rubbish. It's really a bit of fecklessness.[4]

There is another significant difference in eating habits between the classes. It was pointed out in a BBC Audience Research report of 1938 on the subject of what time the British have their meals. For most of the day it found that 'the rich and poor . . .

march fairly well in step, but at tea-time the ranks divide – a dichotomy which extends throughout the evening. For one section of the community high tea is the main evening meal, followed late in the evening by a light supper. For the rest there is an afternoon tea, followed by dinner which is the main evening meal'.[5] It remains true today that many manual workers and their families tend to eat their evening meal one or two hours earlier than most middle-class families.

A nice illustration of the different eating habits which still persist between the classes was provided in the 'Life In the Day of' feature which appeared in the unofficial newspaper produced by *Sunday Times* journalists during the suspension of the main paper in 1979. In the first issue the subject was Mr Marmaduke Hussey, managing director of Times Newspapers, educated at public school and Oxford and a former officer in the Guards. Describing a typical evening meal, he said that he and his wife often had a simple supper of bacon and eggs. The subject of the feature in the second issue, Mr Reg Brady, a printer who left school at fourteen and pointed out 'I live in a council flat – I'm not one of the rich bourgeoisie,' revealed that 'Last night we had filleted steak, potatoes in their jackets, and two bottles of Blue Nun. I drank most of it, my wife prefers scotch. We don't often have a sweet. Later on, at 9.30 or 10, we have a snack – last night it was cheese on Ryvita with gherkins, beetroot and pickled walnuts.'[6]

Drinking habits also differ between the classes. Although Reg Brady's tastes show the danger of generalizing, it is on the whole true to say that while the middle classes tend to drink wine with their meals at home, the working classes are more likely to drink beer or spirits at the local pub or club. If they do drink wine, they tend to prefer sweet or sparkling white and rosé, while the middle classes are more likely to favour drier white and red wines. Sweet mixed drinks, like Bacardi and Coke, Brandy and Babycham, gin and orange, Pernod and lime and port and lemon are regarded as distinctly lower middle class, or worse.

Politics, religion and recreations also distinguish the classes, although not as much as they used to. In their important study, *Political Change in Britain*, David Butler and Donald Stokes showed that the close alignment between social class and political allegiance which had been so strong a feature in twentieth-century Britain was beginning to break down in the 1960s. Subsequent events have confirmed this trend. The latest review of recent British voting habits produced by Professor Richard Rose of the Centre for the Study of Social Policy at the University of Strathclyde is entitled *Class Does Not Equal Party* (1980).

Table 2, which is based on polls conducted after the general elections of 1964 and 1979, shows that there has been a significant swing away from the Conservatives by the top two social classes, who are traditionally thought of as their natural supporters. It also shows a smaller swing away from Labour on the part of the working classes. However, it remains broadly true that a majority of the middle classes support the Conservatives, just as a majority of the working classes support Labour. In the last general election two and a half middle-class votes were cast for the Conservatives for every Labour one.

Attitudes to political issues also vary between the classes. Polls have consistently shown, for example, that the middle classes are more enthusiastic supporters of the European Economic Community. They are also more liberal in their attitudes to such issues as race and immigration, capital punishment, and the Third World. Working-class and lower middle class Conservatives are noticeably tougher and more right-wing than others. It is significant that Tory opposition to the present Government's tough monetarist policy is coming predominantly from upper middle class 'wets' inside and outside the Cabinet. The instincts of a sizeable minority within the middle classes lead them to support the Liberal Party, which obtained more votes than the Labour Party from those in higher managerial and professional jobs in the 1979 election, and which has been described as 'a vehicle for a lot of very nice and very decorous spokesmen for the caring middle class'.[7]

While religious belief seems to be spread fairly evenly throughout the population, church-going is a predominantly middle-class activity. A survey in 1973 found that 22 per cent of married men in Classes I and II, and only 7 per cent of those in Classes IV and V, had been to church twelve or more times in the previous year.[8] Traditionally, the Church of England has been favoured by the upper middle classes and Nonconformist

TABLE 2

Social grade of head of household by party identification, 1964 and 1979
SOURCES: Butler and Stokes 1964 Cross-section survey
British Election Study May 1979 Cross-section survey

PARTY:	Higher professional and managerial 1964	1979	diff.	Lower professional and managerial 1964	1979	diff.	Skilled/ supervisory non-manual 1964	1979	diff.	Lower non-manual 1964	1979	diff.	Skilled Manual 1964	1979	diff.	Unskilled/ Semi-skilled manual 1964	1979	diff.
Conservative	66	53	(−13)	67	56	(−11)	57	63	(+6)	49	44	(−5)	28	29	(+1)	25	30	(+5)
Labour	12	20	(+8)	15	25	(+10)	20	18	(−2)	26	31	(+5)	57	51	(−6)	61	50	(−11)
Liberal	14	21	(+7)	13	12	(−1)	16	12	(−4)	17	15	(−2)	9	11	(+2)	10	11	(+1)
Other/none	8	6	(−2)	6	7	(+1)	7	8	(+1)	8	10	(+2)	6	9	(+3)	3	9	(+6)
'Swing' to Cons.	−10·5%			−10·5%			+4%			−5%			+3·5%			+8%		

Reproduced from Ivor Crewe, 'The Electoral Decline of the Labour Party',
in D. Kavanagh (ed), *Labour Party Politics* (London, 1981).

churches by the lower middles. One subtle way of establishing a man's middle classness is to ask him to sing a hymn like *All Hail The Power of Jesu's Name* and find out whether he uses the Anglican (Miles Lane) or Nonconformist (Diadem) tune. A recent National Opinion Poll found that the highest level of membership of the Church of England is still in Classes A and B, and the highest concentration of Nonconformists in Class C1. The Roman Catholics, however, who are the fastest growing denomination in Britain, are strongest in Classes D and E.

Recreations and holidays are yet another area of life which reflect social distinctions. Surveys have shown that in their leisure time the middle classes are more likely than the working classes to read books, go to the theatre, watch cricket or rugby union and play squash or tennis, and less likely to watch television, gamble, watch football, boxing, horse-racing or greyhound racing. They are also much more likely to be involved in voluntary organizations and activities outside their work. On holiday, they tend to be more adventurous and individualistic. One possible definition of middle classness might be a preference for walking in Exmoor or exploring provincial France to spending a week in Butlin's camp in Minehead or going on a package holiday to the Costa Brava.

It is, however, in the privacy of their own homes that people show their social position most clearly. Step into any house in the land and it does not take long to establish its occupants' class. Indeed, it may only be necessary to step through the front gate. The middle classes do not, on the whole, have plastic gnomes or other decorative ornaments in their front gardens, nor fancy pictorial numerals or name signs outside their houses, although if they have recently risen from below they may well have reproduction carriage lamps at the door and a two- or three-tone chime on the front bell. It would, in fact, be possible to construct a fairly accurate class profile of the population entirely on the basis of the sound of their doorbells. One Conservative MP, on the evidence of years of canvassing, has already established a set of political guidelines: 'Chimes are Tory, shrill bell old-fashioned Liberal, none at all usually Labour.'[9]

The everyday sights and sounds of home life give a good

indication of the various levels of middle classness. The strains of BBC Radio Three emanating from hi-fi equipment rather precariously balanced between piles of books and dusty Staffordshire figures are a sure sign of an upper middle-class home, just as the sound of Mantovani on Radio Two from a music centre meticulously placed between simulated-leather-bound volumes of the *Reader's Digest* condensed classics suggests lower middle classness. Somewhere in between comes the kitchen with herb charts on the wall, and a coffee grinder on the working surface, with an old transistor radio permanently tuned to Radio Four.

Matters of taste are another good social indicator. Sending out silver-printed wedding invitations with decorative embellishments, or using a commercially made card or a floral notelet to express sympathy on a bereavement would be regarded as rather vulgar and ostentatious in upper middle class households. An undertaker recently commented: 'Among the middle classes it's a matter of keeping down with the Jones's. It just isn't the done thing to have a showy funeral. Our biggest funerals almost always come from people living in council houses.'[10] According to Professor Alan Ross, putting cherries on top of grapefruits and cocking the little finger when taking tea are equally non-U practices, while Sir John Betjeman, in *How To Get On In Society*, made similarly disapproving noises about using fish knives and pastry forks and having simulated log fires.

One of the best examples of the differences in taste between the middle and working classes is the choice of names for their children. The Christian names most frequently occurring in the births column of *The Times* are simple English ones like James, Edward, William, John and Nicholas for boys, and Elizabeth, Sarah, Jane, Mary and Victoria for girls. If the *Daily Mirror* had a births column, it would probably include a large number of Waynes, Craigs, Sharons and Traceys, American influenced names which jar on middle-class ears.

Good manners, like good taste, are something that the middle classes are inclined to feel are not distributed equally by Providence among social classes A to E. One of my friends defines middle classness as 'things like my mother always insisting that we got up when Daddy came into the room'.

Public schools in particular have traditionally stressed the importance of good manners. The motto of Winchester College is Manners Makyth Man, while a notice on the board at Clifton College reminds boys that they must not have their hands in their pockets as they walk through the Memorial Arch which commemorates the dead of two world and several imperial wars. In a recent BBC television documentary series on Radley College, the headmaster, Mr Denis Silk, was seen telling the new boys in Chapel:

> Some of you may be blessed with good brains, others not. That doesn't matter twopence. What does matter is the courtesies we show one another. It matters to me that you should not talk to people with your hands in your pockets. It matters to me that you've got polished shoes, that your top button is done up. I wonder how many of you have got clean finger nails. You come here for one thing – to acquire the right habits for life.[11]

Whether the middle classes actually have better manners than the working classes as a result of this intensive training is, of course, another matter. It is true that they are less likely to beat their wives or commit criminal offences, but in other areas of behaviour their record is less unimpeachable. Those who equate middle-class morality with purity and constancy in marriage have to face the fact that the working classes commit less adultery and have a lower divorce rate than their social superiors. Admittedly, the middle classes have sex less often, but in more varied positions, and with the woman apparently enjoying it more – and that surely cannot be as a result of anything taught at public schools.

Ultimately, the most important and characteristic feature of the middle classes are their distinctive values. It is impossible to compress them into a neat package. Two of the most famous old boys of my school, Colin Cowdrey, the cricketer, and E. M. Forster, the novelist, could be said to represent essentially English middle-class values. Yet the difference between the straightforward conservative, muscular Christianity of the one and the bohemian, liberal, humanist sensitivity of the other could hardly be greater. Complex and even contradictory as they are, however, there is a distinct set of values which are recognized by their champions and their detractors alike as lying at the heart of English middle classness.

To many people thrift is the single most important and characteristic middle-class value. Patrick Hutber singled it out as such in his book, *The Decline and Fall of the Middle Class*. As the comments noted earlier about shopping habits indicate, the middle classes see themselves as careful and provident with money and the working classes as feckless and prodigal. The commonly held view is that the middle-class family will scrimp and save, doing without holidays abroad or a colour television, in order to be able to send their children to public school or to build up capital to pass on to them, while the working class family will spend all its money as soon as the wage packet is brought home on food, drink, cigarettes, consumer goods and entertainments.

There is, in fact, strong factual evidence to support that view. The middle classes do save a higher proportion of their earnings. Studies have shown that as the working classes have become more affluent, they have continued to regard their money as something to be spent rather than saved. Furthermore, they have spent on consumer goods like televisions and cars, and on luxuries like drink and cigarettes, rather than on buying a house or increased pension entitlement. They have not, on the whole, taken on traditional middle-class commitments, like mortgage repayments, life insurance premiums and school fees, which involve postponing instant gratification for more long-term benefits.

A second value commonly attributed to the middle classes is that of ambition both for themselves and for their families. It is, of course, closely related to thrift. One of the commonest reasons for saving and doing without holidays or other luxuries is to enable children to be sent to independent schools. Seeking ways of defining middle classness in its leading article in January 1975, *The Times* concluded that 'the fundamental proposition of the middle class' was as follows:

> I want to lead as successful and creative a life as I can, because I believe that will be best both for me, and for society. I want my children to have the best chance to lead a similar life, because that will be good both for them and society, according to their particular talents. I hope to give my children as good a family life and as good an education as they can get, and if possible to leave

them sufficient money to have some extra security and some extra opportunities.[12]

Those may seem universal goals. Indeed, the Director of Education for Gwent in Wales was prompted to write to *The Times* suggesting that on this definition the entire population of his county was middle-class. Nonetheless, although most parents have ambitions for their children, it is true that among the middle classes these ambitions tend to be stronger. A survey in Liverpool in 1972 found, for example, that 92 per cent of parents in the Registrar General's Class I wanted their sons to remain at school until eighteen or later, compared with only 27 per cent of those in Class V. Significantly, it also found that a slightly higher proportion of those in Class III NM (70 per cent) than in Class II (68 per cent) wanted to see their sons stay on, apparently confirming the continuance of a traditionally strong lower middle-class trait, epitomized in the intense family pressure to get a bright boy first into grammar school and then to university.[13]

Having an ambitious attitude towards one's job is also traditionally regarded as a sign of middle classness. According to the same leading article in *The Times*, 'any man who sees his career as a progress rather than a static occupation has inevitably acquired the central attitude of middle class life'.[14] Obviously it is much easier to be ambitious in a job which has a career structure and rising pay scales than in the typical manual job where there is no ladder of promotion and the prospect of diminishing rather than increasing earnings after the age of forty. It is not surprising that studies of manual workers have generally found them to be lacking in ambition.

The counterparts to the virtues of thrift and ambition are the vices of meanness and ruthlessness. The middle classes are attacked by their critics for being selfish, acquisitive, materialistic and competitive, while the working classes are seen as more generous and easy-going. A recent Labour Party booklet on public schools talked of 'the bought is best philosophy of the British middle class' and socialist opponents of Mrs Thatcher accuse her of exemplifying the cold hard-heartedness of the bourgeoisie.[15]

It is true that there is a ruthless side to the middle classes.

Those in entrepreneurial and managerial positions are often highly competitive and materialistic, just as they were in the days of Dickens' Gradgrind and Bounderby. There is considerable evidence that middle-class children are more competitive at school than working-class children. However, recent research suggests that manual workers are now, if anything, more acquisitive and materialistic than non-manual workers.[16] Certainly the behaviour of many trade unions, obsessed with differentials and making leap-frogging pay claims to keep one step ahead of other groups of workers, hardly suggests that the middle classes have a monopoly of selfishness and competitiveness.

It is also true that if there has been one element within the middle classes which has been competitive and materialistic, there has been another equally strong element which has exhibited the opposite characteristics. There is a strong strain of selfless idealism and social concern in English middle classness. From it have sprung most of that noble company of idealists and reformers who have so greatly enriched the nation's history. These often rather saintly figures have predominantly come from professional families where the values of Christian compassion and open-minded tolerance are very different from those that prevail among some of the entrepreneurial middle classes. If anything, this idealistic and non-materialistic strain seems to be increasing. It is even displacing ambition as the motive force of a growing number of middle-class children who are seeking less well paid but more socially useful jobs than their parents.

Just as it encompasses both materialism and idealism, so middle classness involves both high cultural values and philistinism. Both those qualities have traditionally been associated with the English middle classes. Matthew Arnold berated the dull, provincial Nonconformist values of Victorian businessmen, and there are still some today who would rather read the *Financial Times* than any novel and who would prefer an evening in the golf club bar to a night at the opera. But there is another element within the middle classes which puts a high value on culture and which gives the nation most of its music, books, theatre and art, both directly through its own creations and indirectly through its patronage.

There has, in fact, always been a tension between the values of the professional and the commercial middle classes as marked as any differences they may jointly have from working-class values. It is nicely brought out in Margaret Drabble's novel *The Ice Age*, whose central character, Anthony Keating, is the son of an Anglican clergyman:

> Throughout his childhood Anthony had listened to his father and mother speaking slightingly of the lack of culture of business men, of the philistinism and ignorance of their sons, of commercial greed, expense accounts, business lunches. Under the massive yellow sandy shadow of the cathedral wall, the Keatings sat safely in their extremely attractive, well-maintained eighteenth-century house (it went with the job) and listened to good music, and laughed over funny mistakes in Latin proses, and bitched about the Canon's wife who had a pronounced Lancashire accent.[17]

Another characteristic popularly and rightly associated with the middle classes is reserve. They are not inclined to open up conversations with their neighbours on trains or buses, and lack the spontaneous friendliness of the working classes. The 'street parties' held to mark the Queen's Jubilee in 1977 in the roads and drives of suburbia were very much more formal and self-conscious affairs than those in the East End of London. It is not so much that the middle classes feel themselves aloof from such things, but rather that they have a certain reticence, particularly strong among the upper-middles, which makes them wary of showing their emotions or letting themselves go. Maintaining a stiff upper lip, and not wearing your heart on your sleeve, are still regarded as virtues.

Independence and individualism are also commonly seen as middle-class values. Shortly before the 1979 election a leading trade unionist predicted that Mrs Thatcher would not win the votes of the working classes because her values were different from theirs. When asked to explain what he meant, he replied, 'working class values are collectivist'.[18] On the whole, manual workers look to their trade union to represent their interests and place more emphasis on collective strength and bargaining than on individual action or initiative. Trade union leaders often invoke the language of class solidarity in their fights against employers or the Government. The middle classes have traditionally lacked this collectivist attitude and sense of class consciousness and have rather prided themselves on their independence and looked to their own individual efforts to improve their lot.

However, this may be another value that is changing. The traditional individualism of the middle classes has undoubtedly sprung at least in part from the nature of their jobs. Typically, in the past, they have worked on their own, or at the most in small teams. However, the development of computer technology and the trend towards open-plan offices has collectivized the working lives of many in the middle classes. After long being shunned, trade unionism is being espoused by many white-collar workers. Individualism can no longer be said to be the dominant middle-class value that it once was.

In one respect, however, it remains a distinctive characteristic. The middle classes still generally have a strong sense of individual responsibility and of personal service to the community. There is a noticeable difference of attitudes in Britain towards the subject of 'do-gooding' and voluntary charitable activity to help less well-off members of the community. There is a strong working-class feeling, reflected in the Labour Party and the trade union movement, that it is much better for the state to provide for the needs of society and a deep-seated suspicion of voluntary action. Both a leading trade unionist and a front-bench Labour politician have told me that in their working-class childhoods they would not even put a penny in a charity collecting box because they regarded voluntary work as something done by condescending middle-class ladies to make them feel good when they went to church on Sundays and as a positive hindrance to the creation of a comprehensive Welfare State.

The middle classes, by contrast, tend to feel that despite the existence of much state provision for the disadvantaged, voluntary effort and personal charity still have a vital role in society. Their sense of social responsibility manifests itself in widespread involvement in voluntary work. Whether they are the formidably competent ladies who organize coffee mornings and bring-and-buy sales and run the meals on wheels service, the young mothers who staff pre-school playgroups and teach English to immigrants, or the long-haired radicals who run urban renewal projects and community action schemes, the vast majority of those who together put in sixteen million hours of voluntary work every week in Britain (the equivalent of what would be done by 400,000 full-time staff) are indubitably middle-class.[19] So also is that small army of enthusiasts who spend their Saturday mornings accosting strangers and stabbing pins into their lapels with little paper flags attached.

The values of individual responsibility and public service are also expressed in a general middle-class commitment to doing things which need to be done without fuss or bother. The doctor will continue working beyond the time that he is officially supposed to stop if he still has patients to see. The teacher will undertake duties which are not strictly laid down in her contract of service. The chemist will open his shop at inconvenient times and the small businessman work into the night to finish a job. Although this traditional willingness shows some sign of diminishing as trade union attitudes take a greater hold on society, it has not disappeared. At the centre of middle classness there is still a strong sense of personal responsibility, an acceptance that if something has to be done, you should get on and do it without standing on your rights and making an issue out of it.

A sense of personal responsibility and public service is not, of course, confined to those in the Registrar General's Classes I to III NM, any more than are the other values characterized in this chapter as middle-class. But it is among the middle classes, and more particularly among the professional middle classes, that it is most widely found. Like the others, it is a value that has deep historical roots and which has developed and changed over the centuries in the long process of evolution which has created the English middle classes of today.

4

The Rise of
the Middle Classes
Origins to Mid-Victorian Heyday

The middle classes are as old as urban civilization. They existed in the city states of Ancient Greece where they were commended by Aristotle for preventing either the very rich or the very poor from becoming dominant. 'It is manifest,' he wrote in his *Politics*, 'that the best political community is formed by citizens of the middle class, and that those states are likely to be well-administered, in which the middle class is large, and larger if possible than both the other classes.'[1]

Aristotle's conception of the middle class as comprising those between the very rich and the poor has been commonly accepted until fairly recent times. It shows clearly the extent to which the middle classes are an urban phenomenon. In primitive agrarian societies there is virtually no one between landowner and peasant. It is only with the growth of towns that intermediate mercantile and professional communities develop. Significantly, the word bourgeois is derived from the burgs or strongholds which in ninth and tenth century Germany provided a refuge from danger for townsmen who lacked the impregnable castles of the nobility and could not disperse into the countryside like the peasantry.

In England the earliest members of the middle classes were the traders and professional men who lived and worked in the expanding towns of the later Middle Ages. The merchant, the miller, the haberdasher, the doctor of physic, the man of law and the clerk of Oxenford who figure in Chaucer's *Canterbury Tales* (1387) were all representatives of this newly emerging group. They belonged to an age which was coming out of feudalism and where social and personal relationships based on contract and cash payment were replacing those based on vassalage and kinship.

For many historians it was these new relationships which gave the middle classes their main characteristic: a ruthless, competitive individualism which contrasted with the co-operative and communal values of medieval life. Karl Marx wrote, 'The bourgeoisie, whenever it got the upper hand, put an end to all feudal, patriarchal, idyllic relations, pitilessly tore asunder the motley feudal ties that bound man to his "natural superiors" and left remaining no other bond between man and man than naked self-interest and callous cash payment.'[2]

It is true that the new urban middle classes were competitive. They operated in a market economy where they had to sell their skills or their goods to live. Their individualism derived from the nature of their work which they tended to perform alone rather than in groups. It is doubtful, however, whether life was quite so idyllic before the bourgeoisie came on the scene as Marx and others have imagined.

The sixteenth century saw important developments among both the professional and mercantile middle classes. The professions began to organize themselves along recognizably modern lines. The Inns of Court were developed to train barristers and to establish the legal profession as independent from the state. Physicians established their own college in 1518, and the less exalted barber surgeons followed suit and formed a company in 1540. The development of substantial mining, iron making, shipbuilding and woollen textile industries greatly increased the number of those engaged in manufacturing and trade. In 1568 the Royal Exchange was opened as a place where the growing number of merchants in London could meet to transact business. Meanwhile, much of the land released by King Henry VIII's dissolution of the monasteries was coming into the hands of merchants and small farmers who rapidly established themselves as the 'new gentry'.

There has been much debate among historians about the position of these new gentry. Socially, they came below the nobility, but in a society where land was still the main determinant of status, they were clearly above landless merchants and professional men. They had the vote under the terms of a statute of 1430 which made the qualification for the franchise the possession of a freehold property with a value of at least forty shillings a year.

William Harrison, who wrote *An historic description of the Island of Britayne* in Holinshed's Chronicle (1577), laid down a clear hierarchy among the middle classes with the gentry at the top, the merchants in the middle and the yeoman, mostly farmers to the gentry, at the bottom. In fact, the social structure in Tudor England was very fluid with considerable interchange between the landed gentry and those in commercial and professional occupations. Harrison noted that the sons of the gentry were often apprenticed to trade or went to the Inns of Court, as did the sons of yeomen, while merchants and lawyers often bought enough land to take them into the ranks of the gentry.

Then, as now, however, it was essentially the quality of being a gentleman rather than the possession of a particular level of income or property which established a man's true social status. Harrison observed that gentlemanliness was not just confined to landed proprietors; it was also found among lawyers, teachers, physicians and soldiers. It did not, however, extend as far as merchants. The feeling that still lingers among the English middle classes that trade is not quite the proper occupation for a gentleman has deep historical roots. A treatise of 1586 noted that 'The practice (of trade) consisteth of most ungentle parts, as doubleness of tongue, violation of faith.'[3]

The sixteenth century also saw the development of a movement that was to help create a distinct outlook and a self-confidence among the new middle classes of Europe, the Protestant Reformation. In the words of R. H. Tawney, in his classic work on *Religion and the Rise of Capitalism*,

> Calvin did for the bourgeoisie of the sixteenth century what Marx did for the proletariat of the nineteenth. He set their virtues at their best in sharp antithesis with the vices of the established order at its worst, taught them to feel that they were a chosen people, made them conscious of their great destiny in the Providential plan and resolute to realize it . . . Puritanism was the schoolmaster of the English middle classes.[4]

Historians are divided about the extent to which Protestantism did, in fact, encourage the development of capitalist society in early modern Europe. What can be said with reasonable certainty, however, is that the new Puritan religion, particularly as it was developed by Calvin, stressed and sanctified certain values which were of obvious benefit to the rising middle classes, among them thrift, self-reliance, individual conscience and participatory government. It also gave them the moral earnestness, the concern with respectability and propriety, the preference for plain living and high thinking and the censoriousness over the failings of others which have, in varying degrees, remained with them to this day.

Certainly it was among the professional and mercantile middle classes that Puritanism found its most fervent adherents. It was lawyers, merchants and small craftsmen who endowed the Puritan lectureships and filled the dissenting conventicles in Elizabethan and early Stuart England. The certainty of personal salvation and sense of spiritual and moral superiority engendered by Puritanism played an important part in the growth of middle-class confidence that was the prelude to the mid-seventeenth century challenge to the prevailing aristocratic hold over government and society.

The English Civil War and the events which led up to it have been described by Christopher Hill and other Marxist historians as a bourgeois revolution. The struggle in the first half of the seventeenth century was not just between Parliament and the King. Puritans were protesting against the exclusive hold of the Anglican Church Establishment. Merchants and manufacturers were rebelling against the closed corporations, monopolies and other restrictions on economic activity that remained from feudal times and against the domination of government by landed interests. The rising numbers of lawyers and educated new gentry were rebelling against their exclusion from office and the rule of Court favourites. Oliver Cromwell, John Hampden and John Pym were perhaps the first middle-class political leaders in England. When civil war finally broke out, the battle lines were drawn according to class. As an anonymous but not impartial observer noted in 1645, 'The king's cause and party were favoured by two extremes . . . the one, the wealthy and powerful men, the other, of the basest and lowest sort; but disgusted by the middle rank, the true and best citizens.'[5]

The result of the Civil War, and of the subsequent convulsions which culminated in the Glorious Revolution of

1688, was by no means a total victory for the middle classes. Political power and influence remained firmly in the hands of the landed aristocracy. In social and economic terms, however, the second half of the seventeenth century brought clear gains to the middle classes. The last remaining feudal encumbrances to the free operation of the market which had been swept away during the Commonwealth and Protectorate were not re-introduced at the Restoration. A government less dominated by the Court brought career opportunities in a new expanding civil service. Commercial life flourished as London developed as a major international banking and insurance centre with the founding of the Bank of England (1694) and Lloyd's marine insurance agents (1688).

The intellectual climate of the age also favoured the up-and-coming professional middle classes. The atmosphere of religious tolerance, which followed the passing of Toleration Acts in the 1660s and the Revolution Settlement of 1688, and the patronage of an enlightened monarch encouraged the development of all branches of learning and prompted the establishment of the Royal Society dedicated to pursuing experiment and research. One of those most actively involved in the society was Christopher Wren, the son of a clergyman, whose subsequent work was greatly to enhance the prestige of the architectural profession. Another was Isaac Newton, educated at a grammar school in Grantham, whose work had much the same effect on the scientific profession.

One of the most important legacies of the intellectual ferment of the seventeenth century was the political theory that was to become almost an article of faith for the English middle classes. A distinguished Canadian political scientist, Professor C. B. Macpherson, has called it the theory of possessive individualism, encompassing both the notion that what makes a man free is his freedom from dependence on the will of others and the conviction that every man is the sole proprietor of his own person and capacities and owes nothing to society for them.[6] Elements of this theory were clearly represented in the speeches of Roundhead leaders like John Hampden and Oliver Cromwell, but it was given its fullest expression in the writing of the philosopher, John Locke.

Locke is perhaps the nearest that the English middle classes have had to their own philosopher. Like them, his approach was urbane and rational, avoiding enthusiasm and excess. He preached the virtues of tolerance, consent, individualism and private property rights, the basic elements of liberal democracy. He also sought to establish the legitimacy of a society divided into two classes, those with property and those without. This he did by arguing that in his original state of nature man's rationality was expressed in his capacity to appropriate land by his industry. It therefore followed that those left without property when all the land had been appropriated were not fully rational and could legitimately be subordinated to others. In thus providing a moral basis for a class-divided society, Locke added an important element to the growing confidence of the middle classes.

Another aspect of that growing confidence is illustrated in the life and writings of an exact contemporary of Locke, Samuel Pepys. Pepys' career was a spectacular example of upward social mobility. The son of a London tailor, who although impecunious had connections with the gentry, he won an exhibition to St Paul's School and a place at Magdalene College, Cambridge, and then, thanks to a well-placed relative, gained employment as a clerk in the Navy Office. Firmly ensconced in the expanding civil service, he was able to lead a comfortable life in London, with servants, frequent entertaining and regular visits to the theatre and concerts.

Pepys had many of the characteristic vices of the middle-class parvenu. He was obsessed with money and material possessions, a terrible snob and a shameless social climber. Longing for a knighthood and coveting his invitations to grand social functions, he loved gossip and tittle-tattle. But he had many of the bourgeois virtues as well. He was generous-minded, tolerant, devoted to his family, assiduous in his attendance at church every Sunday and affected by a deeply puritanical strain which led him into frequent bouts of self-reproach and genuine moral anguish over exhibitions of coarseness and lewdness by his friends or contemporaries. The innocent love of life and the preoccupation with its little businesses that spring from every page of Pepys' diaries established a style of humour, peculiarly English and peculiarly middle-class, which was continued in such works as the

Pickwick Papers, The Diary of a Nobody and *Three Men in a Boat.*

If Pepys was one of the first people to write factually about middle-class life, then Daniel Defoe was one of the first to portray the middle classes in fiction. *The Life and Surprising Adventures of Robinson Crusoe of York, Mariner* (1719) is the first well-known work in English literature to have a recognizably bourgeois hero. Other early novelists were to follow in rejecting the knights and nobles of earlier romances in favour of more middle-class subjects. The central figures in Samuel Richardson's *Pamela* (1740), Henry Fielding's *Tom Jones* (1749), Oliver Goldsmith's *The Vicar of Wakefield* (1766) and Laurence Sterne's *Tristram Shandy* (1760) are school-masters, clergymen, farmers and tradesmen.

It is perhaps no coincidence that the English novel, with its characteristically bourgeois qualities of optimism and in-dividualism, should have developed in an age of growing middle-class confidence. Certainly the early novelists played their part in encouraging that confidence. In *Robinson Crusoe* Defoe observed that:

> the middle state or what might be called the upper station of low life . . . was the best state in the world, the most suited to human happiness; not exposed to the miseries and hardships, the labour and sufferings of the mechanic part of mankind, and not embarrassed with the pride, luxury, ambition and envy of the upper part of mankind.[7]

There was good reason for the middle classes to feel confident by the end of the seventeenth century. According to the unofficial census which was carried out by Gregory King in 1688, they made up nearly a third of the population of England. King calculated that 1·2 per cent of the population were in the aristocracy, 67·1 per cent in the lower orders, and 31·7 per cent in the 'middle ranks', in which he included freeholders, farmers, shopkeepers, merchants, the professions and officers in the army and navy. Interestingly, when Patrick Colquhoun made a similar survey of the population in 1814, he assigned almost exactly the same proportions to each class.

It was not until the mid-nineteenth century, however, that the middle classes successfully challenged the hold of the landed artistocracy over government and society. Although they became more numerous and more confident during the eighteenth century, they still lacked the class consciousness which was a necessary condition for collective political action. That consciousness was created largely through the impact of external forces. Some, like the income tax introduced by William Pitt in 1792 to pay for the war against France, had a direct effect in uniting all those with wealth in a common grievance. Others, like the three movements which radically affected English life in the late eighteenth and early nineteenth centuries, played a more gradual but no less important part in forging a common middle-class consciousness.[8]

The first of those movements, the industrial revolution, had spectacular and contradictory effects on the social structure of Britain. It polarized the classes, creating a proletariat of factory workers and a bourgeoisie of entrepreneurs and managers. At the same time it created a more fluid society with greatly increased opportunities for social mobility and progress from rags to riches in one generation. The example of James Watt or George Stephenson dispelled the traditional notion that everyone had their own divinely ordained station in society from which they could never move.

The most direct effect on the middle classes of England's industralization was, of course, to increase their numbers. As William Mackinnon, a Conservative MP, wrote in the early nineteenth century, 'to allude to the extension of machinery is to account for the increase of the middle classes of society'.[9] Industrialization also greatly enhanced the wealth and power of the middle classes. Commercial and manufacturing families like the Gurneys and the Wedgwoods became as rich as most of the landowning aristocracy. They also had a power over many hundreds of clerks and workmen that was as great, if not greater, than that of the landlord over his tenants. Lower down the scale, there were many financiers, merchants and small manufacturers who were comfortably well-off and with positions of considerable responsibility. Yet they remained excluded from political power.

The evangelical revival began in England at much the same time as the industrial revolution with the first gropings by John Wesley and others towards a new vital religion based on intense conviction of sin, dramatic personal conversion and a stern puritanical moral code. Taken up and propagated by the Methodists and by Anglicans like William Wilberforce and Hannah More, evangelicalism was to do for the rising English middle classes of the early nineteenth century what Calvinism had done for the emerging bourgeoisie of Europe nearly three hundred years earlier. It gave them a creed, a confidence and a common consciousness and purpose.

As a religion evangelicalism was tailor-made for the middle classes. It was a reaction against the rationalism and loose morality of the aristocratic-dominated society of the eighteenth century. The attitudes and practices which evangelicals attacked were those which characterized the upper classes: the cult of honour which found expression in such practices as duelling, the penchant for ostentation and frivolity, drunkenness, sexual laxity, blood sports and Sabbath breaking. Many of these vices were also shared by the lower classes. In place of these Regency traits, the evangelicals championed a lifestyle that was eminently bourgeois, based on hard work, plain living, moral propriety and respectable family life.

Many evangelical propagandists specifically aimed their exhortatory tracts at those in the middle classes. One of the first recorded uses of the term 'middle classes' occurs in the title of *An Enquiry into the Duties of Men in the Higher Ranks and Middle Classes of Society in Great Britain* written in 1795 by Thomas Gisborne, an evangelical clergyman and friend of Wilberforce. Hannah More deliberately addressed some of her tracts to 'Persons of the Middle Ranks'. The call to seriousness which she and others made to their countrymen was addressed principally not to the loose living and atheistic aristocracy nor to the immoral and unbelieving populace, but rather to 'that decent class, who while they acknowledged their belief of (religion's) truth by a public profession, are not inattentive to any of its forms, yet exhibit little of its spirit in their general temper and conduct'.[10]

The middle classes responded in considerable numbers to the evangelical call. They enthusiastically joined associations for the reformation of manners and the redemption of fallen women, supported societies which sent missionaries across the world, read the Bible and conducted prayer meetings within their own homes, and performed a variety of good works among the poor. They also became more assiduous and frequent in their attendance at religious services. Manufacturers and small businessmen, particularly those in industrial parts of the country, tended to patronize the Nonconformist chapels, while members of the professions and the upper middle classes went to church, so establishing a social distinction that has continued until today.

Evangelical religion also had a considerable effect on the consciences of the middle classes. It directly inspired much of the charitable activity for which England was justly famed in the nineteenth century. Most of the great philanthropic movements of the time, from Wilberforce's crusades against slavery and the slave trade, through Elizabeth Fry's work for prison reform to the successful campaigns to outlaw child labour in mines and factories, were led and undertaken by middle-class evangelicals. At a less exalted level evangelicalism inspired thousands of middle-class women, for whom there were as yet virtually no career opportunities, to devote themselves to good works among the poor and needy.

There were two distinct ways in which evangelical religion helped the rising middle classes. First, it encouraged them to lose their sense of inferiority to those above them in the social scale. One of the persistent themes of evangelical tract writers was that society should take its values from the bourgeoisie rather than the aristocracy. 'Domestic restraints and family economy are voted bores,' Wilberforce complained in 1800, 'while whatever ways of thinking, speaking and acting become popular in the higher classes, soon spread through every other.' Eight years later an evangelical clergyman expressed the hope that one of the main effects of the religious revival would be that the English middle classes would stand by their own solid values and that 'frivolous imitation of the higher circles would not so frequently meet us in their houses'.[11]

Secondly, evangelicalism exalted middle class careers into callings and at the same time provided a set of rules that were extremely useful for achieving success in them. Gisborne's *Enquiry into the Duties of Men* had separate chapters on business and commerce, politics, the civil service, the armed forces, the law, medicine and the Church. Its whole purpose was to show the serious importance of these various callings and the heavy responsibilities that attached to them. The duties which Gisborne and other evangelical preachers impressed on their middle-class followers – punctuality, probity, attention to the smallest detail – were not just passports to eternal happiness, they were also extremely valuable aids for worldly success in the factory, the counting-house or the office. Evangelicalism helped to effect the change that occurred in nineteenth century England whereby what had been the pastimes of the aristocracy became the serious professions of the middle classes. It was to play an important part in establishing the reputation for honest dealing which contributed to Britain's commercial supremacy and the ethic of disinterested public service which made the British civil service the envy of the world. More immediately, however, it gave the middle classes a new confidence in their position.

Utilitarianism, the third great movement of the early nineteenth century, was just as much a creed as evangelicalism and had almost as pervasive an influence. It was developed by Jeremy Bentham and his fellow Philosophic Radicals as an academic and abstract philosophy based on the 'felicific calculus' with its careful grading of all pains and pleasures. Bentham had an overpowering faith in the power of human reason and a belief that the individual should pursue his own good as he saw it, since in doing so he would, in fact, benefit society and bring the greatest happiness to the greatest number.

Like evangelicals, the utilitarians attacked the prevailing hold of the aristocracy over society and championed the bourgeois virtues of order, discipline and application. Bentham objected to the aristocracy not because they were immoral, but because they were inefficient and their style of government – based on tradition, restriction and influence – impeded the economic and political development of the country.

Utilitarianism had less direct impact on the lives of the English middle classes than evangelicalism. Not many manufacturers or schoolmasters in real life became as narrowly obsessed with facts and as keen to suppress the imaginative and emotional faculties of their charges as Gradgrind, the model utilitarian in Dickens' *Hard Times*, although there were some parents who sent their children to schools like Hazelwood in Birmingham where the bell was rung 250 times every week to signal a particular action. It was rather as an attitude of mind that the Benthamite creed implanted itself into the collective psyche of the English middle classes, producing a proud and perhaps slightly selfish individualism, a hostility to external intervention, and a strong belief in pursuing one's own destiny according to one's own lights.

Like the evangelicals, the utilitarians stressed the importance and worth of the middle classes. In the first issue of their party periodical, the *Westminster Review*, in 1824, James Mill, one of Bentham's closest disciples, proudly proclaimed:

> Of the political and moral importance of this class there can be but one opinion. It is the strength of the community. It contains, beyond all comparison, the greatest proportion of the intelligence, industry, and wealth of the state. In it are the heads that invent, and the hands that execute; the enterprise that projects, and the capital by which these projects are carried into operation. The merchant, the manufacturer, the mechanist, the chemist, the artist, those who discover new arts, those who perfect old arts, those who extend science; the men, in fact, who think for the rest of the world, and who really do the business of the world, are the men of this class. The people of the class below are the instruments with which they work; and those of the class above, though they may be called their governors, and may really sometimes seem to rule them, are much more often, more truly, and more completely under their control. In this country, at least, it is this class which gives to the nation its character.[12]

There were several different conceptions of exactly who the middle classes were in the early part of the nineteenth century. The most common view was that they were the key agents in the manufacturing and commercial life of the country – Mill's 'heads that invent and hands that execute'. A new periodical, the *Monthly Magazine*, which started in 1797, spoke of 'the middle and industrious classes of the country'. The same phrase was later often used by Richard Cobden, the Lancashire calico printer, who became the leading spokesman for the rising commercial and manufacturing interests. This view tended not to include the professions within the middle classes.

Sir Charles Trevelyan, who was to achieve fame as the joint author of the reforms which turned the Civil Service from a field for aristocratic patronage into a proper middle-class profession, spoke rather of 'a class between the clergy and the legal and medical professions and the higher merchants on one side and the work people on the other . . . the class who carry out all our great industrial and marine operations'.[13]

The middle classes were also often defined as the possessors of the real wealth of the kingdom. Henry Brougham, a Whig politician who was a leading advocate of the enfranchisement and political emancipation of the middle classes, defined them in the House of Lords as 'the most numerous and by far the most wealthy order in the community: for if all your lordships' castles, manors, rights of warren and rights of chase, with all your broad acres, were brought to the hammer and sold at fifty years' purchase, the price would fly up and kick the beam when counterposed by the vast and solid riches of those middle classes, who are also the genuine depositaries of sober, rational, intelligent, and honest English feeling'. John Stuart Mill, the philosopher son of James Mill, pointed out that 'the virtues of a middle class are those which conduce to getting rich – integrity, economy, and enterprise – along with family affections, inoffensive conduct between man and man, and a disposition to assist one another, whenever no commercial rivalry intervenes'.[14]

This idea of the characteristic middle class attributes as wealth and industriousness displayed predominantly through manufacturing and commercial occupations remained dominant throughout the nineteenth century. There were two other commonly held conceptions of the middle classes, however. Largely as a result of the impact of evangelicalism, they were generally identified as the most respectable and moral element in society. Indeed the phrase 'middle and respectable classes' was almost as common as 'middle and industrious classes'. In a similar way the influence of utilitarianism created the idea of a link between middle classness and intellectual capacity. In 1798 the *Monthly Magazine* spoke of 'the middle ranks, in whom the great mass of information and of public and private virtues reside'. This conception of the middle classes as the main repositories of intelligence in the nation led to them being identified as the source of public opinion. 'The seat of public opinion,' the Whig politician Sir James Graham remarked in 1826, 'is in the middle ranks of life – in that numerous class, removed from the wants of labour and the cravings of ambition, enjoying the advantages of leisure, and possessing intelligence sufficient for the formation of a sound judgement, neither warped by interest nor obscured by passion.'[15]

All these highly flattering descriptions of the middle classes were put forward with one object: to press their claim for admission into the political establishment. Industrialization, evangelicalism and utilitarianism combined to produce an important common consciousness among the middle classes. They saw themselves as forming the most industrious, the wealthiest, the most respectable and the most intelligent part of the community, yet they were excluded from political power and influence. During the early nineteenth century this new consciousness was focused on a series of struggles to gain full political emancipation, of which the most important was the campaign to get the vote.

The claim of the middle classes to be admitted to the franchise was pressed by manufacturers, utilitarians and evangelicals alike. Gradually they convinced the Whig Party that it was both unfair and dangerous to keep a group with so much wealth, respectability and intelligence excluded from participation in the nation's affairs. The result was the Great Reform Act of 1832 which gave the vote in the boroughs to all male householders paying a yearly rental of £10 and in the counties to all freeholders with property valued at forty shillings a year. Lord Macaulay, one of the leading Whig advocates of the Act, described its object as being 'to admit the middle class to a large and direct share in the representation, without any violent shock to the institutions of the country'.[16]

It is easy to over-exaggerate the scope of the Great Reform Act. It added only about 500,000 men to the electorate out of a total population of about $13\frac{1}{2}$ million and left middle-class women and the lower middle class of small traders and clerks still disenfranchised. Moreover it was a long time before middle-class MPs came to be elected in any significant numbers. Nonetheless, the Act does mark a decisive step in the rise to political power of the bourgeoisie in England. As

Benjamin Disraeli, the Conservative politician, put it, 1832 brought about 'the monarchy of the middle class'.[17] From then on government had to take notice of the interests of this important section of society.

The next two decades saw the manufacturing and commercial middle classes gain in wealth and confidence. The railway mania of the 1840s made rich men of contractors and speculators like Thomas Brassey and George Hudson. On all sides the middle-class attack was joined against privilege and protection. John Bright, a cotton mill owner from Rochdale, Lancashire, led fellow Nonconformists against the system of Church rates which were compulsorily levied on all parishioners regardless of their own religious affiliations. Edward Miall, a Congregational minister, led a crusade for the disestablishment of the Church of England. Edward Baines, a Leeds newspaper proprietor, rallied manufacturers in a campaign against state involvement in the education of the poor and the regulation of conditions in factories on the grounds that these matters were much better left to employers.

The loudest cry of the commercial and manufacturing middle classes in the 1830s and 1840s was for free trade and their greatest battle was against the hold of the protectionist agricultural interest in Parliament. The campaign to abolish the corn laws, which ended triumphantly in 1846, was a direct struggle between the up-and-coming middle classes and the traditional landed aristocracy. The former held that the laws, which kept out foreign wheat even when it was cheaper than the home crop, denied the natural cereal-growing countries of eastern and southern Europe free access to the British market and so restricted their ability to buy Britain's manufactured goods.

It was not surprising that it was those engaged in Britain's largest export industry, cotton textiles, based in the towns and valleys around Manchester, who, led by Cobden and Bright, were in the forefront of the campaign to abolish the corn laws. The agitation was organized in a highly efficient way, with carefully orchestrated public meetings, poster and leaflet campaigns and lobbying of Parliament. Reflecting on its ultimate success, Cobden wrote:

It has eminently been a middle-class agitation. We have carried it
on by those means by which the middle class usually carries on its
movements. We have had our meetings of dissenting ministers; we
have obtained the co-operation of the ladies; we have resorted to
tea parties, and taken those pacific means for carrying out our
views, which mark us rather as a middle class set of agitators.[18]

The Anti-Corn Law League was in many ways the prototype of
that very British and very middle-class institution, the pressure
group. There had been earlier examples, the most successful
being the various evangelical dominated organizations which
were involved in the campaign to abolish first the slave trade
and later slavery itself in the British Empire. But it was in the
1840s and 1850s that pressure groups really became widespread and effective as the Nonconformist manufacturing
middle classes organized themselves to achieve their emancipation and break the hold of the Anglican landed aristocracy
on the institutions of government and society.

Within the professions there was a similar mood of growing
self-confidence as the hold of old aristocratic practices and
prejudices was gradually loosened. During the eighteenth
century the professions had been based on status rather than
occupation. Only the higher clergy, physicians and barristers
were considered members of the liberal professions and they
were recruited almost exclusively from the sons of the
aristocracy and higher gentry. Curates, surgeons, apothecaries
and attorneys (as solicitors were known until 1874) were
regarded as little above tradesmen. Small matters of manner
and style defined membership of a profession. Physicians, for
example, wrote their prescriptions in Latin and left the
dispensing of them to others. Apothecaries, by contrast, who
acted as doctors to the mass of the population, wrote their
prescriptions in English and dispensed them themselves.

It was during the first half of the nineteenth century that the
professions came to assume their modern form as middle-class
occupations based on the mastery and application of some
specialized body of learning tested by examination and
recognized by diploma. Following on from the evangelical
revival, the High Church Oxford Movement in the 1830s
established the Church as a serious professional vocation
rather than just a congenial and relatively idle life for the

younger sons of the nobility. In 1845 the first proper theological college was established at Cuddesdon to train ordinands for their new responsibilities. Several of the great professional associations date from this period. The Royal College of Surgeons was founded in 1800, the Institution of Civil Engineers in 1818, and the British Medical Association started life as the Provincial Medical and Surgical Association in 1832. The Law Society was set up in 1825 and eleven years later it supervised the first examinations ever held for any branch of the legal profession. The Inns of Court followed suit in 1851 when they set up the Council for Legal Education, although examinations for barristers were not compulsory until 1872.

The development of the principle of self-regulation by professional associations of the standards and ethical conduct of their members can be seen particularly clearly in the development of the medical profession. The Apothecaries Act of 1815 gave the Society of Apothecaries power to determine entry into their profession, to hold examinations and to prevent those who were not qualified from calling themselves apothecaries. In 1858 the Medical Act created a register of general medical practitioners who had satisfied one of more than twenty-one existing licensing and examining bodies that they were fit to practise medicine. The register was kept by a General Council of Medical Education (later the General Medical Council) which had the power to strike off those guilty of misconduct. These two measures are generally taken to mark the emergence of the modern general practitioner. They established a model for the development of the professions, with the state recognizing the rights of each profession to rule itself and examine itself with only minimal interference from outside.

Only two professions still remained closed to the middle classes in the mid-nineteenth century. The armed forces and the civil service jealously guarded their systems of patronage and kept themselves as aristocratic preserves. The upper classes' hold over service commissions was to be breached in the early 1870s. The assault on the civil service began earlier with the formation of a pressure group similar to the Anti-Corn Law League. In 1855 a group of professional and business men under the chairmanship of Samuel Morley, a textile manufacturer, set up the Administrative Reform Association to draw attention to the corruption and incompetence of the prevailing system of government. They called for the disciplines of the counting house to be applied to Whitehall and for appointments to the Civil Service to be made on the basis of merit rather than patronage by means of competitive examination.

The same proposals were made in the report produced by Sir Stafford Northcote and Sir Charles Trevelyan, assistant secretary of the Treasury, in 1855. Both men were strongly influenced by both evangelicalism and utilitarianism in demanding a more efficient civil service and a purer ethic in public life. Their report, which extolled the virtues of industry and merit against indolence and dilettantism, open competition against aristocratic patronage, and efficiency and thrift against waste and extravagance, has been described as 'a manifesto of the rising bourgeoisie in mid-nineteenth-century Britain'.[19]

It was to be some time before official recognition was extended to those other than the three learned professions. The 1851 census classified only clergymen, lawyers and doctors as members of the professions. By 1861 teachers, civil engineers, actors, authors, journalists, artists and musicians were included, and by 1881, architects, land agents, surveyors and merchant navy officers. Although in the mid-nineteenth century, it was still largely of manufacturers and businessmen that people thought when they talked about the middle classes, the professions were beginning to be recognized as an equally important group and did not lack their champions. In 1859 one observer noted that 'They form the head of the great English middle class, maintain its tone of independence, keep up to the mark its standard of morality and direct its intelligence.'[20]

It was not, of course, just middle-class consciousness which developed in early nineteenth century Britain. The advent of the factory system and of wage bargaining produced a new collective sense among the working classes as well. Initially, the two marched together. Philosophic Radicals advocated a universal suffrage and the Anti-Corn Law Leaguers carried working men with them by arguing that repeal would mean cheaper bread. During the 1830s and 1840s, however, the working classes became increasingly conscious of a cleavage of interests between themselves and the middle classes. Still excluded from the franchise, they saw manufacturers in Parliament resisting legislation to improve their working conditions and to increase state provision in the fields of education and health.

Working-class discontent came to a head in the Chartist movement of the 1840s which demanded manhood suffrage, the abolition of property qualifications for MPs and the payment of salaries to MPs. For a time the Chartists co-operated with the Anti-Corn Law League, but when it became clear that the League was not interested in pursuing other working-class demands and was merely using the Chartists to widen the basis of support for its own narrow cause, they broke away, bitter and disillusioned. 'What is our present relation to you as a section of the middle class?' a group of Chartists in the North East asked Leaguers who had requested their co-operation. 'It is one of violent opposition. You are the holders of power, participation in which you refuse us.'[21]

By the middle of the nineteenth century it was clear to perceptive contemporaries that in pulling themselves up to a position where they seriously challenged the influence and power of the ruling aristocracy, the middle classes had increased rather than narrowed the gap between themselves and the working classes. In 1845 Disraeli wrote in *Sybil* of the emergence in Britain of two nations of rich and poor 'between whom there is no intercourse and no sympathy'. Three years later Karl Marx wrote his *Communist Manifesto* to show that the history of all society is the history of class struggle and to call on the workers of the world to unite against the bourgeoisie.

The middle classes were certainly consolidating power fast. Sir Robert Peel, the son of a Lancashire cotton manufacturer, who abolished the Corn Laws and contained the Chartist threat, can perhaps be regarded as the first middle-class Prime Minister of Britain, although two earlier premiers, Henry Addington (1801–1804), the son of a doctor, and George Canning (1827), also have some claim to that title. He also came near to being leader of the first predominantly middle-class British political party. When he found himself deserted by most of his Tory followers for betraying the landed interest over the Corn Laws in 1846, Richard Cobden wrote to him: 'Do you shrink from governing through *bona fide* representatives of the middle class? Look at the facts and can the country be otherwise ruled at all? There must be an end of the juggle of parties, the mere representatives of tradition, and some man must of necessity rule the state through its governing classes. The Reform Bill decreed it: the passing of the Corn Bill has realized it.' A contemporary observer noted that the object of Cobden and Bright was 'to form a middle class administration in contradistinction to the aristocratic element which had hitherto predominated in the government of the country'. Peel did not, in fact, take up the challenge and he died four years later. However, his ablest lieutenant, William Ewart Gladstone, was later to lead a new political party of the kind Cobden and Bright had envisaged.[22]

The Victorian Liberal Party which grew up in the 1850s and became an effective political force in the 1860s was the first distinctively middle-class party in Britain. Admittedly in Parliament and in government it was heavily dependent on Whig aristocrats, but the bedrock of its support were the up-and-coming middle classes who found themselves excluded from the political, social and religious establishment. The pressure groups of the 1840s and 1850s formed the nucleus of the Liberal Party and the demands of the middle classes, for free trade, cheap government, minimal legislative interference in economic and industrial matters, administrative reform, the opening of careers to talent and the removal of the privileges enjoyed by the Church of England, constituted the main planks of Liberal policy.

It is true that the Liberals were also to take up certain working-class causes such as universal manhood suffrage. But that was because they were convinced that a wider franchise would, in fact, confirm and consolidate middle-class rule. Underlying Victorian Liberalism was the assumption not just that the middle classes were the best people to rule the land but also that the working classes accepted them as such. That assumption proved to be correct and was only shaken at the end of the century.

5

The Victorian Heyday

By 1869, the mid-way point in Queen Victoria's reign, middle-class rule had well and truly arrived in England. Gladstone's first Liberal Government was firmly committed to the principles of cheap government, minimal interference by the state and opening up careers to talent. Two of its proudest achievements were to be the enactment of the principles of the Trevelyan-Northcote report so that entry into the Civil Service was established on the basis of competitive examination, and the abolition of the system of purchasing commissions in the Army. It held income tax at only sixpence in the pound. Gladstone regarded even that as dangerously high and in 1874 he was to go to the country on a platform of abolishing income tax completely. Rather surprisingly, an electorate that was frightened about the consequences of so bold a step rejected him.

In his book *Culture and Anarchy*, published in 1869, Matthew Arnold summed up the Liberal dream, which he saw rapidly coming true, as 'the legislation of middle-class Parliaments, the local self-government of middle-class vestries, the unrestricted competition of middle-class industrialists, the dissidence of middle-class Dissent and the Protestantism of middle-class Protestantism'. That was in many ways an accurate description of mid-Victorian England. In politics, as the leading authority on the constitution, Walter Bagehot, commented, 'The sovereign authority is the diffused respectable higher middle class, which on the whole predominates in the House of Commons.' In business, industrialists pursued their aims of profit making and also their philanthropic activities, unfettered by either government interference or strong trade unionism. Like 'the princely merchant in his counting house', they enjoyed considerable status and power in the community.[1]

In society as a whole the values and morals of the middle classes had come to predominate. As early as 1840 John Stuart Mill observed that 'The daily actions of every peer and peeress are falling more and more under the yoke of bourgeois opinion.' By 1867 Bagehot noted that 'The aristocracy live in fear of the middle classes – of the grocer and the merchant. They dare not frame a society of enjoyment, as the French aristocracy once formed it.'[2]

Benjamin Disraeli, who never really liked the English middle classes, indicated the strength of the hold which their moral views had in the country as a whole in an exchange between two aspiring politicians in his novel *Coningsby*:

> 'I tell you what, Mr Taper, the time is gone by when a Marquess of Monmouth was Letter A, No. 1.'
>
> 'Very true, Mr Tadpole. A wise man would do well now to look to the great middle class, as I said the other day to the electors of Shabbyton.'
>
> 'I had sooner be supported by the Wesleyans,' said Mr Tadpole, 'than by all the Marquesses in the peerage.'

It is possible to over-exaggerate the influence and importance of the middle classes in Victorian England. In the opening chapter of his classic work, *The Making of Victorian England*, Professor George Kitson Clark warned of the dangers of attributing to them trends and developments to which many who were palpably not middle-class contributed. He also pointed out that the Victorian middle class was an extremely heterogeneous body, embracing at one end city bankers and large industrialists with incomes from investments and profits of more than £500 a year, and at the other small shopkeepers and clerks with annual earnings of only £50.

Accepting those provisos, however, it is still possible to make certain broad generalizations. The first is that the middle classes were growing rapidly in both numbers and wealth. Charles Booth, the pioneer social scientist and statistician, calculated on the basis of census data that the number of those engaged in middle-class occupations virtually doubled, from 887,000 to 1,640,000, between 1851 and 1881. Perhaps even more significantly, they increased from 10·4 per cent to 13·8 per cent of the total working population. The most spectacular growth occurred in the professions and among clerks, accountants and others engaged in commerce. The economic historian J. A. Banks has calculated on the basis of income tax returns that the middle classes did disproportionately well out of the mid-Victorian economic boom.[3]

The level of annual earnings above which income tax was levied – £100 from 1854 to 1875, and £150 from 1875 to 1894 – gives a reasonable starting point for middle-class incomes. Although most junior clerks in offices and counting houses started below it, at between £70 and £80, they usually rose to salaries of between £100 and £200 with a few senior clerks earning £300. A statistician in 1869 described £300 as a 'small mercantile income' and as the average amount that a doctor might have left after deducting £100 expenses from his gross earnings. £500 was regarded as a reasonable upper middle class income for 'a professional man or tradesman (who) might live in a house at £50 rent and keep three women servants'. Salaries of £1000 and more were exceptional although senior civil servants and judges were at that level.[4]

There were obviously considerable differences between the activities and environments of those who earned only £100 and those with £1000 a year. It is possible, however, to see the emergence of a distinct and common lifestyle among the mid-Victorian middle classes. In many ways, it is the lifestyle which continues to distinguish the English middle classes today – a complex product of physical environment, patterns of behaviour and mental attitudes.

At its heart was home ownership. The possession of a house was one indisputable sign of middle classness. It might be a substantial mansion set in its own large garden, or it might only be a small terraced 'two up and two down'. However humble, it was immaculately kept and proudly cherished and, like Mr Pickwick's residence in Dulwich, 'fitted up with every attention to substantial comfort; perhaps to a little elegance besides . . . the lawn in front, the garden behind, the miniature conservatory, the dining-room, the drawing-room, the bed-room, the smoking-room, and above all the study with its pictures and easy chairs and odd cabinets and queer tables and books out of number'.

Typically, the homes of the urban middle classes were situated, like Mr Pickwick's, in some pleasant residential suburb well away from the offices where their owners worked. The development of an extensive suburban railway network established the middle-class practice of commuting to work every day. While factory workers tended to live close to their work, those in white-collar jobs often lived some miles away.

Houses like Mr Pickwick's also satisfied and confirmed another middle class demand – that their homes should be private. Gardens surrounded by substantial walls or hedges separated them from those of the neighbours, just as curtains and shutters kept out the gaze of vulgar passers-by in the street. As a result, and by deliberate choice, the middle class were much more rooted in their homes than the working classes. Their lives centred on the hearth and the parlour and did not spill out into pubs or on to the street.

Running the home properly became a major preoccupation. It produced the new science of domestic economy expounded most comprehensively by Mrs Isabella Mary Beeton in her book *Household Management* in 1859 and developed by her hundreds of followers. The keeping of domestic servants, a practice which Mrs Beeton took for granted and indeed regarded as central to proper household management, was an essential feature of the middle-class lifestyle, and an important indicator of status. It not only showed a certain level of material prosperity, but also established a clear master-servant relationship within the household with the presence of domestics working in the basement and sleeping in the attic reinforcing the social status of the family living in between. It was not surprising that when he made his famous survey of poverty in York at the end of the century, Seebohm Rowntree took the keeping of domestic servants as marking the division between the middle and working classes.

The expansion in the number of living-in domestic servants in the mid-nineteenth century is one of the surest signs of the growing size and wealth of the middle classes. In 1851 there were 900,000 (13·3 per cent of the working population), and by 1871 1,400,000 (15·8 per cent), the largest single occupational group recorded in the census. A proportion of the increase can be accounted for by families taking on additional servants.

Three (a cook, housemaid and nursemaid) were regarded as necessary for complete household management, although with annual wages of £20 or so each, one was all that many middle-class families could afford.

Although annual summer holidays to the seaside and weekend visits to beauty spots in the country were developing features of this period, home remained the centre for most recreational activities. The parlour poems of Lewis Carroll and Henry Wadsworth Longfellow and the songs of Arthur Sullivan and M. W. Balfe which were recited or sung around the hearth formed a middle-class equivalent to the oral folk traditions of working-class communities. Even today there are many middle-class children who can recite the opening lines of *Father William* and the *Jabberwock* and sing a few snatches of *HMS Pinafore*, although there cannot be more than a handful now who are familiar with *Excelsior* or *Casabianca* (better known by its first line 'The boy stood on the burning deck') which were once part of the standard repertoire of parlour recitals and school concerts.

Those stirring and sentimental verses and ballads, with their undisguised moralism and their comforting certainties, were a part of a middle-class culture which also embraced the music of Stanford and Stainer, the paintings of Landseer and Frith, the essays of Macaulay, and the novels of Trollope and Thackeray. Their work had much in common: it was straightforward, careful, occasionally perhaps a little fussy and florid. Above all, it was clean and decent, suitable for performance, reproduction or reading in the sanctity of the home and in the bosom of the family. They could all say, as Trollope did, that they 'had not written a line which a pure woman could not read without a blush'.

The importance of maintaining propriety in the parlour shows the pervasive hold of middle-class morality, that strange phenomenon that still fascinates observers of English society. It was in the Victorian period that the middle classes took on their high seriousness and concern with moral rectitude. There was, of course, a considerable difference between outward appearance and actual practice. Most middle-class fathers took their families off to church every Sunday. The organizers of the religious census taken one Sunday in 1851, which found that around half the population attended some place of worship, commented that 'the middle classes have augmented rather than diminished that devotional sentiment and strictness of attention to religious services by which, for several centuries, they have so eminently been distinguished'.[5] Surveys of a rather different kind by social historians suggest that at the very least a substantial minority of those same fathers had regular recourse to prostitutes or engaged in secret sexual relations with their servants. Yet that finding only serves to confirm the powerful hold of middle-class morality. Why else the need for the double life, the public profession of high seriousness and the private peccadillo?

Victorian middle-class morality had a number of different roots. Genuine religious conviction played an important part. There was widespread adherence to Christianity and the core of its moral teaching. The demands and experience of work encouraged a distaste for idle frivolity and extravagance, and a respect for hard work, steady application, regulation and sobriety. Class factors were also important. The middle classes had asserted their claim to play a dominant role in society through proving their superiority over both the aristocracy and the lower orders in moral as much as in intellectual or economic terms.

Respectability, in fact, became the great middle-class status symbol. Proper observance of the Sabbath, dignified and restrained behaviour in public, and avoidance of lewdness and vulgarity, were not just matters dictated by religion and prudence. They were also as much signs of social rank as owning your own house or keeping servants.

The institution of family prayers, common among the majority of middle-class families at the time, shows the combination of factors that made the Victorian middle classes so serious. At one level, it was an expression of genuine religious conviction, particularly in evangelical homes where it was the central expression of the family's faith. At another, it reinforced the hierarchy of the household, with the pater-familias firmly at the top. That aspect is well illustrated by the ritual which the writer H. W. Nevinson remembered from his boyhood in the 1860s in a sizeable house in Hampstead. The butler would ring a brass bell at 8.30 each morning. All of the family would then file through one door into the sitting-room and, when they were seated, all the servants would file through another, the housekeeper first and the butler last. Each person in order of seniority would then read a verse of the chosen chapter of the Bible and the head of the household would provide a commentary at the end. In this way, they progressed from Genesis to Revelation, omitting only the Psalms, Levitical laws, genealogies and indecent passages.

Family prayers were also an indication of social class and status. When the Provost of King's College, Cambridge, wrote in a circular letter to undergraduates about morning chapel in 1869 that 'You, most of you, come from homes where family prayers are the custom,' he was making an implied comment about their social as well as their religious position.[6] As the secularist Walter Besant observed of his middle-class childhood in London in the 1850s:

> At that time great was the power and authority of seriousness. To be serious was to be fashionable, if one may say so, in City circles. Respectability was nearly always serious: it was divided into two classes: that which had morning prayers only and that which had evening prayers as well.[7]

If having family prayers was important in establishing middle-class status, then sending sons to public school was even more so. The way in which the public school system was developed to provide a distinctive middle-class education is one of the most interesting aspects of Victorian social history, and one which has left an enduring mark on English society.

In the early years of the nineteenth century there were only nine recognized public schools: Eton, Winchester, Rugby, Harrow, Westminster, St Paul's, Charterhouse, Merchant Taylors' and Shrewsbury. They catered almost exclusively for the upper classes. The middle classes either sent their sons to the local endowed grammar school or taught them at home, if, indeed, they gave them any education beyond the elementary stage. They had little time for what they took to be the outdated classical syllabus and aristocratic overtones of the public schools and tended to prefer the modern subjects offered by Benthamite establishments like the Hills' School at Hazelwood and University College School, London.

What changed this attitude was a growing snobbishness coupled with the reform of the public schools associated with Thomas Arnold, the headmaster of Rugby from 1828 to 1842. Arnold's aim was to make public schools instruments which would fuse the middle classes with the aristocracy, and curb the raw materialism of industrialists and tradesmen by inculcating in them the ideal of the Christian gentleman. His prescription of godliness and good learning fitted the middle classes' demands both for a Christian upbringing for their sons and for an education that would equip them to cope with the new competitive examinations for entry into the professions. Believing that schools should be self-governing republics where boys could learn the values of responsibility and duty in their own world, Arnold also maintained that it was only when separated from their parents that the sons of mill-owners and merchants could have their rough edges rounded off and develop their characters. By 1850 the public boarding school had established itself as the only proper place of education for those who wanted either to maintain or to attain upper middle class status.

The spread of the railways made possible the boarding education that Arnold's work and writings had made fashionable. It was no accident that several of the new schools set up on the Arnoldian model were sited near stations on recently constructed railway lines. They included Cheltenham (1841), Marlborough (1843), Clifton and Haileybury (both 1862). Two schools, Wellington (1853) and Radley (1847) had stations built on existing lines primarily to serve them.

Two specific attempts to establish a national network of public schools show how class-based the whole movement was, although the direct motivation in both cases was religious. In 1848 Nathaniel Woodard, a curate at Shoreham, Sussex, published a 'Plea for the Middle Classes'. He was concerned at the large number of middle-class Dissenters and saw the creation of a network of High Church boarding schools as a way of bringing them into the Anglican fold. At the same time, his plan of campaign showed that he was also extremely conscious of the importance of maintaining class distinctions.

Woodard saw three distinct groups within the middle classes which should be kept separate for educational purposes so that they would not contaminate one another. Accordingly, he set about creating three types of school, each with a different level of fees, a different curriculum and a different leaving age. His first school, started in Shoreham in 1848 but later moved to Lancing, charged fees of £30 a year and was designed to cater for the sons of noblemen, clergymen, professional men and others in the upper middle classes. His second, Hurstpierpoint, was started in 1850 for the sons of tradesmen, farmers and clerks, with annual fees of eighteen guineas. The third was established at Ardingly in 1870 for the sons of shopkeepers, farmers, mechanics and lower clerks, with fees of only thirteen guineas a year. These three schools made up Woodard's Southern division. He hoped to give every region of England a similar tripartite system of boarding schools. In fact, he never managed to complete his network but he did establish several other schools including Taunton, Denstone and Worksop College.

A similarly ambitious and unfulfilled plan to cover the country with public schools was conceived by J. L. Brereton, a pupil of Arnold's at Rugby and rector of a village in Devon. Brereton wanted to establish public schools in every English county together with a county college for more advanced study and a new college attached to Cambridge University at the apex of the whole system. Like Woodard, he proposed three grades of school for the different groups within the middle classes. Although he himself was unable to establish many schools, several were set up along the lines he had advocated, including Framlingham as the East Anglia county school and Bedford County School. In 1865 the Surrey County School was opened in premises less than a mile from the railway station at Cranleigh, 'to provide a sound and plain education in accordance with the principles of the Church of England and on the public school system . . . for the sons of persons engaged in farming, trading and other occupations'. At the school speech day in 1867 Sir Stafford Northcote, Secretary of State for India, commented that it only needed a chapel to make 'this institution what it ought to be, a great Church of England Middle Class College in this part of the country'.[8]

The government took a similar class-based view of education. In 1864 a commission was appointed under the chairmanship of Lord Taunton to examine the state of education 'for those large classes of English society which are comprised between the humblest and the very highest'. It was charged specifically to look at the old endowed grammar schools which existed in many towns and gave free education to local children.

Like Woodard and Brereton, the commission recommended that there should be three types of school in England for the middle classes: proprietary boarding schools aiming to get their pupils to university and catering for the children of the upper middle and professional classes, those with large unearned incomes, businessmen and poorer gentry; day schools to be established in every town with more than five thousand inhabitants with a leaving age of sixteen to prepare the sons of the mercantile classes, larger shopkeepers, rising men of business and substantial tenant farmers for careers in the Army, the legal profession, the civil service and engineering; and finally schools with a leaving age of fourteen catering for the children of small tenant farmers, small tradesmen and superior artisans.

The commission was implacably opposed to mixing different social classes in the old endowed schools. It recommended the abolition of the traditional free places given to local children and their replacement by a system of scholarship based on merit. These recommendations were accepted by the government and the 1869 Endowed Schools Act enabled old endowed grammar schools like Sherborne, Tonbridge and Dulwich, which had been founded to give free education to poor local boys, to become middle-class public boarding schools open to the sons of fee-paying parents throughout the country.

The fate of the endowed grammar schools shows very clearly an aspect of the strength of the English middle classes which is still much in evidence today, namely their knack of taking over and fashioning for their own purposes an institution originally designed to serve those less well-off. In the 1850s the method of entrance to Oxford and Cambridge universities underwent a similar transformation from its original purpose with the poverty clauses which had traditionally governed the award of scholarships and exhibitions being replaced by competitive examination. As a result, it has been calculated that fewer working-class boys went to university in the second half of the nineteenth century than in any period before or since.

The public school system provided a self-contained world where middle-class boys, and a smaller number of girls, grew up uncontaminated by the influences of the opposite sex or the lower orders. Many of the characteristic traits of the English middle classes can be at least partially explained by their early and total immersion in that system. Their reluctance to go into industry or trade, for example, is partly the result of the successful implantation of one important aspect of Arnold's ideal of Christian gentility. 'No person shall be considered as eligible who shall not be moving in the circle of Gentlemen,' Cheltenham's first prospectus for parents announced, 'no retail trader being allowed in any circumstances to be so considered.'[9] Another successful strand of the Arnoldian scheme has ensured that until very recently most members of the middle classes have been considerably more familiar with the classics than with modern science. Their total segregation from girls has made many public schoolboys shy and awkward in their relationships with the opposite sex, while their equal segregation from working-class boys has perpetuated and aggravated the English class system.

Admittedly the public school ethos developed in ways which Arnold had not intended. His ideal of Christian gentility was taken out of the classics and the chapel where he had rooted it and transplanted into the changing room where it sprouted in the shape of muscular Christianity. Similarly, the Arnoldian notion of community became transformed into an intense camaraderie which sometimes bordered on the homosexual. Both processes can be followed in that peculiarly English literary genre, the public school novel, which starts with Thomas Hughes' *Tom Brown's Schooldays* (1857), set in Arnold's Rugby, and still continues today. The favourite during my own schooldays in the mid-1960s, I remember, was *Lord Dismiss Us*, a story of homosexual crushes set in some minor public school on the South coast.

However distorted their original ideals, the public schools still had an enormous and enduring effect in fashioning the future lives of their pupils. The notions of duty and service, team spirit and fair play were carried by the Victorian upper middle classes from the chapels, classrooms and playing fields of their boyhoods into the professional, administrative and commercial careers of adult life. Above all, perhaps, they fired and sustained the Colonial Service which developed as one of the great middle class careers in the latter half of the nineteenth century. Men were inspired to go out and work in the Empire for a mixture of motives – evangelical fervour to convert the heathen, restlessness with the familiar scene at home, desire for gain and glory. At the root of many a young colonial administrator's decision to leave home and make his career abroad, however, lay values which he had learned at his public school.

Some schools, like the Imperial Services College at Haileybury and the United Services College at Westward Ho!, were specifically created to prepare their pupils for careers in the Empire. But others were no less successful in performing the same role. The unmistakable stamp of the public school system is imprinted throughout that distinctive sub-species of the English middle classes, colonial society, with its language of 'pukkah' and 'tiffin', its literature which ranges from Kipling and Henty to E. M. Forster and Leonard Woolf, and its curious customs of playing croquet and cricket in the sticky heat of the Tropics and building Anglican churches in the midst of Muslim cities or heathen jungles.

Not everyone looked favourably on the public schools, however. Matthew Arnold, Thomas's son, felt that the whole system involved the middle classes in paying for social advantage rather than real education. He saw an urgent need to establish in England what every other civilized country had, a state system of secondary education which would develop the intellectual and spiritual capacities of the whole population.

Matthew Arnold was one of a small band of intellectuals who criticized the dominant ethic of the English middle classes in their mid-Victorian heyday. These critics were the precursors of the *Guardian* readers on the 8.23 train from Poundford. They were themselves solidly bourgeois in their origins and lifestyle, none more so than the man who saw himself engaged in 'holy warfare' with the middle classes, the socialist artist and poet William Morris, who was only able to devote himself to his crusade against capitalism because of an annual unearned income of £900 which he inherited at the age of twenty-one as the result of his businessman father's successful speculation in mining shares.

These critics' first charge against the middle classes – and by that term they, like others, tended to mean those in industry and commerce rather than in the professions – was that they were narrowly materialistic. 'Your middle class has an enjoyment in its business, we admit,' Arnold wrote in 1866 in his essay *My Countrymen*, 'and gets on well in business, and makes money, but beyond that?' In the same essay he listed the three qualities that went to make up 'a natural, rational life in the modern world' as 'the love of industry, trade and wealth, the love of the things of the mind, and the love of beautiful things'. He went on, 'Of these three factors of modern life, your middle class has no notion of any one, but the first.'[10]

Others made the same point. John Morley, a Liberal journalist and politician, wrote a scathing essay on *Middle Class Morality* in which he observed that 'the great pursuit of the English middle class is the search after money, and next to this, the search after position. The average member of the middle class first wants to be very rich, and then he wants to know lords.' Thomas Carlyle denounced the middle-class gospel of mammonism with its belief that financial dealing was the most important form of relationship between human beings. 'Can the middle class regenerate themselves?' William Morris asked rhetorically. 'I doubt it: their own creation, the commerce they are so proud of, has become their masters.'[11]

These critics objected to the middle classes' acquisitive pursuit of wealth on both moral and intellectual grounds. They argued that the competitive business ethic led to selfishness and exploitation of other men who were regarded simply as tools for profit-making.

They also complained that the middle classes' concentration on material things turned them away from matters of the mind and the spirit. This was the central theme of Matthew Arnold's *Culture and Anarchy* which designated the middle class as philistines:

> Philistine gives the notion of something particularly stiff-necked and perverse in the resistance to light and its children; and therein

> it specially suits our middle class, who not only do not pursue
> sweetness and light, but who even prefer to them that sort of
> machinery of business, chapels, tea meetings and addresses . . .
> which makes up the dismal and illiberal life on which I have so
> often touched.[12]

John Morley inveighed in similar vein about what might be
called the Gradgrind mentality of the middle classes, keen to
banish all imagination and fantasy from their lives and
demanding instead only the useful and practical:

> Their contempt for ideas, being measured by the ignorance of
> them, is enormous and profound. They look upon disinterested-
> ness as the dream of sentimental novelists. A man who would
> sacrifice a thousand a year for a theoretic principle is a fool who
> will justly end his days in the lunatic department of a workhouse.
> A poet is a person who writes for young ladies, and manufactures
> ornaments for the dining-room walls. Historians, biographers,
> and essayists are over-rated and over-paid people who supplement
> the work of the cabinet-maker who supplied the bookcase.[13]

No less objectionable to their critics than the philistinism of the
middle classes was their puritanism. 'Drugged with business,'
Arnold observed, 'your middle class seems to have its sense
blunted for any stimulus besides, except religion; it has a
religion narrow, unintelligent, repulsive.'[14] John Stuart Mill,
in other respects a champion and admirer of the middle classes,
was exceedingly unhappy about this one aspect of their make-
up. His great essay *On Liberty* warned his contemporaries of
the serious danger that the middle classes would impose their
puritanical ideas on drink, Sunday observance and sex on the
community as a whole.

How justified were these criticisms? It is certainly true that
many manufacturers and traders were interested in making
money, but they often genuinely believed that this was the best
way of furthering the general good of the community. In
building up their businesses they were creating jobs and
improving general living standards in a direct way.
Materialistic the Victorian middle classes may have been, but
they were certainly not indifferent to the needs of those less
well-off than themselves. *The Times* reported in 1855 that
charitable giving in London alone exceeded the national
budgets of Denmark, Portugal, Sweden or the Swiss Con-

federation, while a survey of middle-class families in the 1890s found that on average they expended 10·7 per cent of their income on charity, more than they spent on servants' wages, rent, clothing or any other item except food.

It is true that many employers resisted the idea that the state should act to protect their workers. They did so partly out of self-interest but also because they had a temperamental aversion to legislative intervention and compulsion and a preference for voluntary action and self-help. There were manufacturers and mill-owners who treated their workers cruelly but there were many more who looked after them, and encouraged them to look after themselves, not because of any directive from the state but because of their own sense of responsibility and duty.

It is true also that the middle classes were inclined to be philistine, to prefer *Punch* or Macaulay's history to Goethe or Hugo, parlour songs and ballads to Beethoven or Keats. But philistinism in that sense is the state of most of the people most of the time and it is possible to argue that there was, in fact, a higher level of cultural interest and awareness among the Victorian middle classes than among any comparable group before or since. They sustained a serious quarterly periodical literature, the like of which certainly does not exist in our own day, and in the absence of television, radio and gramophones, they were participators rather than passive spectators or listeners. There were few middle-class homes which did not possess a copy of Palgrave's *Golden Treasury of Songs and Lyrics* and a collection of pieces by Chopin or Mendelssohn on top of the piano.

The Victorian middle classes also took a leading part in political, religious, philanthropic, sporting and social activities, both locally and nationally. They were the mainstay of the mass of voluntary organizations that sprang up in the nineteenth century to champion every conceivable cause, relieve every single distress and right every possible wrong. There were plenty of real-life equivalents of Miss Clack in Wilkie Collins's *The Moonstone*, stalwart supporter of the Mothers' Small Clothes Conversion Society which existed, 'as all serious people know, to rescue unredeemed fathers' trousers from the pawnbrokers and to prevent their resumption, on the part of irreclaimable parents, by abridging them immediately to suit the proportions of the innocent son', and of Mrs Pardiggle in Dickens's *Bleak House* who proudly listed her activities to all new acquaintances: 'I am a school lady, I am a visiting lady, I am a reading lady, I am a distributing lady, I am on the local linen box committee and many general committees, and my canvassing alone is very extensive.' It has been calculated that over half a million middle-class women were actively engaged in charitable and philanthropic work.[15] Theirs may have been lives of tea-meetings, chapel services and committees that Matthew Arnold so despised, but they were certainly not dull or inactive.

The philistinism of the middle classes arose from the same roots as their puritanism. They were unsure of their position, still climbing the social ladder, and so anxious to appear respectable, to play safe and to avoid dangerous excesses and enthusiasms. If they were rather suspicious of using their imagination and letting their minds soar too freely above the matter of fact, then that was partly because their work, and often their leisure time activities as well, demanded a constant attention to facts and solid application to the task in hand. It was not surprising that Richard Cobden should feel that there was more to be learned from the latest issue of *The Times* than from the works of Thucydides, just as it was not surprising that Samuel Morley, on the basis of his own rise to the position of hosiery magnate and knitwear king, should feel that life was one long competitive examination.

The uncertainty of their own position, and their experience of climbing the social ladder, inevitably made many rather class conscious. In the eighteenth century there had been an easy intimacy between the upper and working classes. High-born ladies had happily shared their beds with their maids on their travels. In the more self-conscious, puritanical atmosphere of the Victorian age the classes became more segregated and separated. Domestic servants used different staircases and washing facilities from their masters and mistresses. Accents became more distinguishable as the new middle classes dropped the regional inflexions of their parents in favour of the smoother pronunciation that they were taught at public school.

But if they were increasingly aware of their distance from the working classes, they were equally aware of their distance from the aristocracy. There was not as yet the desire to create an impression and ape the lifestyle of the upper classes which became a feature of the bourgeoisie at the end of the century. Most mid-Victorian manufacturers and merchants led sober, unostentatious, relatively simple lives, and shared John Bright's dislike of 'society, smart people, hot rooms, elaborate meals, and ceremonious observances'.[16] Those who were employers often lived in close proximity to their own workers. Only twenty-nine of the nine hundred and four mill-owners in Lancashire in the middle of the nineteenth century did not live in the same town as their mills. In the industrial areas of Britain at least, the great geographical and social gulf which was later to separate the classes was not yet fully apparent. Capitalists and labourers still worshipped in the same chapel, belonged to the same local Liberal association and took part in the same voluntary societies.

It was, indeed, noticeable that the harshest criticism of the Victorian middle classes came from those themselves within them and not from those below. At a time of rising prosperity it was still the fondest hope of every artisan that he, or at least his children, might rise into their ranks. 'Denounce the middle classes as you may,' a campaigner against the Corn Laws told a slightly hostile Chartist gathering, 'there is not a man among you worth a half-penny a week that is not anxious to elevate himself among them.'[17]

Even among their sternest critics there was a certain respect for their power and potential. Matthew Arnold conceded:

Mean and ignoble as our middle class looks, it has this capital virtue, it has seriousness. With frivolity, cultured or uncultured, you can do nothing; but with seriousness there is always hope . . . In a transformed middle class, in a middle class raised to a higher and more genial culture, we may find, not perhaps Jerusalem, but, I am sure, a notable stage towards it. In that great class, strong by its numbers, its energy, its industry, strong by its freedom from frivolity, in that class, liberalized by an ampler culture, admitted to a wider sphere of thought, living by larger ideas, with its provincialism dissipated, its intolerance cured, its pettiness pumped away, what a power there will be, what an element of new life for England.[18]

The middle classes were, in fact, to take their critics' strictures very much to heart. By the end of the nineteenth century they were well on the way to abandoning mammon worship and profit-seeking, shunning careers in business or industry for more gentlemanly callings, and casting off at least some of their philistinism and puritanism. In doing so, they became both weaker as a social force and more class conscious than they had been in their mid-Victorian heyday.

6

The Middle Classes
Lose Confidence

In an essay published in 1893, William Morris reflected that the real social product of the Industrial Revolution had been 'the final triumph of the middle classes, materially, intellectually and morally'. In the next revolution, he predicted, 'The middle class will in turn be absorbed into the proletariat, which will form a new society in which classes shall have ceased to exist.' Karl Marx had earlier sketched a rather different but equally pessimistic scenario for the future of the middle classes, that as 'the rich become richer and the poor poorer', they would be ground out 'between the upper and nether millstone'.[1]

These two fears – that either they would become proletarianized in a new classless society, or be squeezed out altogether by the combined might of those above and below – began to haunt the English middle classes during the last quarter of the nineteenth century. They were heightened by a sense that the heyday of the bourgeoisie was over. They were no longer the up-and-coming class advancing economically and they were also losing their social and political ascendancy. From 1880 onwards there was a steady fall in their relative economic position compared with that of other classes. The enfranchisement of two million working men in 1884 confirmed the trend begun in 1867 of widening the electorate to include the labouring masses. Although the middle classes remained the main repository of political power and authority, the claims of the numerically much stronger working classes were increasingly challenging their supremacy. 'It is the end of an epoch,' Lord Randolph Churchill observed in the late 1880s, 'the long domination of the middle classes, which had begun in 1832, had come to its close.'[2]

The one group within the middle classes that was in fact still up-and-coming at the end of the century only served to underline fears about proletarianization. The growing army of clerks who staffed the banks, insurance houses and trading companies which boomed in the new commercial revolution was precariously perched between middle-class and working-class status.

Between 1850 and 1910 clerks were by far the fastest growing occupational group. Their numbers rose from less than a hundred thousand to nearly a million and they increased from 0·8 per cent to 10·5 per cent of the total working population. In terms of their earnings it was doubtful if this growing army of clerical workers recruited as Britain turned from being an industrial to a service economy could be properly regarded as middle-class. Most were on salaries of between £75 and £100 a year, which put them on much the same level as manual workers with an average weekly wage of between 30 and 60 shillings. Some were even poorer, like Bob Cratchitt in Dickens's *A Christmas Carol* who received only fifteen shillings a week and had to make frequent visits to the pawnbroker to keep going. It was hardly surprising that a mid-nineteenth-century work, *The Social Position and Claims of Clerks and Book-Keepers Considered*, concluded that most of them could not meet the four essential requirements of middle classness: saving, providing children with a good education, giving to charity, and keeping servants.

Yet although in strict economic terms they belonged to the working classes, in lifestyle and in social pretension, the clerks were part of the middle classes. The tasks which they performed at work, filling in invoices, entering figures in ledgers, keeping wages sheets, copying letters and selling tickets, were not actually manual even if they were routine. Their uniform of white collar and black coat indicated their distance from the overalls and shirtsleeves of the manual worker. It also confirmed that it was with the middle classes that they worked, albeit in a rather servile capacity, handling their money in banks, keeping their accounts and representing them as commercial travellers.

For this new lower middle class, respectability was even more important than it had been for the mid-Victorian businessmen. It was essential for job success. The first handbook for clerks published in 1878 listed the qualities they required as 'patience, perseverance, courtesy, cheerfulness, and perhaps more than any other quality, a humble distrust of self and a deferential respect for the judgement of others'. It went on to add that the model clerk should be 'quiet and unassuming' in his clothing, should eschew eccentricities and individualistic manners, and pursue 'rational recreations', rather than theatre going or habitual novel reading which were 'as hurtful to the mind . . . as habitual dram drinking is to the body'.[3] Thus was the characteristic deference, conventionality and philistinism of the lower middle classes established. It was not surprising that William Morris should describe the new species as 'ill-housed, ill-educated, crushed by grovelling superstitions, lacking reasonable pleasures, entirely devoid of any sense of beauty'.[4]

Respectability was not only the passport to job success, it was also the way in which a group as marginal as the white-collar workers proved themselves members of the middle classes. It was by cultivating respectability that they maintained their distance from the masses. Hence the importance, after marrying and forsaking the cold comforts of a respectable lodging house or the YMCA, of moving to a home of one's own, however small, and however overlooked, in a suburb like Clapham, Peckham, Walthamstow, Kilburn or Battersea, where the poet Richard Church's parents struggled to maintain 'a small margin of safety between their respectable little home and the hungry ocean of violence whose thunder never left our ears'.[5]

Other manifestations of this craving for respectability were a horror of getting anything on credit, regular attendance at church or chapel, and a shunning of working-class institutions like public houses and trade unions. This was all part of upholding a morality and lifestyle that was thought to be middle-class and which was defied by those below. Bernard Shaw observed that when he was an estate agent's clerk in the 1870s, he would never have contemplated joining a trade union, had one existed:

> Not only would it have been considered a most ungentlemanly thing to do – almost as outrageous as coming to the office in corduroy trousers, with a belcher handkerchief around my neck –

but, snobbery apart, it would have been stupid, because I should not have intended to remain a clerk. I should have taken the employers' point of view from the first.[6]

The members of this new lower middle class were intensely class conscious. George Gissing, who worked as a clerk in Manchester, built several of his novels around the snobbery of white-collar workers. In *New Grub Street* (1891), the hero's wife leaves him after he tells her that he has taken rooms in Islington. She regards this as about as far as a consciously middle-class person can sink, and protests that such a move would degrade her. It is a curious irony that a hundred years later a move to Islington would indicate rising social status and 'gentrification'. In 1896 Alfred Harmsworth created a newspaper for the new class of office workers which brilliantly exploited their class consciousness. The *Daily Mail* was a penny paper that sold for a halfpenny, a popular paper that looked like a quality. It has remained ever since a faithful barometer of lower middle class taste – conventional, conservative, and titillating without ever quite becoming vulgar.

The classic picture of the lifestyle of this new class at the end of the nineteenth century is, of course, George and Weedon Grossmith's *Diary of a Nobody*, first published in book form in 1892 after being serialized in *Punch*. Mr Pooter, the City clerk who chronicles his dull but wholesome life at the Laurels, Brickfield Terrace, Holloway, has all the attributes of the species. He is over-keen to please his superiors at work, ever concerned to show his superiority over tradesmen, extremely careful with money, shocked at his son's loose and extravagant ways, and very prudish about verses in songs. He has an intense pride in his home and a desire to beautify it with such tasteless monstrosities as the plaster of Paris stag's head which he buys to hang on the wall of the hall. He is also determined to be accepted in society, and attributes deep social significance to such trivial matters as the vicar's request to take round the collecting plate at church. Two events stand out as the high-points in his life. One is his invitation to the Lord Mayor's Ball at the Mansion House for the representatives of trade and commerce, an experience somewhat marred when he discovers his ironmonger is also present and when his own name is left out of the list of those attending printed in the *Blackfriars Bi-Weekly News*. The other is the presentation to him by the Principal in his firm of the freehold of his house in recognition of his sterling services.

The emergence of the Pooters in such large numbers made the established middle class more snobbish than they had been. 'Lower middle class' became a term of abuse almost worse than working class. Sir Joseph Porter in Gilbert and Sullivan's *HMS Pinafore* (1878) felt compelled to remind Captain Corcoran that he 'occupied a station in the lower middle class' while the peers in *Iolanthe* (1882) were even more demeaning with their command: 'Bow, bow, ye lower middle classes, bow, bow ye tradesmen, bow ye masses.'

This new snobbishness and class consciousness was only one aspect of a more fundamental transformation which the middle classes underwent in the last two decades of the nineteenth century. It is not too much to say that they reversed the outlook of the generation of Cobden and Bright. Instead of being interested primarily in making money, they became concerned with spending it. Shunning the occupations, and often also the politics and religions of their fathers, they opted for an easier, more self-contained existence and cultivated the aristocratic lifestyle which had once been so despised.

The change is neatly encapsulated in George Gissing's novel, *The Year of the Jubilee* (1894). The old generation is represented by the Barmby sisters, puritanical, provincial, 'who dwelt as remote from anything metropolitan as though Camberwell were a village in the Midlands', and the new by Samuel Bennett Barmby, better educated, bent on pleasure and more sophisticated in his tastes and interests.

This transformation was the result of both economic and social change. As Britain moved from being an industrial to a service economy, and as limited liability companies and amalgamations of businesses grew more common, it was inevitable that the middle classes should move from en-trepreneurship into management and administration and from independent ownership into salaried employment. As a result their attitudes and priorities altered. They no longer needed to strive to assert themselves against the dominance of aristocratic wealth and the landed interest. Their battles were largely over and they could now sit back and enjoy the fruits of their own past toil.

Simple generational factors also played their part. Those brought up in successful and comfortable homes and educated at public schools in the 1860s and 1870s were bound to have outlooks and expectations radically different from their fathers who were in many cases self-made men born into working-class families in the 1830s and 1840s. They were, in fact, the first generation to display those characteristics that have been regarded as the hallmark, and the curse, of English middle classness ever since: a strong distaste for working in industry, a remoteness from the mass of the population, and a rather smug conservatism.

One of the ways in which this new spirit showed itself was in the choice of where to live. The sons of many of the mill-owners and manufacturers of Lancashire and Yorkshire forsook the modest homes where their fathers had lived in close proximity to their workers and instead bought secluded suburban villas or houses in the country. Those in commerce and in the professions likewise left town centre residences for the suburbs. In 1879 John Carvell Williams, a Congregationalist and Liberal MP, warned of 'that modern political evil which I may designate as suburbanism. That means in a large number of cases respectability, which is incompatible with enthusiasm, great apathy, and sometimes downright snobbishness, and a recantation of principles firmly held in days gone by.'[7]

This retreat into the suburbs was only the symbol of a much wider retreat by the middle classes. It was but one aspect of a change of attitude which also led Nonconformists to become Anglicans and employers to stop taking a personal interest in their employees and appoint welfare officers to do the job instead. In leaving city and town centres to the poor and inarticulate, the middle classes were abandoning their traditional role as leaders and organizers of the working classes and mainstays of local community life. They were exchanging the vice-presidencies of charitable institutions, debating societies and Liberal clubs for the less demanding and more private leisure pursuits of sitting at home, reading and gardening. Beatrice Webb, who regarded this decline in voluntary charitable activity the most striking social change within her lifetime, lamented on a visit to Liverpool in the 1890s that the bourgeois families who had formerly dominated local government and philanthropic activities in the city 'are petering out, and the sons are not worthy of the fathers . . . The present generation of rich folk want to enjoy themselves, find nothing to resist, no class or creed interest to fight for, so that they have ceased to consider anything but their pleasures.'[8]

In one sense, the new direction being taken by the middle classes brought them closer to the values championed by their critics. They were certainly less narrowly interested in money-making, less provincial and puritanical than they had been. Yet the ideals with which Matthew Arnold and others had hoped to imbue the English bourgeoisie were still very far from being realized. Far from cultivating them, the public schools had, in fact, succeeded in creating a new kind of philistinism. Muscular Christianity had taken over from Christian gentility as the ideal which they fostered in their pupils.

It was not the cultural and intellectual pursuits of the aristocracy that the middle classes were seeking to take up, but rather their outward trappings of rank and position. Gilbert and Sullivan characteristically caught the new mood well. In *The Gondoliers* (1889), the Duke of Plaza-Toro turns the snobbishness of the middle class to his own pecuniary advantage by forming himself into a limited company to dispense 'small titles and orders for mayors and recorders'. In *Ruddigore* (1887) Sir Ruthven Murgatroyd warns:

> Ye well-to-do squires, who live in the shires,
> Where petty distinctions are vital,
> Who found Athenaeums and local museums,
> With views to a baronet's title –
> Ye butchers and bakers and candlestick makers
> Who sneer at all things that are tradey –
> Whose middle-class lives are embarrassed by wives
> Who long to parade as 'My Lady',
> Oh! allow me to offer a word of advice,
> The title's uncommonly dear at the price.

The fact was that the middle classes were becoming, as the *Manchester Guardian* put it in 1900, 'by natural inclination and in the strict meaning of the term, Conservative'. The 'pineries

     The English Middle Classes

and vineries' of the suburbs were filling up with 'sleek citizens who pour forth daily from thousands and thousands of smart villas, read their *Standard*, and believe that the country will do very well as it is'.[9] Safely installed in their suburban privacy, the middle classes cast off their old radical Liberalism and rallied behind the Tory notions of protectionism and imperialism. Thus was born a political alliance which has lasted until our own day.

At the same time the working classes were also experiencing a much greater class consciousness and forging a new political alliance. Their enfranchisement, begun in 1885 and completed in 1918, gave them a new confidence and independence just when their experience at work was leading them to lose their sense of identification with and hopes of emulating the middle classes. Increasingly they rejected the Liberal Party and demanded their own separate Labour Party.

The polarization of politics along class lines was one of the most striking and enduring features of late nineteenth century British history. Previously, the upper and middle class electorate had determined their political allegiance according to interest, ideology, religion and even occupation. Land-owners, Anglicans, lawyers and brewers were traditionally Conservative, while manufacturers, Nonconformists and teetotallers were more likely to be Liberals. Now, however, the arrival of a mass electorate produced a new and clear cleavage along class lines. Even the new electoral system of single member constituencies introduced in the 1884 Reform Act encouraged the trend since the boundaries tended to be drawn so as to create single-class seats, with middle-class suburbs separated from working-class inner city areas.

This political cleavage was part of a more fundamental polarization that was taking place throughout society. The trend towards larger scale industrial activity and factory-based mass-production brought workers together in bigger numbers and increased their remoteness from employers. The development of a 'shop floor' mentality was further encouraged by the emergence of a new kind of trade unionism in response to the worsening economic position and the changing pattern of work in the 1880s and 1890s. A more aggressive, collectivist, narrowly economic outlook came to replace the deference, the individualism and the pride in traditions and standards of work of the old craft unions which had hitherto predominated.

A parallel movement took place among employers. In the face of the economic difficulties, and as part of the same move towards larger scale factory production, small entrepreneurs and owner-managers increasingly sold out to and became absorbed by big corporations. A new breed of salaried managers arose, less intimately bound up with both their businesses and their workforces than the old proprietors had been. Just as collectivism became the dominant ethic of the workers, so corporatism became that of their bosses. The growing militancy of trade unions was matched by the emergence of an equally aggressive stance on the part of employers who forsook their traditional individualism and joined forces in cartels, restrictive associations and communal lock-outs. For the first time it was not just Marxists who began to talk about the two sides in industry and to see the future in terms of inevitable class conflict.

Although there was increasing concern among the middle classes at the turn of the century that they were about to be squeezed out of existence by the combined forces of capital and labour, they were still doing very well for themselves economically. More than 3,750,000 people (10 per cent of the total population) belonged to families enjoying incomes of between £160 and £700 a year. Although their earnings came increasingly from salaries and less from fees and profits, they managed to preserve their differentials from the working classes. An annual income of £160, until 1914 the point at which income tax started to be levied and which could be taken as the minimum middle-class salary, was twice the average annual wage in the country as a whole. Those in the higher professions earned more than four times the average national wage, managers two and a half times as much, and those in the lower professions nearly double. Clerks were more precariously situated, earning one and a quarter times the national average, exactly the same figure as for skilled manual workers.

Living-in domestic servants were still a common feature of many middle-class households. The 1901 census found them in more than 80 per cent of the households in upper-middle-class

Hampstead and Kensington, over 60 per cent of those in Ealing and Westminster, and over 50 per cent of those in Paddington, Marylebone and Chelsea.

Middle-class culture and values still seemed to predominate in the nation as a whole. The national heroes of the Edwardians, both in real life and in fiction, were the clean-limbed, clean-living, public-school-educated upper-middle-class Englishmen who took part in imperial adventures and stalked the pages of G. H. Henty's historical novels. The most admired and keenly cultivated national virtues were those so powerfully expressed in Rudyard Kipling's *If* and Henry Newbolt's *Vitaï Lampada* (better known by its first line: 'There's a breathless hush in the Close tonight'): fair play, the stiff upper lip, and the kind of team spirit that was shown on the public school cricket pitch or rugger field.

One indication of the dominant hold which these values had on the population as a whole was the extraordinary popularity of public school stories in magazines read primarily by lower middle-class and working-class children. Talbot Baines Reed, author of *The Fifth Form at St Dominic's* which began in the *Boy's Own Paper* in 1881, and Frank Richards, who created Billy Bunter's Greyfriars in *The Magnet* and *The Gem*, which started in 1909, wrote of a world of fagging, house matches and tuck boxes that was almost entirely alien to the readership at which they were primarily aiming. Yet their public school stories remained among the most popular reading matter for boys of all backgrounds until the Second World War.

Outwardly, at least, the middle classes still exuded a considerable self-confidence. It is there in the slightly self-satisfied faces that stare out from so many of the photographs of our Edwardian great-grandfathers. It is also a marked feature of the most celebrated of the fictional portrayals of the Edwardian middle classes, John Galsworthy's Forsyte family. Jolyon, the epitome of the new commercial and managerial middle classes, rejoices that:

> They are half England, and the better half, the half that counts. It's their wealth and security that makes everything possible; makes your art possible, makes literature, science, even religion possible. Without Forsytes, who believe in none of these things, but turn them all to use, where should we be? My dear sir, the Forsytes are

the middlemen, the commercials, the pillars of society, the cornerstone of convention; everything that is admirable.[10]

Yet even in that expression of apparent confidence and certainty there is perhaps an underlying note of doubt and unease. It is almost too self-justifying and also concentrates too much on a narrow economic view of the middle-class function in society. It was precisely because of that economic function that the middle classes were vulnerable to attack. In the first decade of the twentieth century they felt themselves to be the victims of a mounting assault both from a government which seemed dangerously infected with the doctrines of socialism, and from the forces of organized labour who were apparently ready and willing to embark on class warfare.

The actions of the Government hit the middle classes hardest. For most of the latter half of the nineteenth century the government of Britain had been carried out fairly clearly in their interest. However, the advent of a mass electorate brought an increasing need to appeal to and placate the working classes. Already in the latter years of Victoria's reign a trickle of legislation had begun which positively discriminated in favour of the working classes, in the fields of housing, of education and terms and conditions of work.

On the whole, these measures had not caused great alarm to the bourgeoisie. They did not involve the use of taxpayers' money and they did not hit too directly at the rights of traditional middle-class groups like small businessmen and professionals. One measure did, however, cause concern. The Workmen's Compensation Act of 1897 made employers liable to pay compensation for injuries sustained by their employees at work. Several businessmen took that as a serious assault on the traditional freedom of contract between employer and worker and saw it as a dangerous precedent in terms of Government support for the interests of organized labour.

The Liberal Government of 1906 to 1914 seemed to extend this trend dangerously far. One of its first measures, The Trades Disputes Act, gave trade unions total immunity from all legal action by employers for damages suffered as a result of industrial action. Even more worryingly, Asquith and Lloyd George committed themselves to the principle of redistributive taxation and cheerfully took the middle classes' money directly to subsidize the working classes. The 'People's Budget' of 1909, which increased income tax from one shilling to one shilling and twopence in the pound and introduced a new super tax on high incomes to finance a non-contributory old age pension for manual workers, was greeted by the *Daily Mail* with the banner headline: 'Plundering the Middle Class'.

The 1911 National Insurance Act confirmed the drift of Government policy. Although the unemployment and sickness benefit and the free medical attention which it provided involved a contributory element, they were paid for largely by middle-class tax-payers and employers. The benefits, on the other hand, were limited to those who earned less than £160 a year. The middle classes had no particular objection to being excluded from these new benefits – they were still much too proud of their independence and sufficiently well-off to spurn any dependence on state assistance. They were, however, increasingly unhappy about the burden that they were being asked to shoulder for the benefit of the working classes.

Their feeling that the Government was bending too much to the twin evils of socialist ideology and trade union pressure was enhanced by the general social atmosphere of the time. The years immediately before the outbreak of the First World War saw the first real flexing of those trade union muscles which have continued to be such a feature of life in Britain ever since. Demoralized by a serious fall in real wages, incensed by the increasingly aggressive response of employers to their demands, and egged on by the first of a new breed of militant leaders, the working classes engaged in an unprecedented series of strikes, demonstrations and protests which periodically threatened to turn into a full-scale general strike.

It was not surprising in the circumstances that many in the middle classes became confused and frightened. Feeling themselves equally distant from the aggressive capitalism of the large corporations that were taking over small businesses, and from the militant syndicalism of union leaders like Thomas Mann and Ben Tillett, they looked on in horror and bewilderment at the increasingly violent clashes which followed lock-outs and strikes. It was no wonder that many a suburban dweller felt that the revolution was not far away and was prepared at any moment 'to find the crowd behind the red flag, surging up his little pleasant pathways, tearing down the railings, trampling the little garden'.[11]

Some responded to the growth of socialism and trade union power by setting up middle-class defence organizations, an expedient to which recourse has been made ever since whenever particular danger has threatened the bourgeoisie. In 1906, the year of the Trade Disputes Act and of the first appearance in Parliament of the infant Labour Party (then known as the Labour Representation Committee), a group of businessmen, self-employed workers and shopkeepers, together with Conservative and Liberal MPs, set up the Middle Class Defence League. The League soon had forty-five branches and made an impact in the 1907 London County Council elections when it helped to secure victories for several moderate candidates.

Further such organizations sprang up during the next few years. In 1908 an Anti-Socialist Union was set up to co-ordinate attacks on the increasingly socialistic tendency of the Liberal Government's legislation. It vigorously attacked Lloyd George's 1909 budget, campaigned for profit-sharing in industry and spawned offspring like the Nonconformist Anti-Socialist Union and the Civil Service Anti-Socialist League.

Middle-class alarm at the 'People's Budget' directly inspired the creation of another defence organization, the United Kingdom Property Owners Federation. The president of that body summed up the feelings of its members when he wrote in 1913 that:

> By far the greater bulk of the property owners were people who by thrift had acquired a little property on which to live in the latter years of their life. Year by year, owing to the socialistic tendencies of the times, they, who were really the backbone of the country – the middle classes – were singled out for ever increasing burdens which, unless they combined against them, would wipe them out altogether.[12]

Without some kind of political representation, the middle-class protest groups were unlikely to make much impact on either the Government or the unions. Although individual Liberal and Conservative MPs were sympathetic to the movements, their parties as a whole were moving away from representing predominantly middle-class interests. While the Conservatives were becoming increasingly identified with the new class of plutocrats, the Liberals were showing themselves to be governing primarily in the interests of the working classes, partly in an effort to scotch the further development of the infant Labour Party which was already making significant electoral gains. In a lecture in 1907 on the theme *How the Middle Class Is Fleeced*, George Bernard Shaw pointed out that the poor bourgeoisie

> has nowadays fallen into an extraordinary state of neglect and contempt. It was not even represented in Parliament. The aristocratic party had a chamber to itself, and the plutocratic class had the Commons very nearly to itself, and the labouring class had the rest . . . The middle class man was beginning to have a hard struggle. Why? He had been beaten in political organization by the working class.[13]

One attempt was, in fact, made to create a new political party that would represent the middle classes. In 1911 Lord Robert Cecil, an idealistic High Church Tory who had broken with the Conservative Party because of its 'sordid attempt to ally imperialism with state assistance for the rich', attempted an amalgamation of the Middle Class Defence League, the Anti-Socialist Union and other similar bodies with the older established Liberty and Property Defence League, an anti-interventionist body to which were affiliated such groups as the Association of Principals of Private Schools and the Society of Licensed Victuallers. He hoped to create what he called a citizens' union which would attract mass support and lead to the creation of a new centre party in Parliament. However, his scheme came to naught and the various middle class defence organizations collapsed. The very qualities of individualism and independence which they had been formed to foster proved a barrier to collective action.

There was another reason why these ventures failed. A substantial element within the middle classes was only too happy to swim with the tide and enjoy for itself the new benefits provided by the state and by trade union membership. For a growing number of white-collar and professional workers employed in the public sector, a policy of higher taxation and more government did not hold the horrors that it did for small businessmen. Those working in large and impersonal organizations similarly found combination in trade unions a much less unattractive proposition than entrepreneurs and independent professional men had. The early years of this century saw the beginnings of that fundamental divergence of interests between entrepreneurs, managers and clerical workers, and between those working in the public and in the private sectors, which has been a major stumbling block to the achievement of a single middle-class consciousness ever since.

In its origins middle-class trade unionism was a fairly gentlemanly affair. Because of its proletarian connotations, the word 'union' was itself generally eschewed in favour of some more respectable term like 'association'. The first president of the Association of Teachers in Technical Institutions, formed in 1904, expressed the general view of his members when he said that 'it should become in no sense a trade union of teachers, but that our labour of love should be for the benefit of technical education'. He added, 'teaching is one of the great professions' as if to reiterate that professionalism was incompatible with full-blooded trade unionism.[14]

Other early white-collar workers' associations took the same line. The United Kingdom Commercial Travellers Association specifically denied that it was a trade union and confined itself to lobbying for weekend railway concessions and uniform hotel charges. The National Association of Local Government Officers, founded in 1905, also left wage bargaining to individuals and concentrated on educational and leisure activities. Nonetheless, however tentative and respectable their collectivism might be, there could be no denying that those middle class workers who were joining trade unions were deserting the traditional bourgeois values of individualism and independence. It is an appropriate note on which to enter the twentieth century.

7

The Middle Classes Start Feeling Guilty 1900–1950

The two trends which the middle classes first perceived as threatening their position in the 1900s, the growing socialism of the state and the increasing power of trade unions, both continued through the first three quarters of the twentieth century. The responses with which they were met also remained the same. Some fiercely resisted their advance, others enthusiastically embraced it, and the majority accepted it with a sense of resignation which was engendered partly by a distinct feeling of guilt.

It was in the Edwardian age that the English middle classes as a whole first started feeling guilty about their comfortable and privileged position in society. That feeling expressed itself in two distinct ways: it acted as a spur to positive social action to help the less fortunate, and it produced a mood of rather uncomfortable and apologetic embarrassment. Both those manifestations of a guilty conscience have been marked characteristics of English middle classness in the twentieth century.

John Galsworthy caught the new mood nicely when he had Jolyon observe to the elderly Soames that self-consciousness was the feature which distinguished the Edwardian Forsytes from their Victorian forbears.

> Self-consciousness is a handicap, you know, and that's the difference between us. We've lost conviction. How and when self-consciousness was born, I never can make out. My father had a little, but I don't believe any of the old Forsytes ever had a scrap. Never to see yourself, as others see you, it's a wonderful preservative.[1]

Hilaire Belloc, one of the sharpest observers of English middle

classness in the early twentieth century, summed up the same
mood in one of his poems:

> The Rich arrived in pairs
> And also in Rolls Royces
> They talked of their affairs
> In loud and strident voices.
>
> The poor arrived in Fords,
> Whose features they resembled;
> They laughed to see so many Lords
> And Ladies all assembled.
>
> The People in Between
> Looked Underdone and harassed,
> And out of place and mean
> And horribly embarrassed.

In part, the middle classes' new sense of unease was simply a
reaction to the over-confidence and certainties of their
Victorian parents. But it also resulted from the fact that they
were being made aware for the first time of the conditions in
which many working people lived and of the stark contrast that
these afforded with their own comfortable surroundings. The
pioneer social surveys carried out in the late 1880s and early
1890s showed the extent of the poverty and suffering that still
persisted in a supposedly rich and civilized nation. In separate
surveys of London and York, Charles Booth and Seebohm
Rowntree found that 30 per cent of the population were living
at or below the poverty line and on the verge of hunger. Their
disturbing revelations shocked many of the middle classes into
social action.

One of the first manifestations of this newly awakened social
conscience was the settlement movement which colonized the
poorest parts of London and other cities with public school
boys and Oxbridge undergraduates. The first settlement was
established in 1869 by Edward Thring, the headmaster of
Uppingham School. By 1900 there were twenty-four settlements in London alone, most of them in the East End,
established and staffed by public schools, Oxbridge colleges
and churches. Inspired partly by traditional Christian
philanthropy and voluntaryism and partly by more secular,
socialistic ideals, the settlement movement was also a direct

response to the middle-class retreat from the cities. The idea of a settlement, according to a Congregational minister who founded an early East End mission, 'is to bring back to a poor neighbourhood, from the suburbs or other source, those who shall supply the place left vacant by the exodus of the well-to-do'.[2]

Two of the largest and best known East End settlements, both of which are still flourishing today nearly a hundred years after their foundation, epitomize the two different channels into which the middle-class feeling of guilt flowed and which made it such a potent force for positive social action. Oxford House in Bethnal Green and Toynbee Hall in Stepney were both founded in 1884 as a result of meetings held in Oxford colleges inspired by the publication of *The Bitter Cry of Outcast London*, a Congregational minister's dramatic account of the poverty and suffering in the capital. Both had the aim of settling, or colonizing, a particularly deprived area with active and idealistic undergraduates. In their style and future development, however, they were very different.

Oxford House sprang directly out of the High Church movement which had spread through Oxford fifty years before and which had produced a revival in the Church of England of the social gospel and the doctrine of good works. The idea of the House was conceived in Keble College, the living monument to the Oxford Movement, whose first warden, Edward Talbot, provided the direct inspiration for the settlement. It was first and foremost a religious community. The daily services in its chapel were central to the life of its residents, most of whom were undergraduates or recent graduates in theology.

Toynbee Hall had a rather different pedigree. It was conceived in Balliol College, the nursery of secularist idealism and the ethic of public service. Although the founder, Samuel Barnett, was an Anglican clergyman, he belonged to the liberal Broad Church school which laid less emphasis on doctrinal niceties. From the first Toynbee Hall was seen not so much as a religious mission as a centre for social work and social observation.

In their subsequent history, these two settlements have continued to exemplify two different strands of the middle-class social conscience. Oxford House long retained its High Church, public school atmosphere. Until the Second World War the undergraduates living in the House were served dinner by waitresses and were regularly to be seen in the streets of the East End clad somewhat incongruously in hunting gear on their way to follow the hounds. Many of its residents, who included the writer A. P. Herbert, have been hearty, colourful figures who have endeared themselves to the local population by their warmth and humour. Today the House is actively involved in voluntary and community projects in the area.

Toynbee Hall, by contrast, has arguably had less direct impact on the lives of local inhabitants and a much greater influence on the welfare of the nation as a whole. There the style of living has been plainer and less flamboyant, and the residents, while perhaps not quite so colourful and well-loved as those in Oxford House, have had a much more significant impact on the formation of social policy. They include Hubert Llewellyn Smith, the civil servant largely responsible for drafting some of the most important social legislation enacted by Liberal Governments before the First World War, William Beveridge, the architect of the modern Welfare State, Clement Attlee, Prime Minister of the 1945 Labour Government, and R. H. Tawney, the economic historian and pioneer of the Workers' Educational Association.

Tawney, who spent three years living in Toynbee Hall after his education at Rugby and Balliol, epitomized the best features of the middle-class social conscience. The son of a member of the Indian Education Service, he was early imbued with the notions of duty and service. His life combined the spontaneity and compassion of Christian voluntaryism with the broader more theoretical perspectives of socialism. Like many middle-class socialists, he became a fervent advocate of equality and a fierce critic of the institutions and privileges of his own class.

Among others to be affected by a sense of guilt at this time were a group of advanced Liberals who came together out of a common disillusionment with the middle-class bias of their party's policies. Without exception, they were themselves solidly bourgeois in their origins. Sidney Webb, a civil servant, was the son of an accountant, and his wife, Beatrice, the daughter of an entrepreneur who had made a fortune from cotton, timber and promoting railways abroad. Graham Wallas, the Webbs' first and closest ally in the Fabian Society which they formed to give expression to their new-found socialist beliefs, was the son of an Evangelical clergyman and had been educated at public school and Oxford. L. T. Hobhouse, who like the rest of the group clung on to Liberalism and shrank from embracing the full socialist creed, had a similar background. J. A. Hobson, who described himself as 'born and bred in the middle of the middle class of a middle sized Midland industrial town', was the son of a newspaper proprietor.[3] J. L. Hammond was the son of a Yorkshire vicar and had been educated at Bradford Grammar School and Oxford. His wife, Barbara, was the daughter of the headmaster of Haileybury School who had himself been involved in the early days of Toynbee Hall.

Although the members of this group, and particularly the early Fabians, spoke more enthusiastically than many working-class leaders about collectivism and the need for the redistribution of wealth, and described themselves as 'intellectual proletarians', they remained unmistakably middle-class in their attitudes. They had a strongly élitist streak, believing that the new socialist order would only come with government by experts, and never really trusting the masses. Their lack of sympathy with popular prejudices and their commitment to giving the common people what was good for them rather than what they wanted showed their adherence to the traditional bourgeois Protestant ethic.

The curious mixture of socialism and élitism which inspired the early Fabians has continued to be a feature of the middle-class left in Britain during the twentieth century. So also has an obsession with the class system and with the evils of the middle classes in particular. The Webbs and their friends set about making their own class feel guilty: Sidney attacked its prevailing individualism and opposition to state action to help others, while Beatrice bitterly criticized her own father for failing to think 'in terms of general principles' and lacking 'a clear vision of the public good'. The Hammonds meanwhile reinterpreted Victorian history to show how much the working classes had suffered at the hands of their employers. In so doing, they established a powerful school of British historiography which has glorified the working classes and denigrated the middle classes.

The impact of the First World War enhanced the middle classes' sense of guilt. There was a realization that decisions by upper class generals had sent thousands of men to the horrors of the trenches and gas attacks. The war shattered for ever the prevailing optimism and liberalism that had underpinned the heyday of the bourgeoisie. It was also a great social leveller, finally ending the ascendancy of the landed aristocracy and greatly exalting the status of the ordinary man in the street.

The middle classes were hard hit in the economic slump which followed the war. Inflation reduced the value of earnings and savings and drove up rates and taxes. The publication in 1922 of official statistics showing that middle-class families were becoming smaller led to headlines in the papers proclaiming, 'The Dying Middle Class' and 'Middle Class Vanishing. Taxes Hit the Backbone of the Nation'.

As always in times of adversity, some people fought back. A new defence organization, the Middle Class Union, sprang up immediately after the war was over, inspired by the conviction that, as one correspondent to *The Times* wrote, 'The Radical draper and the Conservative butcher must now unite and show the retired major and dyspeptic socialist doctor that their interests are all the same.' The chairman told members at its first meeting: 'If you are properly organized you can possibly hold up capitalists, or you could even hold up the Government. You must see to it that you are not squeezed.'[4]

Within eighteen months of its formation, the Union had over two hundred branches. It was particularly strong in London and on the South coast. In Brighton Conservatives and Liberals stood down to give Middle Class Union candidates a clear field against Labour in local elections between 1918 and 1924. In its election literature the Union variously defined the middle classes as 'all those outside organized Labour and organized Capital', 'the unfortunate consumer – the majority of the tax-paying public' and simply as 'the great majority of the British public'. It ultimately decided on a wider image and a national appeal, changing its name in 1922 to the National Citizens Union, and proclaiming,

'People have different views as to who constitute the middle classes, but the real point is that the term comprises all who place the cause of the nation above the cause of a particular section.' The change of name and style, however, was not enough to prevent it disintegrating, like all other middle-class protest groups, a few years after its foundation.[5]

Most people in the English middle classes, in marked contrast to their counterparts in Germany, reacted to the privations brought about by the post-war slump with remarkable docility. This was particularly true of the lower middle classes who were hardest hit by the inflation of the 1920s and who also found themselves downgraded both officially and in the eyes of their contemporaries. The 1921 census demoted to Class II half a million clerks who had been placed in Social Class I in 1911. The 1931 census further demoted them to Class III and also showed that 70,000 clerks were unemployed. It was the beginning of the progressive devaluation of clerical work that has gone on ever since. In other respects too, the white-collar workers of the 1920s did not enjoy the status or relative wealth of their fathers in the 1880s. Pooter's living-in servant must have seemed like a distant dream to most clerks in the 1920s.

In fact, it was to be neither the capitalists nor the Government that the middle classes took on in the mid-1920s, but rather the trade unions. During the General Strike of May 1926 it was middle-class volunteers, many of them coming straight from university and public schools to man railway engines and drive buses, who kept goods moving and so helped to persuade the trade unions to give in. The good-natured, schoolboyish enthusiasm with which they took to their temporary jobs as railway firemen or lorry drivers concealed the fact that one class had been used to defeat another.

The General Strike engendered a sense of middle-class superiority in terms of moral values and attitudes. In the midst of the strike, Dr W. R. Inge, the dean of St Paul's Cathedral, remarked, 'The middle classes are the most down-trodden in the community. They have to work hard and pay exorbitant taxes. Yet they never grumble and never strike.' Another Anglican clergyman observed,

English middle-class people would do anything rather than accept what members of the working class not only expect but clamour for – state aid, free education, free this and free that. Rather than accept those things, and in order to maintain their independence, they were prepared to suffer almost incredible privations.[6]

It was perhaps partly this sense of their own superiority and pride that kept the middle classes from more definite action in defence of their economic privileges. There was also the fact that life was still pretty good for many of them. The 1920s saw a considerable consumer spending boom, with the middle classes in the van buying the vacuum cleaners and other gadgets that were to make the disappearance of the living-in servant less grim to bear. It was also the decade of the 'bright young things', when many in the middle classes abandoned their usual cautious respectability if only because they believed like the later Forsytes that the only thing to do was 'to have a good time because we don't believe anything can last'.

It is possible to take stock of the position of the middle classes at the beginning of the 1930s. There were still two and a half million families (just over 20 per cent of the population) who enjoyed a weekly income of between £4 and £10, and half a million families with living-in servants. If they were suffering deprivations, these were only relative as a letter to *The Times* in 1930 from a correspondent who simply signed himself 'Middle Class' makes clear:

> The result of any increased taxation in my individual case is that I shall have to reduce my servants by half. I now have eight dependent on me and in order to requite good and faithful servants I have made large inroads on capital. Alas! I have passed the margin of safety, and the moment that my income is still further taxed I shall have no alternative but to reduce my establishment of servants . . . domestics, servants, gardeners, grooms and chauffeurs, the majority faithful servants, must go to swell the total of unemployed.[7]

A sizeable and growing minority among the middle classes felt only guilt and embarrassment when they compared their own relatively easy lives to those of others. In 1919 another correspondent to *The Times* had written:

> The plight of the middle classes is undoubtedly partly due to a disposition for the last twenty or thirty years to aim at a standard

of living which has been far too high, to seek expensive pleasures, and to neglect the more irksome duties of citizenship. In the Victorian era, which it is now the fashion to despise, the middle classes lived far more simply and frugally. They did not frequent costly restaurants, went to the theatre once a month, travelled comparatively little, rarely sought a continental holiday and were more interested in domestic life than they are in these insurgent times. Their existence was perhaps comparatively dull, and lacking in excitement, but was less feverish, and possibly happier. The motor car and champagne standard was not dreamed of in the last century.[8]

With the advent of the 1930s, there were increasing signs of a loss of self-confidence among the middle classes. Leading writers and thinkers of the decade, like George Orwell, D. H. Lawrence, Bertrand Russell and Aldous Huxley, attacked the morality and values of the bourgeoisie and extolled those of the working classes. Tawney followed up his book *The Sickness of an Acquisitive Society* with a powerful work, *Equality*. The *News Chronicle* pricked the consciences of its Liberal-minded, bourgeois readers with strong leading articles on the wrongs of the world. Victor Gollancz built the fortunes of his publishing house on the Left Book Club. There was even a new type of boys' comic, represented by *Wizard, Champion, Hotspur, Rover* and *Modern Boy*, which although they still used the public school settings of *The Gem* and *The Magnet*, devoted more space to stories of the Wild West, war and crime.

Their increasing sense of guilt had an important effect on the political beliefs and activities of many in the middle classes. Concern about the effects of the depression and the rise of fascism in Europe pushed several to the left. The more passionately committed and romantically inclined went out to Spain to fight with the communists in the Civil War. At home, the effects of middle-class guilt can be seen very clearly on two trios of ex-public schoolboys. At Oxford, at the end of the 1920s three young men who came from similar civil and imperial service backgrounds, and who had been to Winchester together, found themselves attracted to socialism and to careers in the Labour Party. Hugh Gaitskell, Richard Crossman and Douglas Jay joined Labour because they realized how privileged their own lives were compared to those of others, and they were to display as politicians that same mixture of socialism and élitism which had distinguished the early Fabians. They also exhibited some extraordinary manifestations of middle-class guilt. Gaitskell, for instance, felt so uneasy about his own privileged position when he met working-class people that as an undergraduate he travelled first-class on the railways to avoid the embarrassment of meeting them. At Cambridge a few years later, Kim Philby, Guy Burgess and Donald Maclean were for much the same reason to find themselves equally attracted to communism, with consequences that are all too well known.

The Second World War further intensified the middle classes' guilt feelings. Evacuation of children from the big towns and cities made many middle-class suburban and country dwellers aware for the first time of the poverty in urban areas. Although horrified at what they regarded as the feckless behaviour of the lower orders, they were also genuinely shocked at the conditions from which the children had come. This is borne out by the robust comment of a member of the Derbyshire Women's Institute: 'I had no conception such awful people existed, but we are to blame that we allow the Government to have such housing conditions. These children should have a chance to be brought up as decent citizens. Under present conditions they cannot.'[9]

The war prompted a general feeling that middle-class institutions and privileges had had their day and that when peace finally came there would and should be a natural tendency to create a classless society. *The Times* looked forward in its leading articles to the reconstruction of society on a more equal basis. In a pamphlet of 1943, *The Problem of the Public Schools*, Tawney turned his attention to the inequalities perpetrated by one particular institution that has perhaps provoked more middle-class guilt than any other. The following year the Government passed an Education Act which, while admittedly not touching the independent schools, dismantled one of the class barriers which still straddled the state sector by abolishing fees for secondary schools and throwing them fully open to talent.

It seemed a logical extension of these aspirations when in 1945 the votes of the middle classes were apparently decisive in bringing to power the first majority Labour Government in Britain. Admittedly, to a certain extent the result of the election was simply a consequence of social changes over the past twenty years which had produced a new lower middle class salariat with no natural attachment to the Conservatives. Indeed, the *Economist* commented that 'The great paradox of British politics in the past quarter century – the faithfulness of the Tories to the propertyless lower middle class – is at an end.' However, 1945 also showed a new spirit among the old-established middle classes. The *Spectator* defined the middle class as 'those two million or so electors who put Labour into power in 1945 and could equally well put it out again in 1950'.[10]

In fact, a careful analysis of the election by J. Bonham suggests that a certain amount of caution is needed in interpreting the significance of the middle-class vote. While it was true that the seats which swung to Labour included a significant number of white-collar suburbs like Dulwich, Chislehurst, Wimbledon, Bexley and Harrow, the Conservatives continued to maintain a substantial majority of the total middle-class vote. Among the lower middles there had been a substantial shift to Labour, but among the upper middles there were still four Tory voters for every socialist.[11]

The middle classes as a whole were not quite sure what to make of Britain's first fully fledged Labour Government, nor was it quite sure what to make of them. At one level deep-seated class antagonisms welled up on both sides. Frightened by the sound of 'The Red Flag' being sung on the floor of the House of Commons by the new intake of MPs, 'some anxious middle class ladies', in the words of Maude and Lewis, 'rang up their solicitors and stockbrokers to enquire whether it was the end of all things'.[12] Their worst fears must have been confirmed when Aneurin Bevan, speaking shortly after the election of the new Government on the theme of the two nations in Britain, described the Tories as 'lower than vermin' and Emmanuel Shinwell announced that the working classes were the only people who mattered and he didn't care 'two hoots or a tinker's cuss' for anyone else.

There was another side to the new Government, however. The new Prime Minister, Clement Attlee, was after all a much more characteristic specimen of the bourgeoisie than his predecessor, Churchill, even down to the fact that he had become a socialist as a result of his experiences as a resident in the settlement run by Haileybury School in the Limehouse area of London's East End and later at Toynbee Hall. He was, in fact, a product of the middle-class social conscience, just like his personal assistant, Douglas Jay. Other leading members of the 1945 Labour Government had also derived their socialism partly from the public service ethic of public school and Oxbridge. Hugh Dalton, the Chancellor of the Exchequer, was the son of an Anglican clergyman and had been educated at Eton and King's College, Cambridge. Stafford Cripps, President of the Board of Trade, was a barrister educated at Winchester and New College, Oxford.

Senior ministers in fact went to considerable efforts to persuade the middle classes that they were not ranged against them in inevitable class conflict. Herbert Morrison told the 1947 Labour Party conference:

> The middle classes have, for some time past, been experiencing a painful and difficult reduction in their living standards . . . many of them voted for us two years ago, but whether they did or not, if they stand the strain with no undue grousing but with patience and understanding, then they are our partners in the great social enterprise on which we have embarked.[13]

In fact, the strain which the middle classes were required to bear was a considerable one, in some ways more considerable than many of them probably realized at the time. In the first place, they were experiencing for the first time a Government that was inevitably committed, by its history, its ideology and the nature of its support, to favour another class. In its handling of the economic difficulties that followed the war, Attlee's Government deliberately sheltered the working class from the full brunt of inflation and austerity and let a heavier burden fall on the shoulders of the better-off. The overall effect of this policy was clear. As an American observer remarked, 'For the first time in British history the brunt of an economic crisis is not being borne by the workers. The Labour Government has been cushioning the workers, from whom its votes come, against the crisis.'[14]

There was a second less perceptible way in which the 1945

Labour Government was antipathetic to the middle classes. In its social welfare legislation it finally abandoned middle-class principles of selectivity, voluntaryism, and charity and in their place it substituted the principles of universalism, state provision and social justice. The setting up of the National Health Service and the provision of compulsory national insurance for all represented the culmination of a trend which had begun with the legislation of the 1906 Liberal Government forty years earlier and which was fundamentally at odds with the traditional middle-class tenets of self-help and self-reliance coupled with voluntary charitable activity to help those in need.

Just how antipathetic the Labour Government was to those values is shown by the following extract from an article written in 1948 by Harold Laski, one of the architects of the new state welfare system:

> We still have a stratum, running from the bottom of the middle class to the summit of the aristocracy, who thoroughly enjoy the power that comes from dispensing patronage, and receiving with all possible profusion, the obedient gratitude of its recipients. It is a stratum which finds in this effort a genuine relief from the hard task of thinking out the meaning of social justice . . . Whenever there is a group in our society whose fate is unhappy through no fault of their own, I am for justice and against charity . . . I think that, in an immense degree, it is socially preferable to deal with the overwhelming mass of these problems without the intervention of gracious ladies, or benevolent busybodies, or stockbrokers to whom hospital is a hobby.[15]

The creation of a fully fledged Welfare State did not simply weaken the middle classes by taking away their traditional role as providers of charity and voluntary effort. It also assaulted their own self-reliance. They were not exempted from the scope of the legislation establishing compulsory national insurance and health service contributions, as they had been in 1911. This seemed to spell the abolition of the great distinction which the middle classes had always drawn between themselves as sturdily independent and self-reliant citizens and the working classes who needed assistance and protection.

The social reforms also offended against another cherished middle-class principle, the independence of professional practice. The creation of the National Health Service involved a prolonged and often bitter wrangle between Aneurin Bevan, its socialist architect, and the British Medical Association, representing doctors. The Association won three significant victories: doctors were to be allowed to continue in private practice, they retained their self-employed status, and they were not to be compelled by the Government to take on any particular patient. There was no denying, however, that the establishment of the National Health Service turned them in certain respects into state servants with ever-greater administrative duties and with their professional independence diminished.

In the long run, the Welfare State was going to prove a good deal more advantageous to the middle classes than they had at first feared. They themselves proved adept at exploiting the medical and other services which had been set up primarily for the sake of the less well-off. In addition the new National Health Service and social service system created a plethora of professional, managerial and clerical jobs and led to the development of a new middle-class industry. In the short run, however, it was not surprising that the initial reaction from the bourgeoisie to what seemed like an assault on some of their most cherished principles and interests was hostile.

The initial traumas suffered by the middle classes as a result of this new legislation were accompanied by wider economic, social and cultural shocks. The continuance of rationing, a falling living standard and general austerity hit the traditionally high consuming bourgeoisie harder than the working classes. Differentials between wage and salary earners, which had been largely preserved for the first forty years of the twentieth century, were narrowing. For example, between 1939 and 1954 the salaries of Class I clerks on the railways increased by only 80 per cent (to £605 a year), while those of engine cleaners rose by 186 per cent (to £6 9s. a month). Meanwhile the running of many upper middle-class homes was transformed by the almost total disappearance of domestic servants who by 1951 were found in only 1 per cent of households in the country. Lord Blake, the historian, has commented of the immediate post-war years that:

They can be seen in retrospect as a sort of twilight period between the era of cheap servants and the era of cheap washing machines. The effect of the disappearance of servants constituted a revolution in the middle-class way of life far more dramatic than anything that followed the First World War; and the effects were more acutely felt at this time than later when prosperity returned, labour-saving devices became the norm, and people had recognized the need to adjust themselves to a change which, they now saw, would never be reversed.[16]

Culturally also, the dominance of the middle classes was being threatened. The war had brought classless American influences into English life. Austerity was hitting traditional upper middle-class style and creating a new uniformity. The novels of Angela Thirkell which were so popular at this time consciously chronicle the end of an era for the middle classes with time-honoured practices being sacrificed to the onward march of socialist equality. There were many who would have agreed with George Orwell in his confident prediction made in *The English People* (written in 1944 and published three years later) that:

The tendency of the working class and the middle class is evidently to merge. It has been accelerated by the war, and another ten years of all-round rationing, utility clothes, high income tax, and compulsory national service may finish the process once and for all.[17]

There were, of course, the usual rallying cries and protests from a section of the bourgeoisie. The *Economist* ran a series of articles in 1948 calling for a new centre party to balance the Conservatives with their big business interests and Labour with their trade union connections. However, it concluded that a new political party would take so long to form that it was better for the middle classes to organize themselves into some kind of pressure group. The Middle Class Union was revived in 1949 and even a Labour MP was moved to remark that 'something would have to be done soon to relieve the burden of the long suffering middle classes if they were not to be completely eliminated'.[18]

To those born into the middle classes in the 1870s and 1880s and coming to the end of their lives at the end of the 1940s, much about their lot must have seemed to have changed for the worse. Their relative standard of living had slipped, their distance from the working classes had narrowed and their lifestyle had become less leisured and easy. The onward march of socialism, collectivism and the nanny-state seemed to threaten not just their economic and political position, but their traditional values of independence, individualism and self-reliance. Yet from our own viewpoint another thirty years on, the position of the middle classes at the dawning of the second half of the twentieth century does not look so bleak. They were about to embark on a decade of affluence, their cultural dominance was by no means over, and they were, in fact, going to benefit more than anyone else from the political and administrative developments that initially they had so much feared.

8

Towards a Classless Society
Embourgeoisement or Proletarianization
1950–1974

Seen in retrospect, the early 1950s seem like a brief Indian summer for the English middle classes. The Conservative Government elected in 1951 was dedicated to maintaining their traditional interests and institutions. Inflation and taxation had not yet begun their task of seriously eroding capital and reducing the living standards of the better off. The physical manifestations of middle-class strength and stability, from the Church and the public schools to tea shops and high-class grocers, showed a confidence and vitality still to be shattered by the tide of secularism and standardization which ushered in the swinging sixties.

In the cultural field, for perhaps the last time, middle-class types and values were dominant. The sporting heroes of the day were the clean-limbed young ex-public school men who broke world records seemingly effortlessly and certainly without ostentation. Roger Bannister, who in 1954 ran the first four-minute mile having taken time off from his studies at Guy's Hospital, Christopher Chataway, the holder of the world 5000-metre record, and Nicolas Stacey, like the others a British competitor in the 1952 Olympic Games, epitomized the amateur tradition in English sport. It was somehow appropriate that they should go on to become respectively a doctor, a Conservative MP and a Church of England clergyman.

Similar types dominated the national game of cricket. The team sent out to Australia in the winter of 1950 to win back the Ashes that had eluded England since the war was made up predominantly of public school and university men. To have picked professionals, even very good professionals like Bill Edrich, would somehow have been out of keeping with the national mood. The most popular cricketers of the 1950s were elegant, unostentatious, upright ex-public school men like Colin Cowdrey, Peter May and David Sheppard.

The same attributes characterized the leading figures in the world of entertainment. In the cinema Kenneth More, John Mills, Jack Hawkins and Richard Attenborough played their way through a series of films set either in the war or in the heyday of the British Empire and displayed impeccable public school accents and manners and a determination to preserve the stiff upper lip. BBC radio, although coming to the end of its golden age as the dominant cultural medium in the home, still spoke to the nation in an unmistakably middle-class voice and even when the Corporation resumed its fledgling television service after the war it was the comfortably bourgeois face of Richard Dimbleby which viewers first saw flickering on their screens.

Middle-class cultural influences were still strongly felt among the young as well. Those who were schoolchildren in the early 1950s were the last generation to experience the delights of BBC Children's Hour with its high standards and improving but entertaining tone. Even their favourite comics continued to be those with public school stories rather than the more modern ones with tales of war and outer space. Recalling his days at a secondary modern school in Shoreditch, East London, in the early 1950s, the journalist Frank Johnson has written:

> *Rover* and *Hotspur* were still favoured by us. And for Christmas an aunt, who would never have set foot in a public school except as a cleaner, would think it a matter of course to give her nephew *The Fifth Form At St Dominic's*, a morality involving the eventual downfall of Loman, a cad. None of us knew any Latin tags. The language was not taught. Nor, indeed, on the whole was English, so we were not strong on Shakespearian quotations either. But the phrase 'Flashman: You are a bully and a liar, and there is no place for you in this school' was understood among us as emanating from the incomparable *Tom Brown's Schooldays*.[1]

Despite this apparent continuing cultural dominance of middle classness there were several people in the 1950s who prophesied that Britain was well on the way to becoming a classless society. One of the most emphatic was R. H. Tawney, who argued in an epilogue to a new edition of *Equality*, published in 1952, that the strikingly inegalitarian character of British society was about to be overcome. The programme of social democratic reform introduced by the Labour Party after the war, he argued, had produced distinct advances 'towards the conversion of a class-ridden society into a community in fact as well as name'.

It was not only socialists who looked forward to the early transformation of Britain into a classless society. The Conservative Governments which ruled the country continuously from 1951 to 1964 were committed to a similar goal. They did not tamper with any of the basic components of the Welfare State. These were, in fact, the years of the 'Butskellite' consensus (the term was derived from marrying the names of R. A. Butler, the Tory architect of the 1944 Education Act and Chancellor of the Exchequer from 1951 to 1955, and Hugh Gaitskell, the leader of the Labour Party) when the dominant elements in both major political parties pursued broadly the same overall policy. While Labour politicians might stress the positive role of the state slightly more, and Conservatives the benevolent effects of greater industrial productivity and profitability, both were agreed that economic growth and greater material affluence would inexorably lead to a better and more equal society from which class differences and antagonisms would gradually disappear.

The very continuation of the Conservatives in power for so long seemed to confirm the truth of these optimistic assumptions. They won three successive general elections by picking up a substantial vote from the working classes, who, it seemed, agreed with the famous remark of the Prime Minister, Harold Macmillan, in a speech at Bedford in 1957 that 'some of our people have never had it so good'. After the triumphant conclusion of the third election in 1959, Macmillan gave voice to another widely held sentiment when he declared emphatically: 'the class war is obsolete'.

Sociologists developed a theory to explain why increasing numbers of the working classes had apparently deserted their traditional loyalty to Labour. The embourgeoisement theory, as it became known, was first clearly stated by Dr Ferdinand Zweig in a book called *The Worker In An Affluent Society* published in 1961. He argued that because of general economic advance, which had brought them an increasing level of real income and expenditure and more material possessions, and as a result of better education, the working classes were becoming more middle-class in their lifestyle and values. As this process continued, he asserted, they would develop a greater interest in their families and their children's education, see their role more as consumers and less as workers, and generally become less collectivist and class-conscious in their attitudes.

There was certainly no doubt about the fact of the economic advancement of the working classes in the period between the mid-1950s and the mid-1970s, nor about the effect that this had in reducing differences within society. One after another the products of the new age of mass-produced affluence, baths, washing machines, telephones, motor cars, holidays abroad, ceased to be the exclusive possessions and symbols of the well-to-do middle classes. The statistics gathered together by the Government for their publication *Social Trends* dramatically illustrate the extent of this egalitarian revolution. In the mid-1950s, only just over half the homes in Britain had their own baths, less than 10 per cent had televisions and only 8 per cent refrigerators. Twenty years later all three items were to be found in more than 90 per cent of homes.

It is much more doubtful, however, whether this new found affluence led the working classes to change their attitudes and behaviour in the ways that Zweig suggested. Certainly many in the middle classes thought that it had simply given the lower orders new opportunities to indulge their fecklessness and proletarian tastes. This view received some support from an important sociological study carried out in 1964 by a group of sociologists led by Dr John Goldthorpe and published five years later under the title, *The Affluent Worker*.

Goldthorpe carried out his investigations among car workers in Luton. They were among the most highly paid manual workers in Britain and therefore could be expected to show signs of embourgeoisement if Zweig's theory was correct. In fact, the survey found that they retained their proletarian attitudes and lifestyle. They continued to hold the traditional working-class view of their jobs simply as a way of making money. When asked to name the greatest single source of satisfaction in their work, the overwhelming majority said pay. When a group of white-collar workers was asked the same question, the nature of the job proved the most popular answer and only a small minority mentioned money. The Luton car workers saw their increased earnings as something to be spent quickly on consumer goods, luxuries and entertainments rather than saved and put towards a house, private education for their children or other longer-term goals.

Goldthorpe also suggested that the political attitudes and behaviour of the working classes had not changed as much as had been thought. About 80 per cent of the Luton car workers had voted Labour in the 1955 and 1959 elections and intended to do so again in 1964. They still saw themselves as working-class and were strongly committed to trade unionism and to an 'us-them' view of politics and society. The only way in which they had seemingly moved closer to a middle-class lifestyle as a result of their affluence was in becoming more family and home-centred and less community orientated. This process, however, seemed to have narrowed rather than widened their perspectives. Goldthorpe found that the dominant charac-teristic of the affluent workers was what he described as 'instrumentalism'. By this he meant that they increasingly saw their work, their trade union and the political party for which they voted simply as instruments to further their own immediate material ends. There was no sign that they were adopting the traditionally broader perspectives of the middle classes.

But if the working classes were not, in fact, becoming 'embourgeoised', that did not necessarily mean that society was not becoming more classless. It was equally possible that the middle classes were becoming 'proletarianized', and that was precisely what several sociologists and commentators saw happening in the late 1950s and early 1960s. The trend towards amalgamation and take-over in business and industry meant that many employers were becoming employees and large numbers of white-collar workers found themselves working for large and impersonal organizations. In 1956 an American sociologist, W. H. Whyte, described these developments in a book, *The Organization Man*, and suggested that they were leading the middle classes in the United States to give up their traditional entrepreneurial initiative and drive and adopt a more passive, collectivist mentality. The beginnings of the same phenomenon in Britain will be explored later in this chapter. First, however, it is necessary to turn to the so-called consumer revolution which overtook Britain in these years and which brought in its wake a fundamental 'proletarianization' of society as a whole.

The roots of this revolution lay in the economic boom that had enabled the working classes to afford washing machines and cars. With their increased affluence those in the lower social classes dominated the market for goods and services. As a result their tastes largely dictated what would be sold in shops and what would appear on the new medium of television. High-class grocers and butchers gave way to supermarkets selling packaged 'convenience foods'. Tea shops were replaced by coffee bars and 'fast food' outlets. Hotels installed televisions in their lounges and restaurants introduced canned music to cater for the new mass market.

Initially the middle classes reacted against many of the manifestations of this revolution. They spurned the supermarkets and stuck to their traditional small shopkeepers. They refused to have television in their homes. They deplored the development of hire-purchase and easier credit facilities which seemed to assault the principles of thrift and of not paying for something until you could afford it. The bolder spirits tore up the credit cards that were sent to them by their banks with the slogan 'Take the waiting out of wanting'. They resisted the pressures of advertising and in 1956 set up the Consumers' Association to fight for the preservation of quality and high standards. The Association's magazine, *Which*, became something of a bible in many middle-class households in the 1960s.

It was not long, however, before the middle classes realized that the new order had its advantages, even if it offended against some of their traditional values and prejudices. Supermarkets were cheap; credit cards were undeniably useful; it was important to have television if only for the children's sake; and even convenience foods had their advantages. Gradually, and without really realizing it, the middle classes were giving up their position as arbiters of the nation's taste and were allowing themselves to be influenced, if not actually dictated to, by those below them on the social scale.

Similar changes were taking place in other areas of life. In sport, the middle-class amateur heroes of the early 1950s were being displaced by working-class professionals. One of the new breed, Gordon Pirie, the long-distance runner, devoted a chapter of his autobiography, *Running Free*, published in 1961, to 'the hypocrisy of British amateurism' in which he criticized 'the Oxford school of British athletes' exemplified by Bannister and Chataway for their dilettantism.

The decline of traditional middle-class values was particularly marked in the game of cricket. In 1959 Yorkshire elected its first non-amateur captain. Four years later the Marylebone Cricket Club ruled that the traditional distinction between gentlemen and players in the game should be abolished. Henceforth, all those playing in first-class matches would be paid. The leading batsmen of the 1960s, Ken Barrington, John Edrich and Jim Parks, even had a different stance at the wicket from that of May, Cowdrey and Sheppard. Instead of facing with their shoulder square to the bowler, they turned to face mid-on. They did not play the classic offside shots and elegant cover drives of the public school men. They were more concerned with notching up a high score than with the style of their play. Batting and bowling averages became more important and team spirit less so, as such innovations as commercially sponsored one-day tests and man-of-the-match awards drove out the old Newbolt spirit of 'Play up, play up and play the game'. Brian Close, a working-class professional, was brought in to captain England in the last test of the 1966 series against the West Indies after two captains in the old amateur tradition, M. J. K. Smith and Colin Cowdrey, had failed to win any of the earlier games.

Similar changes were taking place in the cultural sphere. Even that most bourgeois of all art forms, the novel, was seemingly being proletarianized. One of the best sellers of 1957 was John Braine's *Room At The Top*, an earthy story of a northern working-class boy's life and loves. The following year Alan Sillitoe drew on his own experiences of working-class life in Nottingham to produce the equally successful *Saturday Night and Sunday Morning*, and in 1960 Stan Barstow, the son of a coal miner, wrote another celebration of working-class life, *A Kind of Loving*. In the theatre John Osborne achieved considerable fame and success with his play *Look Back in Anger*, which featured a working-class family in South London hurling abuse at the hypocrisy and pretension of the middle classes.

The cinema underwent a similar revolution. In the mid-1950s, Lindsay Anderson, a young film maker, commented that 'a young actor with a regional or cockney accent had better lose it quick . . . for where are his chances of stardom?'[2] Five years later it was clipped public school accents that needed to be discarded as directors cried out for working-class realism in such films as *A Taste of Honey, Billy Liar*, and the adaptations of the three novels already mentioned. The new stars included Albert Finney, the son of a Salford bookmaker, Peter O'Toole, the son of an Irish immigrant from Leeds, Michael Caine, whose father was a fish porter at Billingsgate, and Terence Stamp, the son of an East End tugboat captain.

The major new cultural phenomenon of the 1950s and 1960s, pop music, was distinctly proletarian from the beginning. Tommy Steele, the first British rock and roll idol, who became a national celebrity within weeks of his début in the basement of a Soho coffee bar in 1956, was a seaman from Bermondsey. The four young men who were to burst into the hit parade in 1962 as the Beatles came from equally strong working-class backgrounds in Liverpool. Although several of the managers and promoters of pop groups were to come from the middle classes, the great majority of the song writers and the members of the groups themselves were working-class. Their music had a distinctively proletarian sound and its success reversed the usual pattern of cultural influence by spreading from the working to the middle classes.

The pop craze went some way towards establishing a single proletarian youth culture in Britain. The Mersey sound beat out at public school dances and debs' coming out parties as well as in juke boxes and works canteens. Admittedly class differences still persisted among those who took up the new culture. The middle-class beatniks of the 1950s with their sloppy jumpers and duffel coats were as different from the working-class teddy boys in their winkle pickers and drainpipe trousers as the bearded and beaded hippies of the 1960s were from the mods and rockers. Yet in dress, taste and outlook, the young of different social backgrounds were coming closer together as generation began to vie with class as the great social divider.

Television, perhaps the major cultural influence of the 1950s and 1960s, was not so much proletarian as classless. Admittedly in certain respects it maintained the traditional middle-class dominance of national culture. Even when commercial television arrived in 1955 its newscasters, Robin Day, Christopher Chataway, Aidan Crawley and Geoffrey Johnson Smith, presented the same impeccably upper middle-class image and enunciated their vowels as properly as the men from the BBC. In the areas of drama and light entertainment, however, the personalities who appeared on the screen were less clearly socially defined. The accents of Hughie Green and Bob Monkhouse seemed to hover somewhere in the middle of the Atlantic, while David Frost, educated at Cambridge and the son of a Methodist minister, produced a voice that was flat, ugly and which seemed consciously to reject his middle-class background. By its very nature as a medium bringing the same images into millions of different homes television fostered the development of a classless mass culture. *Coronation Street* was watched and enjoyed as much in the lounges of suburbia as in the living-rooms of the back to back terraced houses in the north that it portrayed.

Both pop music and television offended against certain traditional middle-class values. They had an undeniably vulgar and brash side. Their 'stars' achieved considerable fame and fortune almost overnight without the long grind of building up a business or amassing professional qualifications. The earnings of the Beatles put them firmly in the top of the upper middle-class bracket, yet there were several expressions of outrage in the letters column of the *Daily Telegraph* when they were awarded MBEs by the Queen. Arguably, however, they were no different from those Victorian entrepreneurs who had progressed from rags to riches on the basis of speculation and lucky breaks.

The late 1950s and early 1960s were, in fact, a time of considerable upward social mobility in Britain when many in the working and lower middle classes climbed up into the ranks of the bourgeoisie. Some rose through entrepreneurial flair and applied the traditional virtues of self-help and hard work to exploit the possibilities created by the consumer boom, the spectacular rise in property prices and the reorganization of business and industry. One such was Peter Walker, the son of a capstan lathe operator, who read the *Financial Times* instead of comics as a boy, and rose from being a junior clerk earning £80 a year, with another £10 for making the coffee, to become the joint head of one of the biggest finance companies in the City.

Other made their way in more conventional careers after rising through grammar school and university. There were the so-called meritocrats whose virtues of natural intelligence, hard work and dedication to duty were celebrated in the novels of C. P. Snow, most notably in *The New Men*. By the early 1950s there were several men who shared Snow's background of provincial grammar school and Oxbridge and who were already in commanding positions in the Establishment. They included Oliver Franks, British Ambassador to Washington, and Norman Brook, Secretary to the Cabinet. William Haley, who had left school at fourteen to become a wireless operator, was successively Director-General of the BBC and editor of *The Times*. At a less exalted level, many people of similar backgrounds were becoming engineers, scientists and administrators. Although these occupations put them in the middle classes, there was a sense in which they were outside the conventional class structure. As George Orwell had observed, 'People like radio engineers and industrial chemists, whose education has not been of a kind to give them any reverence for the past, and who tend to live in blocks of flats or housing estates where the old social pattern has broken down, are the most nearly classless beings that England possesses.'[3]

The meritocrats made particular headway in politics where they gradually achieved ascendancy in both the Labour and Conservative parties. It was not a classless régime that they introduced, however, but rather a distinctly middle-class one brought about at the expense of the working-class and patrician politicians who had traditionally dominated the two main parties.

In the Labour Party there was a clear process of embourge-oisement in the 1950s and 1960s as the meritocrats gradually

displaced working-class MPs. The clearest trend noted by
Dr Colin Mellors in his fascinating study *The British MP*
(1978) is what he calls the move from 'men of toil' to 'men of
ideas' between 1945 and 1974. The proportion of manual
workers among Labour MPs fell from 27.6 per cent in the 1945
Parliament to 18.4 per cent in 1964, having held reasonably
steady through the 1950s, and was down to 12 per cent after
the October 1974 election. Among new MPs the fall in the
proportion of manual workers was even more dramatic, from
39.2 per cent in 1945 to only 4.6 per cent in 1974. By contrast,
the proportion of Labour MPs with professional backgrounds
steadily increased from 34.6 per cent in 1945 to 50.8 per cent in
1974.

Statistics on the changing educational background of
Labour MPs confirm this process. In 1945 45 per cent of
Labour MPs had received only elementary schooling. That
proportion was down to 29.7 per cent in 1974. Conversely,
while those with public school education remained fairly stable
throughout the period at around 20 per cent, the proportion
with state secondary and university education went up from
18.7 per cent in 1945 to 24.6 per cent in 1964 and to 40.3 per
cent in 1974. Altogether the proportion of graduates among
Labour MPs increased from 34.2 per cent in 1945 to 55.7 per
cent in 1974.

The extent of this middle-class take-over of the Labour Party
worried some MPs. In his book *The Class Struggle in
Parliament* (1973) Eric Heffer lamented that

> Middle class ideology has permeated the party and too often the
> top echelons of the trade unions also. The trade union movement
> has continued to send its members to the House of Commons but
> certain unions have departed from the selection of genuine 'sons of
> toil' and co-opted lawyers and others on their union-sponsored list
> . . . The Parliamentary Labour Party has become increasingly
> dominated by academics, lawyers, doctors, etc. Genuine grass
> roots trade unionists have become a diminishing group.[4]

The middle-class take-over of the upper echelons of the Labour
Party was, if anything, even more striking. Half of the members
of Attlee's 1945 Cabinet were working-class, defined as those
with fathers who were manual workers and who themselves

had received no formal education after the minimum school leaving age. Only 26 per cent of Harold Wilson's first Cabinet, in 1964, fell into that category, however, and the proportion steadily dropped after successive Cabinet reshuffles until after October 1969 there were none at all. On this particular definition, the 1970 Labour Government had a 100 per cent middle-class Cabinet. The main social division had ceased to be between those with working-class and middle-class backgrounds but between meritocrats, who had risen from the lower middle classes through grammar school and university, and patricians, born into upper middle-class homes and educated at public school. The 1970 Cabinet had thirteen meritocrats and ten patricians, while in 1974 the proportion was fourteen to seven.

The Conservative Party took rather longer to be taken over by the meritocrats. The traditional patrician hold on the party remained and even strengthened throughout the 1950s and early 1960s. The proportion of Tory MPs educated at public schools, after falling slightly from 83.2 per cent in 1945 to 75.9 per cent in 1959, rose again to 78.9 per cent in 1966. When Harold Macmillan, himself a distinctly patrician figure despite his grandfather's humble origins as a Scottish crofter, was forced to give up the leadership through ill health in 1963 he was succeeded by Lord Home, the first hereditary peer to be Prime Minister of Britain since Lord Salisbury at the turn of the century.

Two political setbacks were important in persuading the Conservatives that they must drop their patrician bias and present a more classless image to the electorate. The first was the loss of the traditionally rock-solid seat of Orpington to the Liberals in a by-election in 1962. There were many reasons for the result but its message for the Tories was clear: the middle classes could no longer be relied upon to vote in straight class terms for their traditional friends. A new and more volatile middle-class electorate was growing up with no such 'natural' loyalties.

The second and more important reverse suffered by the Conservatives was the Labour victory in the 1964 General Election which put an end to thirteen years of Tory rule. The new Labour Prime Minister, Harold Wilson, was himself a perfect example of the new meritocratic middle class. The son of an industrial chemist, he had been educated at two northern grammar schools and at Oxford where he had developed a specialist grasp of economics. In his vision of a new classless Britain 'forged in the white heat of a technological revolution' he seemed to speak directly to the new classless breed of scientists, professional workers and technically qualified managers.

It was not long before the Tories realized that they must come to terms with the changes in society. In 1965 Home resigned and the party elected its first ever leader from the lower middle classes, Edward Heath, the son of a master-builder, educated at a grammar school in north Kent and at Balliol College, Oxford. Heath gradually surrounded himself with people whose background was similar to his own. Peter Walker was one of his favoured protégés. During his time as leader the Conservative Party swung gradually but perceptively away from its old patrician traditions and came more under the control of the new meritocrats and businessmen. Although there was only a marginal reduction in the proportion of Conservative MPs educated at public schools (down to 74.6 per cent after the October 1974 election), there was a steady decline in the number with landed backgrounds. On the other hand, the proportion coming from careers in business and industry, having hovered around 35 per cent throughout the 1950s and early 1960s, jumped to 55.5 per cent after the 1970 election and to 62.5 per cent after 1974.

Given how much Wilson and Heath had in common, it was not surprising that the years between 1964 and 1976 during which they presided over the government of Britain had a certain unity. As Prime Ministers both pursued a quest for efficiency, economic growth and centralized interventionist government. Both played down class divisions and sought their erosion through greater material prosperity and the restructuring of society to create a kind of classless corporate state. Both ultimately fell foul of the trade union movement and caved in before its power.

The middle classes as a whole expanded considerably in size during the Wilson and Heath years, as indeed they did throughout the 1950s and 1960s. As Table 3 shows, they grew

TABLE 3

Major occupational groups as percentage of total occupied population
SOURCE: R. Price & G. S. Bain, 'Union Growth Revisited: 1948–1974 In Perspective',
British Journal of Industrial Relations, vol. XIV, no. 3, p. 346.

	1911	*1931*	*1951*	*1961*	*1971*
Employers and proprietors	6·7	6·7	5·0	4·8	2·6
Managers and administrators	3·4	3·7	5·5	5·4	8·6
Higher professionals	1·0	1·1	1·9	3·0	3·8
Lower professionals and technicians	3·1	3·5	4·7	6·0	7·7
Foremen and inspectors	1·3	1·5	2·6	2·9	3·0
Clerks	4·5	6·7	10·4	12·7	14·0
Salesmen and shop assistants	5·4	6·5	5·7	5·9	5·6
All non-manual occupations	25·4	29·7	35·8	40·7	45·3

almost as much in those two decades as they had in the previous forty years. This growth was not uniformly spread across the various occupational groups, however. While there was a marked increase in the proportion of managers and professional workers in the population as the impact of the new meritocracy made itself felt, and a steady rise in the number of clerical workers, there was a sharp fall in the proportion of employers and entrepreneurs. The fact was that the middle classes were moving out of entrepreneurship and ownership into salaried positions as employees.

There were several factors which accounted for this trend. Businesses were amalgamating with small firms being taken over by large ones and independent proprietors replaced by corporate boards of directors and salaried managers. This process went very much further in Britain than elsewhere. The Bolton Report of 1971 found that only 31 per cent of the working population were employed in small firms, a lower proportion than in any other industrialized country in Europe. The retailing business, where so many petit bourgeois entrepreneurs had traditionally been found, was particularly affected. When Angus Maude and Roy Lewis researched their book in 1948 they found that 90 per cent of retail outlets in Britain consisted of single, independent establishments. By 1977 the proportion was less than 60 per cent.

It was not simply pressures for economy of scale that brought about the decrease in the number of independent businessmen. Other considerations had made the owners of grocery shops become supermarket managers and small employers sell out to large companies. The effects of inflation, coupled with the burdens of value added tax and employers' national insurance contributions were making the lot of the small businessman an increasingly troublesome one. It was not surprising that many of them finally decided to follow the advice that George Bernard Shaw had given at the beginning of the century when he called on the middle classes to abandon their obsession with independence for the greater comfort and security that came with being employed, so that 'the builder, instead of being a struggling tradesman, would become a public official with a gold band round his hat, a secure income and a pension'.[5]

The long-term structural change in the British economy from a manufacturing to a service base also played an important part both in increasing the size of the middle classes and in altering the nature of their occupations. A high proportion of the three million new jobs in the service sector which were created between 1951 and 1971 were by their nature middle-class occupations. During those two decades the areas of work which expanded most were education (an increase in jobs of 185 per cent), professional and scientific services (an increase of 131 per cent) and insurance, banking and finance (87.8 per cent). Just under three-quarters of these new jobs were in the so-called public sector of central and local government and nationalized industries.

The expansion of the public sector opened up a whole range of new career opportunities for the middle classes. The civil service, of course, had long been a favourite destination for bright graduates, but the middle classes had tended to shun jobs in local government. Maude and Lewis had observed slightly snootily in 1950: 'While it has never welcomed university graduates with any great show of enthusiasm, it offers reasonably good prospects to secondary school leavers.'[6] During the 1960s and early 1970s this state of affairs changed. Reorganization of local government by Peter Walker and of the health service by another of Edward Heath's ministers, Sir Keith Joseph, created an elaborate career structure and made jobs in such areas as hospital administration appealing for university graduates. The growth of the public sector also encouraged the shift from independent entrepreneurship to salaried employment. Many lawyers, architects and engineers took Bernard Shaw's advice and forsook the uncertainties of independent professional practice for the secure salary and pension of a job with a local authority, government department or public corporation.

One of the most fascinating aspects of the expansion of the service and public sectors was the attempt made to give the new jobs which they had created the status of professions. The 1950s and 1960s saw the rise of a plethora of new professional institutes and registration bodies, each with its own rules and regulations and qualifying examination on the model of the old-established professional bodies. By 1970, when the Monopolies Commission reported on the professions, there were one hundred and thirty such bodies, many of them set up in the previous two decades to confer professional status on such groups as estate agents, personnel managers and advertising practitioners. Local government was particularly rich in such bodies. There was an Institute of Baths Management, which examined its members on the operation of recreational services and engineering and water treatment, and there was even an Institute of Municipal Entertainment, whose qualifying examination could be taken by anyone 'employed in the provision of grant-aided entertainment in a post considered to qualify him for membership'.[7]

These changes in the type and style of their jobs significantly altered the outlook of a substantial proportion of the middle classes. The expansion of jobs in the public sector diminished their traditional hostility to central and local government. For an increasing number of professional, managerial and clerical workers, it was now the source of security and employment rather than of unwanted interference and unwelcome rate and tax demands. In 1975 Roy Lewis computed that there were more professional and managerial workers in the public sector than in the private sector, with only 'a diminishing cadre of self-employed'.[8]

The switch from independent entrepreneurship and professional practice into salaried employment also changed the outlook of many middle-class people. It led to that shift in attitude which W. H. Whyte had noticed in the United States of America whereby the old 'get up and go' Protestant ethic of the bourgeoisie was being replaced with a more leisured, accommodating, collectivist mentality. Fitting into the organization became all-important. That distinctive species 'Corporation Man' was beginning to be found in large numbers in the golf clubs and mock Tudor pubs of suburbia.

Other factors were also leading increasing numbers of the middle classes to identify more with other workers than with their employers. The growing use of computers downgraded the skills and status of many white-collar workers and made their offices more like factories with shift working and the need to organize around the demands of technology. Changes in the organization of companies and in working methods were breaking down the traditional close contact between white-collar workers and their bosses. Mergers and take-overs meant increasingly less contact with those at the top and progressively more extended chains of command. The trend towards open plan offices and grouping people together in large headquarters buildings produced a new sense of collectivism in the previously individualized world of managers and administrators.

As they saw their status and conditions at work declining, it was not surprising that many in the middle classes felt that they were becoming proletarianized. A survey in 1963 found that 68 per cent of lower non-manual workers saw themselves as working-class. There was growing evidence that white-collar workers were losing their traditional deference and adopting the 'them and us' attitude to employers that characterized most manual workers and that the mentality of the shop floor was entering the office. Perhaps the clearest sign of this new mood was the espousal of trade unionism by increasing numbers of middle-class workers.

Historically, as we have seen, white-collar workers had

shunned trade unions as being collectivist, working-class institutions. For marginal groups like clerks in particular membership of a union had been regarded as incompatible with middle-class status. The Clerical and Administrative Workers Union had the same level of membership in 1951 as it had had in 1921, despite the doubling in the number of clerks in the intervening thirty years.

TABLE 4

The Growth of Trade Unionism, 1948–74
SOURCE: R. Price & G. S. Bain, 'Union Growth Revisited: 1948–1974 in perspective', *British Journal of Industrial Relations*, vol. XIV, no. 3, p. 347.

(A) Union membership (000s)

	1948	*1964*	*1970*	*1974*	*% increase*
White-collar	1,964	2,684	3,592	4,263	+117·1
Manual	7,398	7,534	7,587	7,491	+0·1

(B) Union density (%)

	1948	*1964*	*1970*	*1974*	*% increase*
White-collar	30·2	29·6	35·2	39·4	+9·2
Manual	50·7	52·9	56·0	57·9	+7·2

As Table 4 shows, between 1948 and 1974 there was a considerable increase both in the absolute number and also in the relative proportion (union density) of white-collar workers who were in trade unions. Much of this increase took place in those lower middle-class occupations which had traditionally shunned trade unionism. In the twenty-five years between 1952 and 1977 membership of the National Union of Bank Employees jumped from 36,000 to 117,000; of the Clerical and Administrative Workers Union (after 1972 the Association of Professional, Executive, Clerical and Computer Staff) from 40,000 to 150,000; of the National and Local Government Officers' Association from 222,258 to 709,000; of the civil service and Post Office white-collar unions from 300,000 to

530,000; and of the main union representing draughtsmen from 55,000 to 178,000.

Several new unions sprang up to represent middle-class workers. The most significant was the Association of Scientific, Technical and Managerial Staffs (ASTMS) which was formed in 1977 by amalgamating a number of small unions. Under the dynamic leadership of Clive Jenkins, who described his main hobby in *Who's Who* as 'organizing the middle classes', it had by 1977 become the second biggest white-collar union with a membership of 441,000.

ASTMS waged bold and vigorous campaigns to attract members. It grew initially by capturing members of tradition-ally non-militant staff associations in banks and insurance companies. In 1971 it launched a large and successful advertising campaign with posters at railway stations inviting middle managers to join. 'We caught the imagination of the middle classes,' Clive Jenkins triumphantly declared. 'In the past they used to go and see their doctor, lawyer or priest. Now they come and see us.'[9]

However skilful their recruiting tactics were, however, the white-collar unions would never have grown had they not been able to capitalize on genuine and widely felt grievances. Bank clerks forsook their staff associations and middle managers abandoned their sense of identification with their bosses because they felt down-graded, alienated and under-valued. They had been collectivized at work and it was not surprising that they looked to collective action to improve their position, particularly when they saw how much it was helping manual workers. 'There is nothing startling in the growth of middle-class trade unionism,' Clive Jenkins has written, 'it was historically inevitable.'[10]

Natural as it might seem to some, however, the espousal of trade unionism by white-collar workers was regarded as an aberration by many in the small business and professional sectors of the middle classes. To them it seemed a sell-out to proletarian values. It is true that in joining trade unions the new salaried middle classes were abandoning traditional values of independence and individualism and showing the narrow 'instrumentalism' which Goldthorpe had found among the Luton car workers. But they were just as keen as the rising industrialists of the nineteenth century to defend their social position and maintain their economic distance from the working classes. They simply used different methods, seeking the protection of the state and the trade union rather than the sturdy independence of self-employment, and preferring the security of the monthly salary cheque followed by a pension to the less certain rewards of the annual profit and loss account. The growth of the unionized salariat was a challenge to old-established middle-class values and ways, but not as much as the outlook and activities of another group which came into prominence in the 1960s, the radical bourgeoisie.

9

The Radical Middle Class

If the salaried managers and unionized white-collar workers were the counterparts of the up-and-coming industrialists of the mid-Victorian period, then the new radical middle class which also emerged in the 1960s was heir to the mid-Victorian critics of the bourgeoisie. Like William Morris and Matthew Arnold, and from equally comfortable backgrounds, its members bitterly criticized the materialism, the philistinism and the conservatism of their contemporaries. Through their domination of the instruments of mass communication and education, and in particular of television and the universities, they were able to achieve a power and influence that their Victorian forbears had never had.

As with its previous manifestations earlier in the century, the middle-class radicalism of the 1960s was partly a product of guilty feelings. Its harbingers were a group of impeccably upper middle-class young men who had been at Oxford University together in the years immediately after the Second World War and who shared a certain unease about their privileged backgrounds. They included Kenneth Tynan, the son of a millionaire chain store proprietor, Lindsay Anderson, the son of an army officer, Anthony Crosland, the son of a civil servant, Anthony Wedgwood Benn, the heir to Lord Stansgate, and John Grigg, the heir to Lord Altrincham.

In the mid-1950s the members of this 'New Oxford Group', as it has been called, unleashed a series of biting attacks on the prevailing values of the middle classes and their dominant social, political and cultural institutions. The message was the same whether from Kenneth Tynan's plays about the stultifying hypocrisy of 'Loamshire', Lindsay Anderson's attempts to challenge British cinema's domination by public school heroes, Anthony Wedgwood Benn's struggle to remounce his title to the peerage so that he could sit in the House of Commons as a left-wing Labour MP, or John Grigg's irreverent dig at that most sacrosanct of all British institutions when he described the Queen as 'a priggish schoolgirl, captain of the hockey team, a prefect and a recent candidate for confirmation.'[1]

Common to all these outbursts was a strong protest against the dominance of the class system in English society. Perhaps the fullest expression of this protest came in Anthony Crosland's book, *The Future of Socialism* (1956). Crosland pointed out that 'We still retain in Britain a deeper sense of class, a more obvious social stratification, and stronger class resentments than any of the Scandinavian, Australasian or North American countries.' The purpose of his book was to expose this deep sore in the English body politic and to suggest how it might be removed by the application of democratic socialism.

While the politicians in the New Oxford Group, of whom Crosland and Wedgwood Benn were the most prominent, dedicated themselves to creating a classless society through political and economic change in the tradition of the Webbs, those involved in the arts, like Tynan and Anderson, welcomed the new proletarian culture of pop music, working-class novels and realistic cinema. Meanwhile their protest against conventional bourgeois values was being taken up more widely. The movement from entrepreneurship into employment, the development of the public sector and the expansion of education had created a new middle class which was not wedded to the principles of competitive ambition and individualism and much more open to new ideas and cultural influences. From the late 1950s onwards a series of political and social movements gave expression to a new radical consciousness among this group which was to have a profound impact on English politics and society.

The first of these movements was the Campaign for Nuclear Disarmament (CND) which was launched in 1958. From the start it was an overwhelmingly middle-class movement. Of the nineteen people on its executive in its first year, thirteen were in *Who's Who*. A recent survey of over four hundred of the activists in the early years of the movement has found that 90 per cent were from middle-class backgrounds, while Frank Parkin, who wrote a book about CND with the appropriate title *Middle Class Radicalism*, found that 83 per cent who went on the famous march from the Atomic Weapons Research Establishment at Aldermaston to London in 1965 were in professional or other white-collar occupations.[2]

CND had an important effect both in rousing the moral consciousness of the middle classes and in establishing a style of protest which was to continue throughout the 1960s and 1970s. The duffle-coated teachers and clergymen who went on the annual Aldermaston march with 'Ban the Bomb' badges in their lapels were the first in a long line of middle-class demonstrators who took to the streets in an orderly fashion to protest about the horrors of the Vietnam war, the injustices of immigration policy, the evils of racialism and the illiberal nature of the law on abortion. Before the days of CND, protest marches and public demonstrations had been predominantly working-class activities, normally organized by trade unions. Many of the protest marches of the 1960s, however, involved members of the middle classes. Indeed, it is significant that the only two people to have been killed in political demonstrations in Britain in the last twenty years were a mathematics student from Warwick University, Kevin Gately, who died during an anti-National Front demonstration in Red Lion Square in 1974, and a teacher, Blair Peach, who died after a similar demonstration in Southall in 1979.

CND also demonstrated very clearly the stress on moral values which distinguished the middle classes' approach to politics. When Parkin surveyed the 1965 Aldermaston marchers, he found that 65 per cent of those in the Registrar General's top two classes, but only 32 per cent in the bottom three classes, gave priority to moral issues when asked why they were members of CND. Conversely, twice as many in the bottom three classes (48 per cent) as in the top two (24 per cent) gave priority to economic issues. He commented: 'Radical movements with a middle class base tend to be far less orientated to the achievement of economic or material rewards for their supporters. They are instead more typically concerned with issues of a moral or humanitarian nature.'[3]

It was certainly true that the causes for which the radical middle class took to the streets in the 1960s and 1970s were predominantly humanitarian and altruistic. The working classes, by contrast, marched under their trade union banners predominantly to draw attention to their demands for better pay and conditions for themselves or in protest against something which threatened their own interests rather than in support of some minority group or far-off people.

With moral conviction and idealism went a certain fundamentalism and extremism. It was another feature of CND noted by Parkin that the middle-class members tended to be more radical and more in favour of direct action than the working-class members. This characteristic had, in fact, been already noted by George Orwell who observed in 1948 that 'In extremist political parties, it is only the middle class membership that thinks in revolutionary terms.'[4] It was certainly a noticeable feature of the various extreme left-wing political parties that emerged in the 1960s. The 'New Left', as it was called, was overwhelmingly middle-class in its activist membership. The only revolutionary left-wing party in Britain to have a significant working-class following was the old-established Communist Party which was highly conservative and scrupulously constitutional in its approach compared to the various new Trotskyist and Marxist parties. It is not without significance that the three best-known figures on the revolutionary far left in Britain in the late 1960s and 1970s, Tariq Ali of the International Marxist Group, Paul Foot of the Socialist Workers Party, and Vanessa Redgrave of the Workers Revolutionary Party, should all be from impeccably upper middle-class backgrounds.

Many of the new radical bourgeoisie went into the Labour Party where they were similarly distinguished from the more traditional working-class supporters by their extremism. Studies have shown that the displacement of manual workers by teachers, lecturers, social workers and journalists in local constituency associations provides one of the main reasons why the party as a whole moved leftwards during the 1960s and 1970s. These new middle-class recruits were more left-wing and also more interested in influencing policy than the working-class activists whom they ousted. When asked their reasons for being involved in local politics, the former were more likely to reply 'to pursue socialist goals' and the latter 'to help people'.[5]

Within the Parliamentary Labour Party and Labour Governments the same difference of emphasis existed, although on a less clear-cut basis. It was broadly true during the 1960s and early 1970s that it was working-class politicians like Ray Gunter, Bob Mellish and George Brown together with many of the trade union leaders who were on the right of the party, meritocrats like Harold Wilson and Denis Healey in the middle, and upper middle-class 'patricians' like Anthony Wedgwood Benn and Michael Foot, the son of a West Country solicitor, who tended to be on the left. In the best traditions of middle-class radicals, both these two left-wingers did their best to play down their origins, Foot by modelling himself to a certain extent on Aneurin Bevan, his predecessor for the Welsh working-class constituency of Ebbw Vale, and Benn much more systematically by shortening his name to the proletarian 'Tony Benn' and erasing from his entry in *Who's Who* all details of his education.

The second new movement which helped to create a common radical middle-class consciousness was the boom in satirical entertainment which took place in the early 1960s. It began, as far as most people were concerned, in 1961 with the arrival in London from the Edinburgh Festival of a show called *Beyond the Fringe* and the publication of a crudely printed magazine entitled *Private Eye*. Within a year the BBC had climbed on the bandwagon with a weekly Saturday evening programme, *That Was The Week That Was*, which rapidly became compulsory viewing for the new radical bourgeoisie.

To a large extent the satirical programmes and publications that followed in the wake of these pioneers appealed to an exclusively middle-class audience. Certainly those involved in their production were almost all from middle-class backgrounds themselves. *Beyond the Fringe* starred two ex-public school boys from Cambridge, Peter Cook and Jonathan Miller, and two ex-grammar school boys from Oxford, Dudley Moore and Alan Bennett. One of the founders of *Private Eye*, later to become its editor, was Richard Ingrams, educated at Shrewsbury School, with a passion for church organs and the appearance of a rather conservative prep school master. The

That Was The Week That Was team was led by David Frost and consisted mostly of other young graduates. The programme's first executive producer, Alasdair Milne, was a product of Winchester and New College, Oxford.

In taking over the new medium of television to talk largely to their own kind, the satirists established a trend that was to continue throughout the 1960s and 1970s. Careers in the mass media, and particularly in television, replaced politics or the civil service as the ultimate ambition of the bright, socially aware, moderately left-wing middle-class young. Through late night chat programmes, social concern documentaries and colour supplement features they spoke in their own distinctive language primarily to each other and to a much lesser extent to the wider world beyond. Their message was essentially the same as that of the New Oxford Group – a fairly conspicuous parading of a left-wing social conscience, a celebration of working-class culture and vitality and a corresponding attack on conventional middle-class lifestyles and values.

One of the main creations of these new secular missionaries, and the third movement which could be said to have shaped the development of a radical middle-class consciousness, was the so-called Permissive Society. Ostensibly championed as a deliberate flouting of middle-class morality, it was in fact equally, if not more, at odds with the traditional morality of the working classes and it was predominantly among the higher social classes that the new permissive mores were adopted. It applied particularly to sexual behaviour, which was also being revolutionized by what was perhaps the greatest technological breakthrough of the early 1960s, the development of an easy-to-use oral contraceptive which came to be known simply as 'the pill'.

It was extraordinary how quickly members of the Establishment joined the permissive bandwagon. In his 1962 Reith Lectures Professor G. M. Carstairs shocked many of his Home Service listeners by questioning whether chastity and monogamy were the supreme moral virtues. Two years later the Principal Medical Officer to the Ministry of Health suggested that pre-marital sexual experience should not be condemned. In 1967 Lady Helen Brook, the wife of a leading figure in the City, set up the Brook Clinic to give confidential advice on contraception to unmarried women. The following year the Family Planning Association abandoned its thirty-eight-year-old rule that it would only advise married women. Even the churches were not immune from the tide. In 1963 the Quakers produced a discussion document which departed from the traditional Christian teaching that all extra-marital sex was wrong. Three years later a British Council of Churches report on 'Sex and Morality' contained a minority recommendation that individuals should be free to pursue sexual relations with their partners whether marriage was intended or not.

The Permissive Society was given official sanction by three Acts of Parliament in 1967 which legalized homosexual relations in private, made abortion easier and liberalized the divorce laws. Significantly these measures were predominantly championed by young middle-class people with support from the increasingly liberal Establishment and opposed most fiercely by lower middle-class and working-class moralists.

The sexual revolution of the 1960s was, indeed, a predominantly middle-class phenomenon. In some ways it represented a catching up with the working classes, many of whom had traditionally been less inhibited about pre-marital sex. In other respects, however, it went much further. Middle-class homosexuals 'came out' and openly paraded and celebrated their 'gayness' in a way that was still largely impossible for those in the much more conservative and taboo-ridden working classes. Middle-class girls were more likely to go on the Pill. Liberated couples in newly gentrified areas went in for 'open' marriages and wife-swopping, much to the disapproval of their proletarian neighbours. Young middle-class lovers faced with an unwanted pregnancy were more likely to end it with an abortion, those from the working classes to solve the problem in the time-honoured way by marrying. The phrase 'middle-class morality' was beginning to take on a very different meaning from the one that it had had in Victorian times.

The sexual revolution introduced new patterns of behaviour and new tensions into middle-class life. Adolescence became a more exciting, and for parents more anxious, period. Living together rather than marriage became an increasingly common experience for students and young couples. For women the changes which came about in the 1960s were particularly important. The Pill gave them a new mastery over their bodies while at the same time the new atmosphere gave them greatly increased expectations of sexual enjoyment and of personal independence. In middle-class relationships the traditional pattern of male dominance and female submissiveness broke down as the age of the liberated woman dawned.

The idealism and left-wing political activity which followed in the aftermath of CND, the satire boom and the permissive society would not have flourished as they did without the great expansion of higher education in the same period. Between 1954 and 1974 the number of full-time university students quadrupled from 68,000 to 261,000. The females among them acquired qualifications and expectations which led them far beyond the traditional middle-class woman's role of housewife and voluntary worker. More generally, the new intelligentsia proved the perfect breeding ground for the developing radical middle-class culture.

The expansion of the universities had been designed to give greater educational opportunities to the working classes and to breed more scientists and technocrats. In fact, the new universities recruited overwhelmingly from the middle classes and turned out predominantly arts and social science graduates. A distinct student culture emerged in the 1960s, based on left-wing political commitment, permissive attitudes to sex and drugs, and attachment to folk music and the work of certain 'cult' authors. It was as far removed from traditional working-class values as it was from those of the bourgeoisie. The middle-class hippies with their peasant-style clothes, beads, flower patterns and psychedelic bands could hardly have been further removed from the working-class skinheads with their cropped hair, dyed Levis, braces, Dr Martin boots and aggressive proletarian patriotism.

In a way this new youth culture had achieved what the Victorian critics of the bourgeoisie had called for. No longer could it be said that the middle classes were all competitive, money-loving and uncultured. Many a bank manager or industrialist tried vainly to persuade his son to follow in a safe and respectable career instead of 'dropping out' to a commune in rural Wales, doing a doctorate on some esoteric academic subject, or going into the new caring profession of social work.

The new radical middle classness had a considerable effect on the academic life of universities as well as on the values of students. It led in arts and social science departments to a preoccupation with the phenomenon of class and particularly with the sociology, culture and history of the working classes. Sociologists and historians followed the lead given by the Hammonds at the beginning of the century of looking at society with an anti-bourgeois perspective. In 1960 a Society of Labour History was formed to correct the middle-class bias that was thought to exist in previous historical writing. In 1963 E. P. Thompson produced his classic work, *The Making of the English Working Class*, in which he dismissed the Methodist religion in which he had been brought up by his missionary parents as an agent of social control and a form of psychic masturbation. English lecturers found similarly unpleasant things to say about bourgeois novelists.

Although it was the media and the universities which most obviously felt the effects of the new middle-class radicalism other institutions were not immune from its influence. The Church was clearly affected. It responded to a continuing steady fall both in attendance (down by 19 per cent between 1960 and 1970) and in the number of recruits to the ministry (down from 632 to 373 between 1963 and 1973) by striving to make itself 'trendy' and 'with it'. In 1963 the Rev. John Robinson, the suffragen Bishop of Woolwich, produced a best-selling book called *Honest to God* which discarded much traditional theology. Other clergymen keenly welcomed the new permissive morality and espoused left-wing political causes. In 1966 the first of a series of services in modern English was introduced as an alternative to the 1662 Prayer Book.

The civil service also felt the effects of the new radicalism. In 1966 Harold Wilson set up a committee under Sir John Fulton to examine ways of making it more up-to-date and less dominated by upper middle-class public school and Oxbridge entrants. One of the committee's main recommendations was implemented in 1970 when the old tripartite class system was abolished and the separate administrative executive and clerical grades were merged into a single hierarchy.

The professions were also affected by the new movement. An increasing number of young entrants into the old learned professions chose to go into community medicine or neighbourhood law centres rather than into more conventional private practice. Meanwhile the new caring profession of social work was given official recognition by the Seebohm Report of 1968. Until the 1950s social work had predominantly been undertaken by volunteers and those working for voluntary agencies and by hospital almoners. Subsequent legislation had created new jobs in the probation service, child care and family welfare and following Seebohm's recommendations many of these jobs were brought together and a new career of professional social worker was created.

Not even the public schools were immune from the effects of the new movement. *The Public School Hymn Book*, a reliable barometer of upper middle-class confidence, having shed one or two of its more militaristic and imperialistic hymns at each reprinting, finally changed its name in 1963 to the bland and classless *Hymns for Church and School*. A new breed of masters, educated in the values of the new radicalism in the universities, introduced changes both in the classroom and outside it. Out went compulsory corps, fagging and G. M. Trevelyan's *England Under The Stuarts*, and in came community service, 'A' Level sociology, and the Marxist historian Christopher Hill's *Century of Revolution*. Lindsay Anderson's film *If* (1968) powerfully portrayed the assault on the conventional public school values by the new radical youth culture.

It was significant, in fact, that some of the most energetic propagators of the new radicalism of the 1960s were themselves products of the public school system. The originators of *Private Eye* had been at Shrewsbury together in the 1950s, as had Paul Foot. Tony Elliott, who founded *Time Out*, the most enduring of the 'alternative' magazines set up in the late 1960s, and Richard Branson, who after launching a less successful magazine, *Student*, found a more lucrative way of cashing in on the new youth culture when he set up Virgin Records, the biggest independent record company in Britain, were both at Stowe School in the mid-1960s.

It was, however, in the state sector of education that the full blast of the new middle-class radicalism was felt most keenly. The traditions of competition, selection and high academic achievement upheld by the grammar schools came increasingly under attack from progressive educational theorists and egalitarian politicians in the 1960s as the movement for comprehensive education gathered pace.

The background to the comprehensive movement was a series of reports which showed that despite the 1944 Education Act, access to more favoured forms of education was still strongly differentiated along class lines. As early as 1956 a survey by Oxford sociologists, *Social Class and Educational Opportunity*, revealed that despite the creation of free places, the grammar schools were still overwhelmingly taking middle-class pupils and the secondary modern and technical schools were taking those from the working classes. Successive official inquiries confirmed this finding and also showed that there was little appreciable increase in the number of working-class children going to university. The blame was laid on the divisive nature of the tripartite system.

The attack on the grammar schools and the move to replace them with comprehensives was very much a radical middle-class campaign. It was fiercely resisted by the lower middle classes, who had gained so much from the grammar school system, and by many in the working classes. The greatest champions of comprehensive education were almost invariably themselves either grammar or public school products.

The move towards comprehensive reorganization was enthusiastically taken up by Sir Edward Boyle (himself educated at Eton and Oxford) who was Minister for Education from 1962 to 1964 in Macmillan's Conservative Government. When he came into office, ninety local education authorities already had plans to reorganize schools along comprehensive lines. Boyle encouraged other authorities to do the same and persuaded fellow-Tories, including the future party leader, Edward Heath, of the merits of the new system. Looking back later, he saw his main achievement as having been to bring middle-class opinion round to favour comprehensives.[6]

The real architect of comprehensive reorganization, however, was Anthony Crosland, who as Minister of Education in Harold Wilson's first Government produced the famous circular 10/65 which requested all local authorities to submit plans for reorganizing all their secondary schools along comprehensive lines. In *The Future of Socialism* he had outlined his main objection to grammar schools, that they perpetuated class division. 'Our schools,' he wrote, 'have been essentially middle-class institutions and our educational system geared to educating the middle classes, plus a few from below who looked like desirable recruits to the middle class. The remainder were given cheaper teachers and inferior buildings and were segregated in separate schools.' In Crosland's view comprehensive education was the weapon with which to destroy the English class system.

Although the attack on the grammar schools persisted through the 1960s, with several local authorities implementing an all comprehensive system, it lost momentum in the early 1970s. Mrs Margaret Thatcher, Minister of Education in Edward Heath's 1970 Conservative Government, reversed Crosland's circular 10/65. Even Harold Wilson, who returned as Prime Minister in 1974, promised that the grammar schools would be destroyed 'only over my dead body'. When Labour came to power, there were about two thousand comprehensive schools, just over a third of the total number of state secondary schools. It did not look as though the radical middle class was going to be able to achieve its aim of setting up a totally classless system of state education.

One group within the old-established middle classes was strongly influenced by the ideas and activities of the new radical element in their midst. Those in the professions had always been more broad-minded and tolerant, and more open to ideas and cultural developments than others. They also had a strong strain of idealism and altruism which led them to respond positively to many of the new movements of the 1960s. In their own gentle and unassuming way, many of those in the professional middle class were radicalized in this period. They showed their new social and political awareness in a growing concern about poverty and suffering both at home and abroad, an increased interest in the conservation of the environment, and a growing tendency to vote Liberal.

Concern about poverty and suffering and an active

commitment to work for its alleviation had, of course, long been a characteristic of a substantial element within the English professional class. In the 1950s and 1960s, however, this philanthropic impulse seems to have become particularly strong, inspired partly perhaps by the dramatic portrayals on the new medium of television of the effects of economic and social deprivation and partly by a new interest in under-developed countries as the final dismemberment of the British Empire prompted feelings of guilt about past exploitation.

Certainly it was the plight of the so-called Third World which most touched tender middle-class consciences. Oxfam, the organization which had been founded by a group of concerned Oxford dons to help refugees during the war, mushroomed in the 1950s and 1960s to become one of the biggest disaster relief and development agencies in the world. Virtually every town had its own Oxfam group and shop manned by middle-class ladies. In 1958 the growing idealism and commitment to the Third World of many young people was harnessed by the setting up of Voluntary Service Overseas (VSO) which was to send out to work in developing countries thousands of school leavers with a year free before they went up to university.

The founder of VSO, Dr Alec Dickson, is a fine example of the English upper middle-class tradition of altruism and voluntary public service. Educated at Rugby School and New College, Oxford, he helped refugees in the war and dedicated the rest of his life to putting into practice his deep conviction that the better-off have a moral responsibility to help the less well-off. Four years after setting up VSO, he founded Community Service Volunteers to provide opportunities for young people to engage in voluntary work at home. As a result of his initiative, community service came to be either a curricular or extra-curricular activity at many schools.

Concern with conserving the physical environment was both a newer and more widespread manifestation of the growing social consciousness and radicalization of the professional middle class in the 1960s. It showed itself in different levels of commitment. Many bought more books about the country-side, put their names to petitions opposing the destruction of local historic buildings or the building of a new motorway, and joined their local civic society. Some went further, joining with members of the radical middle class in campaigning organizations like Friends of the Earth to save the whale and stop nuclear power stations being built and consciously trying to live a more natural and simple life, with free-range eggs, wholemeal bread, recycled writing paper and a bicycle. An increasing number in both groups gave political expression to their new idealistic, ecology-conscious radicalism by voting for the Liberal Party.

Most other groups in the middle classes were, however, very little affected by the new current of radicalism. Left-wing political idealism and 'alternative' culture did not penetrate far into the executive-type estates and the mock-Tudor pubs of suburbia nor did it seem to evoke a particularly strong reaction. There were admittedly mutterings of disapproval in *Daily Telegraph* leaders, meetings of the Mother's Union and other strongholds of old-fashioned middle-class morality about the horrors of the permissive society. In 1964 Mrs Mary Whitehouse, the daughter of a gentleman's outfitter and the senior mistress at a secondary school in Shropshire, and her friend Norah Buckland, the wife of a Staffordshire vicar, set up the Clean Up TV campaign to fight the tide of secularism and smut which they saw engulfing the media. But in general during the 1960s most of the middle classes did not seem over-concerned about the assault that was being mounted from within their own ranks on their lifestyle and values. By the mid-1970s, however, their attitude had changed. They had had enough and were in a mood to revolt.

10

To the Barricades
The Crisis of the Mid-1970s

From time to time, as we have seen, the English middle classes go through a fit of collective anger and despair. Such a mood came over them in the mid-1970s when a combination of economic, social and political factors led some of them to feel that their species was in serious danger of extinction. Of these, the economic factors were the most important, and the most directly damaging. A combination of high inflation, high taxation and Government pay policy had hit small businessmen and professional and managerial workers disproportionately hard and eroded their traditional differentials from manual workers.

The middle classes are always hard hit by inflation. As savers they experience a fall in the value of their investments, and as high income earners they suffer from the phenomenon known as fiscal drag which means that they are pushed into higher tax brackets and have to pay a higher proportion of their income in tax. Both these phenomena occurred during the period of high inflation between 1970 and 1975. Yields from investments like unit trusts and building society accounts fell in real terms. At the same time fiscal drag meant that a senior manager who had paid only 25 per cent of his income in tax in 1965 was paying 42 per cent ten years later. The Royal Commission on the Distribution of Income and Wealth calculated that between 1969 and 1975 the real value of salaries after tax had fallen by 17 per cent at the £10,000 level and by 25 per cent at the £20,000 level.

The effects of inflation on middle-class savings and earnings were compounded by a range of fiscal exactions made by both Labour and Conservative Governments. The most severe were perhaps those introduced by the Labour Chancellor, Denis

Healey, in his April 1974 budget when he raised the basic rate of income tax to 33 per cent (the following year it went up again to 35 per cent), increased the top rate on earned income from 75 per cent to 83 per cent and on investment income to 98 per cent, and also lowered the starting point for the surcharge on investment income. Labour's commitment to bring about 'a fundamental and irreversible shift in the balance of power and wealth in favour of working people and their families' seemed one step nearer fulfilment.

The Conservatives themselves had earlier been responsible for a new fiscal exaction which caused almost more anger among one section of the middle classes than anything that Labour did. The introduction of value added tax in 1973 imposed on more than a million small businessmen and shopkeepers with a turnover of more than £5000 an enormous amount of tedious and time-consuming paperwork. Another fiscal innovation, the Capital Transfer Tax introduced in 1975 to replace the old system of estate duty, appeared to many to threaten the possibility of passing on a business from father to son. The self-employed were also angered by the introduction of a new Class 4 graduated national insurance contribution which came into force in the same year.

The economic position of many in the middle classes was further weakened by the effects of the successive pay policies imposed by both Conservative and Labour Governments during the early and mid-1970s. By giving flat rate rises across the board to everyone, they narrowed differentials and favoured the lower paid. They were also conceived primarily in the interests of manual workers, providing opportunities for extra earnings through greater overtime and self-financing productivity schemes, neither of which are normally open to those in professional and managerial occupations. Under the first phase of the 1974 Labour Government's policy, while the pay of workers generally rose by 14 per cent, doctors' incomes, for instance, increased by only 2.3 per cent.

Overall, the combined effect of inflation, taxation and pay policy was to produce a fall in the standard of living of many people in middle-class occupations at a time when other workers were generally still gaining ground. The following figures worked out by Professor Newbould of the University of

Bradford[1] show changes in real income after tax between 1965 and 1975 for various middle-class occupations and for manual workers:

	%
University professor	−19
Senior manager (chemical company)	−14
Senior manager (oil company)	−12
Senior manager (nationalized industry)	−12
Senior manager (food company)	−11
Senior civil servant	−8
Senior hospital administrator	+1
Senior manager (clearing bank)	+2
Senior accountant (in practice)	+2
Average manual worker	+13

As well as coming nearer to them in level of earnings, some of the middle classes were also beginning to experience for the first time deprivations traditionally associated only with the working classes. We have already noticed the introduction of shift working in offices and the diminution of status and independence caused by take-overs and mergers. The re-organization of businesses also meant that the spectre of redundancy was beginning to haunt executive boardrooms. Recognizing this new situation, the Department of Employment in 1973 set up a new agency, Professional and Executive Recruitment, to act as an employment agency for the unemployed middle classes. In its first four years the number of people on its books rose from 23,000 to 74,000.

The sense of grievance among the middle classes was considerably increased by what they took to be the prevailing attitudes of both the Conservative and Labour Governments of 1970 to 1976. In the eyes of many, there was little to choose between Wilson and Heath. Both seemed committed to corporatism and more bureaucracy, and to governing the country through consultation with the trade unions and the representatives of big business without any reference to those in between.

Edward Heath's 1970–74 Government was blamed for causing massive inflation, introducing value added tax, expensively reorganizing the health and local government services and imposing a savage freeze on salaries and professional charges. It seemed radically to depart from the principles of minimal government and non-interference and it was not surprising that there was a substantial middle-class defection from the Conservatives in the February 1974 election. The proportion of those in social Classes A and B voting Conservative dropped by 16.1 per cent from 1970, while those in C1 dropped by 8.2 per cent and those in C2 by 8.6 per cent.

The actions of Harold Wilson's 1974–76 Government provoked ever greater anger. Not only its fiscal policies, but the whole of its legislative programme seemed designed to favour the working classes at the expense of the middle classes. Despite Wilson's promise that he would fight to keep them, not only grammar schools but also direct grant schools were sacrificed on the altar of comprehensive reorganization. The Secretary of State for Education rejected a proposal for education vouchers on the grounds that they would favour 'articulate and enterprising middle-class families at the expense of those less well informed and less well-off'. The freedom and independence of doctors was threatened by moves to prevent those in the National Health Service from practising privately and to abolish pay beds in hospitals. The 1975 Rent Act seemed to favour tenants and penalize landlords. The Government's labour legislation angered employers and non-unionized workers by its apparently partisan nature. The 1974 Trade Unions and Labour Relations Act seemed to put trade unions above the law and made them immune from civil actions for damages. It also allowed unions to operate 100 per cent closed shops. The Employment Protection Act of the following year also seemed to favour the worker and, for example, put the onus on the employer in case of an appeal against dismissal. Like the provision in the Equal Opportunities Act, about rights to maternity leave, it caused particular annoyance among small businessmen.

Almost more alarming to many in the middle classes than the actual measures taken by the successive Conservative and Labour Governments in the early 1970s was the language used by politicians of both parties. Not surprisingly, it was from the Labour side that the most threatening statements came. Eric Heffer wrote his book, *The Class Struggle in Parliament*, in

1973 to attack the Labour Party of the 1960s for being too middle-class and to remind the party in the 1970s that 'Because we live in a class society, based upon private ownership, there is a fundamental struggle between those who own and control industry and those who do not. In other words, the class struggle is a reality.' In the same vein, Michael Meacher, a young Labour MP, complained in an article in the *New Statesman* in January 1974 that class politics had ceased to be respectable when Labour had 'escaped from class to nation'. Now, however, he felt that espousal of class politics was again 'just waiting to be exploited'. Bryan Magee, a right-wing Labour MP, predicted ominously in *The Times* seven months later that under the newly elected Labour Government Britain was going to become a more uncomfortable and unpleasant place for the middle classes as the glaring injustices of what he called 'our caste system' were rectified.[2]

From Labour politicians such sentiments could perhaps be expected. But anti-bourgeois rhetoric was also coming from the mouths of leading Conservatives. Mr Heath had already offended many small businessmen by talking in office about the 'unacceptable face of capitalism'. Following his two defeats at the polls in 1974, several of his staunchest supporters voiced sentiments which seemed even more calculated to alienate their traditional supporters. Declaring that 'It would be quite wrong for the Conservative Party to retreat into the bunkers and bolt-holes of narrow middle-class politics,' Peter Walker warned that if the Tories abandoned their 'one nation' tradition and forgot the working classes, they 'would swiftly deteriorate into a small, middle-class party similar to those Scandinavian right-wing parties that have remained almost perpetually out of office'. Nicholas Scott, a leading Conservative back-bencher, argued equally forcefully that the Tories 'must resist the view that we are the party of the last ditch defence of the bourgeois ethic'.[3]

It was in the mid-1970s that the trend by the radical bourgeoisie of using 'middle class' as a pejorative term reached its height. The General Synod of the Church of England rejected a motion calling for the abolition of the closed shop in industry after speakers had expressed the fear that support for it would offend trade unions and show the Church to be 'a middle-class preserve'. In the educational world, intelligence tests and GCE 'O' and 'A' Level examinations were attacked as middle-class devices which perpetuated social division. Even the Duke of Edinburgh was sufficiently caught up in the contemporary tide to express publicly his worry that his own award scheme for young people had too middle-class an image.[4]

The strength of middle-class values in Britain was increasingly being blamed for the nation's ills. Reversing Matthew Arnold's criticism, commentators maintained that the public school system, the persistence of classical education, and the tradition that the professions were socially superior to trade, were instrumental in explaining why bright British graduates did not go into engineering or industry. A report by the Government's Central Policy Review Staff (the so-called Think Tank) on Britain's Diplomatic Service in 1977 criticized the service for its over-high standards and its conservatism 'in the sense of a sort of middle-classness in the prevailing values'.

There was a parallel assault on the middle-class hold on the media. Independent television finally dared to introduce working-class accents into the sacred preserve of children's television and with Miss Janet Street-Porter, star of a number of programmes aimed at teenagers and young people, it introduced an accent which was the antithesis of all the clipped vowels and beautifully articulated consonants that had gone before. In the BBC as well 'middle class' was becoming a dirty word as an internal memorandum to producers from the Head of Current Affairs Magazine Programmes, Radio, in May 1976 shows:

> May I ask you all for a determined effort to make sure you have a really representative range of voices in your programmes. At the moment it is undoubtedly a stumbling block that people switching on to us occasionally in ordinary households in far flung parts of the United Kingdom react adversely to the preponderance of southern middle-class voices. Stretch every nerve to have less backward looking or nostalgic items and to get a really representative range of ordinary people of every kind of region and class into our programmes.

In industry too the general climate of egalitarianism was making the middle classes feel unloved and unwanted. The growing stress on worker participation, which was given added weight by the recommendations of the Bullock Committee set up by the Labour Government in 1976, was making it increasingly difficult for managers to manage. Those in middle management posts felt particularly frustrated as they saw trade unionists gaining direct access to bosses whom they themselves seldom if ever met.

It was no wonder that in the face of this real erosion of their living standards and power and this barrage of criticism of their values, the middle classes felt beleaguered and threatened. Bryan Magee wrote in his article in *The Times* that 'It is natural that as the middle class loses its special position, and perhaps its identity, more and more of its members will honestly think civilization is falling apart.' The sense of impending disaster that hung over many middle-class institutions in the mid-1970s is clearly evident in a letter sent out to old boys and parents by a preparatory school in the South East appealing for funds for new buildings: 'With the socialists in office this may seem an odd time to show confidence in the future; however, there are two alternatives, to sell up or to fight on until the bitter end when parents will no longer have the right and freedom of choice.' It went on to compare the threat that the school was facing now with the one it faced in the two world wars.

There was certainly general agreement in the media both at home and abroad that the English middle classes were suffering an unprecedented crisis in the mid-1970s. In December 1974 I wrote an article in *The Times* which was entitled 'The Question Mark Hanging Over the Future of the Middle Classes'. A subsequent leader in the paper in January 1975 on 'The Anger of the Middle Class' thundered that 'Many people in the middle class feel all the resentment and anxiety of being boxed in' and warned the Government to recognize 'the danger of a middle-class revolt'. An independent television documentary in June 1975 was entitled *The Mangling of the Middle Classes* while the American Magazine *Newsweek* devoted the cover and much of the contents of its issue of 1 November 1976 to 'Britain's Battered Middle Classes'. In the same month Morley Safer, an American commentator, told the audience of a CBS *Sixty Minutes* programme on the state of Britain: 'The rich still eat their strawberries and cream . . . The workers are lazy . . .

The middle class has nowhere to turn, having been bled white by high taxes and 20 and 30 per cent inflation. Middle class values are a joke.' At the end of 1976 Patrick Hutber, city editor of the *Sunday Telegraph*, brought out his book *The Decline and Fall of the Middle Class and How it Can Fight Back*.

In his book Hutber summed up a general feeling of many who wrote on the subject that the middle classes were acquiescing in their own destruction through a combination of traditional reticence, good manners and feelings of guilt:

> Never has a section of society more enthusiastically co-operated in its own euthanasia. If the characteristic attitude of the middle class has to be summed up in a single phrase, it would surely be the words, 'I'm awfully sorry but you're treading on my foot.' There in a single sentence you have a very mild reaction to intense discomfort, combined with a very strong desire not to kick up a fuss . . . No French aristocrat could have gone to the guillotine more serenely than the British middle class has gone to its economic doom. Taxed, squeezed, vilified, they have smiled wanly and changed the subject.[5]

One of the many letters which appeared in *The Times* on the subject gave a rather different and more dramatic explanation for the phenomenon that the journalist Auberon Waugh had described in a television programme as 'the deafening silence of the middle class':

> It is said that T. H. Huxley placed a frog in a saucepan of lukewarm water and each day increased the temperature of the water by half a degree. Eventually the frog died, but the process was so gradual that at no time did the frog make an attempt to jump out. In such a way the middle class is being deprived of life without complaint or resistance . . .
>
> That the middle classes are the scapegoats for the country's economic ills is quite obvious, and will remain so until those classes are ready to exercise their lungs in their own defence.[6]

This call to arms was a commonly sounded theme. The central message of Hutber's book was contained in the last six words of its title. Its chapter headings included 'How to save your school'. 'How to scare your council', and 'Agenda for action'. In 1976 Roy Lewis contributed an article to *The Times* asking quite simply: 'When are the middle classes going to fight back?'

In fact, the middle classes were reacting to the assault on

them, but not on the whole in ways that those who encouraged them to fight had in mind. Some were simply opting out and leaving Britain for more congenial climes abroad. The mid-1970s saw a quickening in the 'brain drain' of doctors, engineers and high-flying executives to the United States and other countries where they could make substantially more money.

Others, particularly in managerial and white-collar clerical jobs, continued to find as they had in the 1960s that it was better to swim with the tide than to try and resist it. The shift from self-employment and entrepreneurship to salaried employee status and the growth of white-collar trade unionism both quickened in the mid-1970s. One of the more interesting results of the latter phenomenon was a growing challenge to the traditional domination of the trade union movement by manual workers. The 1975 Trades Union Congress (TUC) was enlivened by a spirited attack by white-collar unions on Mr Jack Jones, leader of the largest manual workers' union, the Transport and General (TGWU), and the architect of the flat rate pay policy of 1975, for failing to take account of the interests of middle-class workers and by a powerful speech from Terry Casey, secretary of the National Association of Schoolmasters, reminding Congress that 'better paid trade unionists are every bit as worthy . . . every bit as necessary to our society' as the less well paid.[7]

In many ways the most militant response came from those in the professions. They had particular reason to be angry. Worse affected than most other groups by successive Government pay policies, they were also faced by a decline in their status and their traditional independence because of changing working conditions and public attitudes. The medical profession experienced this combined assault in a particularly acute form. The power of hospital doctors had been diminished by the growth of worker participation which had led in many cases to porters and cleaning ladies having a say in matters which had previously been left entirely to consultants. There was also a strong feeling among doctors that the Labour Government wanted to turn them into salaried servants of the state and rob them of their independence. Engineers and surveyors were also becoming increasingly worried about their declining public status and the growing readiness of clients to sue them for negligence, while many architects were in financial difficulties as the building boom of the 1960s and early 1970s came to an end.

The sense of frustration was well brought out in a letter to *The Times* in March written by the heads of twelve leading professional associations. After outlining the particular problems that inflation caused to members of the professions and pointing out that many had already emigrated, it went on to warn of the consequences of a continued failure by the Government to listen to their case:

> Most worrying of all, and most insidiously damaging to the national well-being, is the danger of an internal retreat to a condition of indifference or self-protectiveness in which the traditional practice of professionals to put service before self-interest is eroded and the opportunity for leisure tends to be put above the satisfaction derived from rendering more than the minimum expected. The nation cannot afford to squander – deliberately – such an expensively produced and precious resource, especially in these difficult times. We ask the Government to give appropriate weight to these considerations and in doing so to consult the professions as necessary, before a difficult situation becomes even worse.[8]

Their feeling that they were being left out of the consultations which the Government was having with both trade unions and employers' representatives on such subjects as pay policy and labour legislation led several professional associations to join together in discussions about establishing a common forum. Several attempts were made in the mid-1970s to establish a body which would do for the professions what the TUC did for workers and the Confederation of British Industry (CBI) did for employers. Eventually at the beginning of 1978 seventeen associations, including the British Medical Association (BMA), the United Kingdom Association of Professional Engineers and the Association of Polytechnic Lecturers, who between them represented 250,000 professional and managerial workers, joined forces to set up the Managerial and Professional Staff Liaison Group.

At its first meeting with Government ministers, when it pressed for a restoration of differentials in the next round of pay policy, and reductions in income tax and national insurance contributions in the next budget, the group was told politely but firmly that the workers whom it represented had no industrial muscle and that if they were treated fairly there would be a wages explosion. It was hardly surprising that many in the professions had already decided that the only way they were going to get fair treatment was by demonstrating that they did indeed have some muscle and by emulating the tactics of industrial workers.

The trade unionization of the professions was one of the most striking social phenomena of the 1970s. It took place in various different ways. Several old-established professional associations, including the BMA, the British Dental Association and the Royal College of Nursing, turned themselves into trade unions as they were obliged to do to take advantage of the new labour legislation. New unions, like the Association of Management and Professional Staffs (AMPS) and the British Union of Social Workers (BUSW), were set up to represent those working in specific professions. Meanwhile existing general white-collar unions took in an increasing number of new members from the professions. By the late 1970s Clive Jenkins claimed that ASTMS was recruiting ten thousand new members a year from professional occupations.

Very few professions were immune from the trend. In 1975 the Council of Engineering Institutions recommended that its members should join trade unions and in the following two years the proportion of chartered engineers who were unionized increased from 37 to 44 per cent. Many speech therapists, physiotherapists and other professional workers in the health service joined the Medical Practitioners' Union, which was part of ASTMS, while a growing number of nurses joined the Confederation of Health Service Employees. Many of the growing band of architects, surveyors and scientists working for central or local government joined NALGO or the Institute of Professional Civil Servants.

Trade unionism even crept into the law and the Church. A legal workers' branch of the Association of Clerical, Technical and Scientific Staff, itself part of the TGWU, was set up in 1976 to represent solicitors' articled clerks, who were traditionally badly paid and enjoyed poor conditions of service. In the same

year a group of industrial chaplains in the Manchester area felt
that they could no longer duck the question 'And what union
are you in then, brother?' which was increasingly being put to
them. They looked round for an appropriate union to join and
found sanctuary in the ever-willing arms of ASTMS. By 1979
the ASTMS clergy group was about eighty strong and had put
forward demands for a minumum wage and better expenses. A
year earlier the Society of Authors had applied to be registered
as a trade union after a poll had shown that 68 per cent of its
members had decided that even the most individualistic of all
the professions would benefit from collective action.

The professions were not particularly enthusiastic in their
espousal of trade unionism. Some were forced into it by closed
shop agreements at their place of work. Others accepted it as an
unfortunate necessity which had been forced upon them by the
Government's labour legislation and its apparent tendency to
ignore the interests of those who were not unionized. Sensing
this general mood of reluctance, the specialist professional
unions stressed their differences from the militant manual
workers' unions affiliated to the TUC. AMPS's recruiting
literature made much of the fact that its membership was
restricted to professional people. 'What would a broom-pusher
know of professional ethics?' it asked rhetorically.

There were many people, however, who remained convinced
that trade unionization, in whatever shape or form, was
fundamentally incompatible with the traditional independence
and commitment to ethical standards of the professions.
Writing in *The Times* review of the first twenty-five years of
Queen Elizabeth II's reign, Paul Johnson took the unionization
of the professions as the single most important step in the
period towards the proletarianization of the middle classes.
The decision of certain professional trade unions to affiliate to
the TUC caused particular concern to those who valued the
traditional political independence and impartiality of the
professions. All the civil service unions took this step in the
1970s, including the First Division Association which
represents those of Assistant Secretary level and above. So did
the Hospital Consultants and Specialists Association and the
Association of University Teachers (AUT). The letter of
resignation sent by Sir Max Beloff, Gladstone Professor of

Public Administration at Oxford University and subsequently Principal of University College, Buckingham, and for thirty-seven years an AUT member expressed the feelings of many:

> I have been increasingly aware of the fact that the AUT which, when I joined it, was regarded as a professional association concerned with its members' common interest in their profession and with the services that this profession might render to the community, has increasingly taken the form of a simple pressure group concerned exclusively with the material benefits that it can secure for its members.
>
> This development from a political body to a mere trade union was completed by the decision to affiliate to the Trades Union Congress. It is to my mind incompatible with the whole idea of academic independence that the members of the profession, irrespective of their view, should be part of an organization which is closely linked to a particular political party.[9]

It was not just the institutional aspects of working-class trade unionism that the professions took on in the 1970s but also something of its militancy and readiness to disrupt society in the pursuit of narrow self-interest. At the beginning of the decade the author of a book on the middle classes could write with confidence that 'When the threat to withdraw labour occurs in the professions, as with doctors and teachers, it all seems a little unreal.'[10] Within the next five years both hospital doctors and teachers had withdrawn their labour in pursuit of pay claims, not admittedly in an all-out strike but by working to rule and refusing to do certain duties that they normally performed. Senior civil servants had taken part in a one-day strike and professional scientists working for the Government had pursued a policy of non-co-operation. At the end of the decade social workers went on strike for periods of up to a year.

The instrumentalism that Goldthorpe had found among the car workers of Luton seemed to be entering into the very heart of the middle classes. It might be understandable that junior hospital doctors were insisting on an industrial-type contract which gave them a forty-hour week, but there was no doubt of the profound change that this and other demands indicated in the attitude of those in the professions. As a correspondent to *The Times* in 1975 pointed out, it signalled a departure from their historic willingness to shoulder the risk of their calling without limitation of liability, 'for if the price does not justify the risk, the risk will be reduced if the price cannot be increased'.[11]

There was one group among the middle classes who did not join in the general move towards collectivism and who displayed their anger at the twin assaults of inflation and socialist legislation in a more traditional form. For most of the self-employed and small businessmen joining a union or becoming a salaried employee were equally impractical and unacceptable options. They responded to the crisis of the mid-1970s just as their fathers and grandfathers had responded to earlier crises, by setting up defence organizations to fight the tide of corporatism and socialism which they felt was threatening to engulf them.

The most curious of these organizations were the so-called 'private armies' which were assembled by a handful of retired servicemen in the Home Counties. The biggest was probably Civil Assistance, set up in July 1974 by General Sir Walter Walker to provide support for the Government in the event of a general strike. It claimed to have a hundred thousand men ready to respond to the call for action. The following month Colonel David Stirling launched GB75, an army of 'apprehensive patriots' who would be trained to operate power stations and keep other essential services going in the event of a strike. In September a third organization emerged in the shape of the Middle Class Volunteer Reserve, founded by Wing Commander Rupert Goding. Although this last body stressed that it was not a private army, it issued a warning 'that most of our members are ex-soldiers, sailors or airmen and well trained men who would rise if called upon to do so by the legitimate government'.

These 'private armies' claimed to represent the silent middle-class majority in the country which was fed up with the actions of governments, unions and big business. Goding announced in a newsletter to his members that an extensive canvass of many thousands of people throughout Britain had shown that:

> Over 80 per cent of our population are down to earth decent middle-class law abiding citizens. Of the remaining 20 per cent some 10 per cent did not wish to listen and said they were 'working class', not middle class but devoted Labour supporters dedicated

to their unions and the TUC. The remaining 10 per cent were either greedy wage-rise hunters sheltering under the unions' umbrella and basking in the sunshine of the blackmailing power of the TUC or a very few rich speculators representing 'the ugly faces of capitalism' who of course were really only interested in themselves . . . It is interesting to note that the vast majority (80 per cent of the population) are middle class, unrepresented by their own party which is non-existent and they are bored with both main parties together with their failure to govern firmly and honestly . . . Join the MCVR at once and stop dithering, please. The MCRV will probably be merged with my new Middle Classes Party soon.[12]

In the event, the 'private armies' were a nine days' wonder. Disowned by leading serving officers and politicians, their support quickly evaporated. When he stood as a 'middle-class' candidate against Anthony Wedgwood Benn in the October 1974 General Election, Goding received only 457 votes, less than 1 per cent of those cast. By the summer of 1976 the armies had entirely disappeared.

Of more significance were the various pressure groups which channelled the protests of the self-employed and small businessmen. At first existing organizations were used for this purpose. Following Denis Healey's April 1974 budget the Income Tax Payers' Society, which had been founded in 1921, suddenly found itself flooded with applications for membership. The Smaller Businesses Society was galvanized into action to press for repeal of Capital Transfer Tax and the British Property Federation took on a new lease of life as the focus for landlords' opposition to the 1975 Rent Act. As the combined assault of inflation and socialism continued, however, there was a growing feeling that new, more militant organizations were needed to defend the interests of the middle classes and four were specifically created for the purpose.

The first of these, and the most short-lived, was the National Association of Ratepayers Action Groups (NARAG) which was formed in June 1974 to co-ordinate the numerous local protests which had greeted an exceptional rise in rates that year. NARAG deliberately adopted a more militant line than the National Union of Ratepayers' Associations which for twenty years had been campaigning quietly but unsuccessfully for a reform of the rating system. It was no more successful, however, and within a year had lost much of its initial support, partly because the Conservative Party had shrewdly taken up the ratepayers' cause and also because of fears that it was being taken over by right-wing extremists. In October 1975 five of its six-man executive resigned and the association broke up.

The second new organization, the National Federation of the Self Employed (NFSE) was set up in the summer of 1974 in direct response to the Government's proposal to levy an extra National Insurance contribution on the self-employed. Other measures already introduced by the previous Conservative administration had also caused anger in the ranks of this particular section of the population. The extent to which Edward Heath's 1970–74 Government alienated its traditional supporters among the petite bourgeoisie is illustrated by the comments of one of the Federation's leading members about the events which brought about its formation:

> I consider that history will see the period of the Heath government as one of the most crucial in cementing the acceptance of socialism in Britain. It was at this time that the self-employed came to feel most abandoned . . . their so-called own kind turned on them, they were greatly disillusioned. Had this not been the case, had they not had VAT thrust on them, local government reorganization, the abolition of resale price maintenance, entry into the Common Market, then when the Class Four levy came along, it would not have acted as the catalyst it did.[13]

The NFSE grew rapidly. By the end of 1974 it had ten thousand members and by the autumn of 1975 over fifty thousand. In 1976 it held a Congress of Professional and Independent Workers to which delegates were sent by more than thirty national bodies, including the British Medical Association, the National Farmers Union and the British Legal Association. The Federation's literature suggested that it would soon be on a par with the CBI and the TUC and consulted by Government as the national voice of the independent businessman and self-employed worker. By 1977, however, it was on the wane, with its membership down to forty-five thousand and melting away fast.

The NFSE lost momentum partly, like the NARAG, because its cause was taken over by the established parties. The Liberals discussed the plight of small businesses at their 1975

Assembly, the Conservatives set up a Small Business Bureau and the Labour Government appointed Harold Lever as minister for small businesses with a brief to help that sector of the economy. Like NARAG, also, the NFSE was weakened by damaging disputes as to whether it should adopt wider political aims. Some argued that it should simply concentrate on specific reforms to help the self-employed, others that it should become a more fundamentalist movement calling for a return to a society based on private enterprise and an individualist ethic. A group of members who adopted the latter approach broke away to form a new group, the Association of Self-Employed People. The NFSE was further weakened by the establishment of yet another pressure group in the same field, the National Association of the Self-Employed, which claimed a membership of twenty-seven thousand in 1975.

The third main middle-class defence organization, the Middle Class Association, had more general aims. It was the brainchild of Mr John Gorst, Conservative MP for Hendon. In August 1974 he invited journalists to the launching of the new association. At the last minute, however, the invitation was cancelled because some of his supporters were unhappy about its title. Gorst saw that very worry itself as symptomatic of the dire straits into which the middle classes had fallen: 'My colleagues in Parliament talk of socio-economic groups, or B, C1 and C2, consumer categories, and they blush when you mention middle class. They can't call a spade a spade any more, though they still talk of the working class.'[14]

Several alternative names were considered for the new body. A woman in Northamptonshire suggested SPINUP – the Society for the Protection of Non-Unionized People – and another proposed the Head Workers Union. Gorst turned down SEMI – Self-Employed and Middle Income – because he considered that the latter category would have included coal miners and car workers, and PIMP – People In the Middle – because he feared that it would offend middle-class morality. In the end, after much soul searching, he returned to his original name and formally launched the Middle Class Association in November 1974.

The Association declared its aim to be 'to represent the interests of individuals who are self-employed or in professional, creative or managerial occupations'. Inflation and Government policies, it claimed, had put at stake the survival of this element of the population. Totally rejecting the idea that it should become a trade union, it saw itself rather as a pressure group operating primarily on Parliament to ensure that middle-class interests were looked after and campaigning specifically for the provision of free choice in education and health and the indexation of tax allowances against inflation. Its membership reached a peak of five thousand in 1975, but it enjoyed only a brief existence. After a change of name in 1976 to the Voice of the Independent Centre, it broke up in disarray, with John Gorst resigning because its committee had been taken over by extreme right wingers.

The fourth new organization, the National Association for Freedom (NAFF), had wider, more ideological aims. It was set up late in 1975 to promote a fifteen-point Charter of Rights and Liberties and to fight what its members took to be the growing threat to individual liberty posed by the activities of trade unions, the spread of bureaucracy and the growing march of socialist legislation. By 1977 NAFF had five thousand members and had achieved considerable success, and considerable publicity, in helping to fight various cases in the courts. Among the most notable were an action brought by parents in Tameside, Greater Manchester, to defend their grammar schools, and an action against the Union of Post Office Workers who had 'blacked' mail to Grunwicks, a film-processing firm hit by a prolonged strike. NAFF had rather more impact than the other middle-class protest groups and it continues to remain active today under its new name, the Freedom Association.

The short lives and lack of impact of most of these organizations underline the weakness of middle-class protest. Their membership was drawn almost exclusively from one particular section of the middle classes, the traditional petite bourgeoisie of small businessmen and the self-employed. Even within that section they won the active support of only a tiny minority. Even at their height the NFSE and its two splinter organizations attracted less than 5 per cent of the two million self-employed people in Britain. On the whole members of the professions, managers and white-collar administrative and clerical workers showed no interest in joining the protest groups. Indeed those of them who were employed in the public sector or who had joined trade unions were regarded almost as class enemies and traitors by organizations like NFSE and NAFF.

If the protest groups failed partly because it was impossible to forge a common consciousness among the disparate ranks of the middle classes, then they also suffered from the traditional deference and reserve of the petite bourgeoisie. Mr Gerald Hartup, national branch organizer of NAFF, admitted that one of the reasons why his organization failed to make more impact was because 'It is often very difficult for middle-class people to get out on the streets . . . they're very embarrassed.'[15] Those who joined the defence organizations were overwhelmingly Conservative in their political views (80 per cent of those in the Middle Class Association were either past or present members of the party) and they were hardly likely themselves to adopt the militant tactics that they condemned in the working classes. In Belgium there was a general strike by the self-employed in 1975 which led to the Government introducing reforms of the social security and tax system. The nearest that Britain came to a similar uprising was in the imagination of J. B. Priestley, the distinguished novelist, who wrote a fanciful article in the *Sunday Times* about a general strike by the English middle classes early in 1976. 'It lasted just six days,' he wrote, 'no demands, no settlement.'

Unable and unwilling to organize themselves into a body capable of disruptive action, the middle classes' only hope of relief from their plight seemed to lie in the development of a new political movement. This was already happening in other countries. The angry ratepayers of California had succeeded through Proposition Thirteen in obtaining a considerable reduction in the state's public spending, while in Denmark the newly formed anti-tax Progressive Party was well on the way to becoming the second biggest political group in Parliament.

In Britain, however, it seemed as though the middle classes would look in vain for any political party to take up their cause. Although all three of the major parties had made some gestures to defuse the revolt of the mid-1970s, none appeared prepared to commit itself to an out-and-out defence of traditional bourgeois interests and values. *Newsweek* gloomily concluded its 1976 survey of 'Britain's Battered Middle Classes':

> Perhaps the most telling sign of the impotence that has overtaken the British middle class is the fact that Britain no longer has a credible alternative Government. When former Prime Minister Edward Heath's Tory government was brought down by the labour unions in 1974, it became clear that the only options open to a British Government in the foreseeable future would be variations on an egalitarian socialist theme. If Heath could not successfully achieve even a modest alteration in the national course, there is no reason to think that any other Tory leader can either.[16]

Newsweek had, however, overlooked one very important fact. In February 1975 Edward Heath had been replaced as leader of the Conservatives by Margaret Thatcher, perhaps the most aggressively middle-class figure in twentieth century British politics. Four years later she was to come to power on a programme based boldly and unashamedly on the traditional bourgeois values of self-help, individualism and voluntaryism.

11

The Turning of the Tide
1975–1980

The 1970s were not a decade of unrelieved gloom for the English middle classes. From the depths of their despondency in 1974 and 1975 they rallied to defend their values and fight back against their critics. The social pendulum began to swing away from the egalitarian notions of the sixties and back to more traditional values, pointing the way for the election of Margaret Thatcher as Prime Minister at the end of the decade.

There had, of course, always been traditionalists who attempted to resist the advancing tide of permissiveness, proletarianization and egalitarianism. During the 1960s and early 1970s, however, they had not attracted very much notice, seeming irretrievably committed to the losing side, and remaining apologetic and quietly ineffectual in their protests. From the mid-1970s this state of affairs changed. In the atmosphere of soul-searching and self-doubt which afflicted Britain in the aftermath of the world oil price rise and the near collapse of the national economy, the values of the radical middle class suddenly seemd to look rather hollow and those of the traditional bourgeoisie rather reassuring. It was no longer just a few reactionaries and 'squares' who expressed doubts about the permissive society, comprehensive education, the new theology and classless culture. The middle classes stopped being so apologetic about what they stood for and 'came out' boldly and distinctly.

This change of atmosphere had a marked effect on the fortunes of Mrs Whitehouse's campaign to clean up television. During its early years it had attracted a relatively small following, mostly of middle-class women associated with the Church, and had been regarded by those working in television, and by many others, as rather a joke. By 1976 the movement against the permissive society had become sufficiently powerful to prevent a Danish film-maker from coming to Britain to make a pornographic film about Christ and to attract several thousand people (62 per cent of them from the Registrar General's top two social classes) to a 'Festival of Light' rally in Trafalgar Square, London. The BBC began taking serious notice of Mrs Whitehouse and her supporters and television critics noticed a new puritanism and caution among the programme planners.

In the world of education a similar change of mood took place. What had begun as a small and little-heeded movement of protest against prevailing progressive and egalitarian currents gradually became more assertive and influential. The first 'Black Paper' on education, published in 1969, was generally dismissed as the reactionary and unrepresentative cry of an unenlightened minority. The fourth 'Black Paper', published in 1975, received a good deal more serious and sympathetic attention, not least because no one could dispute the facts on which it based its castigation of the whole drift of British education in the previous two decades:

> Literacy is declining. Half the adult illiterates are below the age of twenty-five. Industry complains of increasing innumeracy. Some 650,000 children play truant every day and teachers flee from city schools because of lesson resistance and insolence by pupils. Adolescent violence increases and universities show signs of student and staff intolerance of free discussion which threatens a new dark age. Genuine cultural participation falls steadily and a non-value pop culture becomes dominant.[1]

There was one particularly striking feature about the fourth Black Paper. Those who contributed to it were not all people well-known for their right-wing and traditionalist views. They included, for example, Iris Murdoch, the novelist, who while not a rabid left-winger was certainly in general terms a progressive, and who wrote as a socialist in defence of the principle of selection in education and in support of the continued existence of grammar and independent schools. There were a growing number of converts from the radical middle class to the values of competition, discipline and high academic standards. Many parents found that their enthusiasm for non-streamed comprehensive schooling waned when their own children had to go through the experience. Quality gradually regained the position from which it had been ousted by equality.

One event probably did more than any other to change attitudes about education and to bring the defenders of traditional middle-class values out of their previous reticence into a positive assertion of what they believed in. That was the ending of the direct grant schools which came about as the result of a circular issued by the Labour Government in 1975. These schools, which had high academic standards and offered a certain number of free places paid for by the state, had provided a passport for entry into the middle classes for many bright working-class and lower-middle-class boys and girls and produced many of the meritocrats who were now ruling the country. The Government's decision to withdraw public funding from them, coming on top of the change-over of many state grammar schools into comprehensives, provoked an outcry from those like the headmaster of one of the schools affected who wrote to *The Times*:

> What is at issue is whether the pro-comprehensives are right to kick away the ladder which in the past enabled so many boys and girls to rise above their humble origins – and let no one tell me how wonderful are the cultural values of a Walworth slum; I know because I was born and lived in one – to a level where they can make the most of their talents and break down the class barriers which divide us. The neighbourhood comprehensive school can rarely, if ever, do what the grammar schools did, drawing pupils from a wide area and a variety of social backgrounds and mixing some of the poorest members of the community with 'middle-class' children. Incidentally, can anyone explain what is so wrong with 'middle-class' values that they have become anathema to the left?[2]

There was a similar reaction in other institutions which had been affected by middle-class radicalism and feelings of guilt in the 1960s. In the Church of England modern theology and left-wing political commitment came increasingly under attack. In his book, *Church and Society in Modern England* (1976), and in the 1978 Reith Lectures, Dr Edward Norman, the Dean of Peterhouse, Cambridge, developed a theme that he had first raised in the 1976 General Synod when he described the bishops and leading clergymen in the Church of England as 'guilty public schoolboys with a left-wing conscience, who are simply terrified of not appearing to be radical and sympathetic to the spirit of the age'.[3]

Ten years earlier, Norman's traditionalist views would have been dismissed as crackpot. In the disillusioned atmosphere of the late 1970s, however, they struck a chord with many middle-class church-goers, who were beginning to have their doubts about the wisdom of many of the dominant trends in the Church over the past decade. In 1979 a petition to save the old language of the Prayer Book and resist the introduction of the new 'alternative series' of modern services was signed by more than three hundred distinguished figures from the world of politics, the arts and academic life.

A similar mood of reaction was growing in the two main political parties. In his book, *The Death of British Democracy*, published in 1976, Dr Stephen Haseler, an active member of the Labour Party, blamed many of the ills of the nation on the effects of the feelings of guilt which had affected leading politicians:

> As most of the leaders of democratic socialism or even progressive Conservatism have been from the middle or upper-middle classes they have suffered, because of the experience of the thirties, from a huge sense of class guilt. They have found it psychologically very difficult to resist the spurious appeals from the Marxists for more 'working-class power'. When confronted with working-class militancy they have wilted, lost confidence in their own social backgrounds and indeed in their individual worth. Consequently, they have given in all along the line, not to genuine working-class power or to equality, but to ruthless cliques who saw their Achilles' heel and used it remorselessly against them.[4]

Similar feelings were also being voiced in the Conservative Party. When Mr Peter Walker delivered his warning about the dangers of the party retreating into the 'bunkers and bolt-holes of narrow middle-class politics', another Conservative MP, Mr Kenneth Lewis, sprung to the defence of the maligned middle classes:

> At least they do not have the politics of the continuous strike or the picket lines. Well, not yet at any rate. But they have taken

much punishment from Governments and continue to do so. We need to beware lest we impose too much on them. And the Conservative Party should be applauding their sturdy forbearance and sense of duty . . .

The standards of the middle class, comprised as it is and ought to be of so many different sections of the community, are good standards in the main. We could do with an extension of such standards today. This 'bolt-hole' would serve us well.[5]

Attacks on the guilt feelings of the middle classes and bold defences of their traditional values became a common theme of both books and newspaper correspondence columns. Patrick Hutber wrote that the middle class 'has nothing to be ashamed of, and deserves a good conceit of itself'. Paul Johnson, former editor of the *New Statesman* and Labour Party supporter, made the same point in his book *Enemies of Society*, published in 1977: 'No one need feel ashamed of being bourgeois . . . the health of the middle class is probably the best index of the health of society as a whole.' Correspondents to *The Times* frequently sounded a similar note. 'The former Lord Stansgate may suffer a terrible sense of guilt about his wealthy, aristocratic antecedents; Mr Michael Foot may want to expiate the sin of being born into a powerful and privileged family,' wrote one of 'the so-called and much maligned members of the middle classes' who was the son of a labourer, 'but why should we suffer for them?' Other papers carried articles with the same theme. 'Why should I feel ashamed of the indisputable fact that we, the middle classes, fill the better schools with our children and the theatres with ourselves?' a contributor to the *Observer* asked in 1980. 'The working people of this country, on the whole, are not interested in educational or cultural improvement.'[6]

Like the contributors to the fourth Black Paper many of those who were most vociferous in their defence of bourgeois values were themselves either converts from egalitarianism and socialism like Paul Johnson and Stephen Haseler or from working-class backgrounds like the direct-grant school headmaster and the labourer's son who wrote to *The Times*. Those who expressed traditional middle-class values most clearly in their own lives, the professions and small businessmen, were not so inclined to trumpet them abroad.

The loss of faith among the radical middle class was particularly striking. There were few more disillusioned figures than the ageing 'trendies' of the sixties, with their denim jackets fading, their hessian wall covering peeling and their once-confident liberal principles in tatters. Had they been right to put their daughters on the Pill at fifteen and give their sons a progressive education that had left them semi-literate? The angst of this particular species is brilliantly captured in Posy Simmonds's weekly strip cartoon in the *Guardian* about the Webers (he a polytechnic lecturer and she an ex-nurse) and their aggressively 'punk' children who loathe their parents' liberalism. Margaret Drabble's novel *The Ice Age* (1977) also deals with this theme. The central character, Anthony Keating, who after a public school education went first into television and then into property speculation, finds himself at thirty-eight with a heart attack, a broken marriage and a sense of the emptiness of the lives that he and his radical middle-class friends have led:

> Oh yes, they had dabbled and trifled and cracked irreverent jokes: they had thrown out the mahogany and bought cheap stripped pine, they had slept with one another's wives, and divorced their own, they had sent their children to state schools, they had acquired indeterminate accents, they had made friends in unthinkable quarters, they had worn themselves out and contorted themselves trying to understand a new system, a new egalitarian culture, the new illiterate visual television age. They had tried: they had made efforts. They had learned to help their working wives to cook and care for the children: they had learned to live without servants, to give elaborate dinner parties without the white cloths and cut glass and silver cutlery of the grandparents, they had learned to survive broken nights with screaming babies, broken nights with weeping, angry, emancipated, emaciated wives. They had learned, academics, teachers, and parents alike, to condemn the examination system that had elevated them and brought them security: they had tried to learn new tricks. But where were the new tricks? They had produced no new images, no new style, merely a cheap strained exhausted imitation of the old one. Nothing had changed. Where was the new bright classless enterprising future of Great Britain?[7]

As with their parents, so with the young, the late 1970s saw a rejection of the permissive, classless culture of the 1960s and a return to the values of competition, ambition and conventionality. On university campuses it was now the lecturers rather than the students who were more likely to have long hair and left-wing views. Applications for courses in sociology plummeted and those for vocational subjects like law and accountancy increased. The number of graduates going into further academic study, teaching and social work fell steadily from 1974–5, with a corresponding rise in the number of those going into business and industry and into conventional professions like law, accountancy and banking. University authorities reported that the levels of drug-taking and sexual promiscuity among students were falling, while opinion polls showed that for the first time ever a majority of the new voters who had reached the age of eighteen between the 1974 and 1979 elections favoured the Conservatives rather than Labour.

The effects of the change in mood were felt by other institutions. Figures produced by the Church of England in 1978 showed the first annual rise in the number of Christmas and Easter communicants since the early 1960s and the upward trend continued in 1979. Public schools found themselves with longer waiting lists than ever before. The proportion of children being educated at independent schools, which had declined steadily through the late 1960s and early 1970s, increased from 4.3 to 5.5 per cent between 1977 and 1980, partly because of the entry of many of the former direct grant schools into the private sector. In September 1979 a new public school opened in Kent claiming to be the first new establishment of its kind for more than fifty years. There was also a boom in private medical treatment. The number of subscribers to the biggest private health insurance scheme in Britain jumped by 5.8 per cent in 1978 after declining in the previous three years.

New middle-class heroes were emerging in the worlds of sport, adventure and popular entertainment. After the commercial vulgarity of Kerry Packer's 'circus', English cricket turned for its salvation to Michael Brearley, a player in much the same mould as the public school heroes of the 1950s. In September 1979 Sir Ranulph Twisleton-Wykeham-Fiennes embarked with three fellow old-Etonians on an expedition round the world via the North and South Poles. Five months later another adventurer in the public school tradition, Lieutenant Colonel John Blashford-Snell was in London to report on his circumnavigation of the globe in the style of Sir Francis Drake. The proletarian figures who had dominated BBC television comedy in the late 1960s and early 1970s, like Steptoe and Son and Alf Garnett, gave way to the quintessentially middle-class Reginald Perrin, marketing manager of Sunshine Desserts, whose rise and fall first delighted audiences in 1977, and the distinctly upper middle-class Audrey Fforbes-Hamilton, star of *To The Manor Born*.

The growing confidence of the middle classes and the reassertion of their values played an important part in the contest for the leadership of the Conservative Party which followed Edward Heath's defeat in the October 1974 election. In January 1975 a letter appeared in *The Times* from two Conservatives who suggested that it was no accident that the 'anger of the middle classes' should occupy the paper's columns simultaneously with the question of the leadership of their party. The present leadership they suggested,

> has chosen to neglect that section of the population which looks to it for representation as do the unions to the Labour Party . . . The politics of appeasement against the class propaganda of the left are the short road to political extinction, and denigratory comments about the 'warrens and bolt-holes of the middle class' from Mr Walker are deeply offensive to large sections of the population.[8]

The letter went on to say that the choice offered in the current leadership contest was not just one of personal style. Mr Heath and Mr Walker had 'thrice denied their natural supporters'. Mrs Thatcher and Sir Keith Joseph, on the other hand, 'have had the courage to defend unfashionable but widespread beliefs. They at least have the merit of articulating and defining the aspirations and fears of the non-unionized classes.' There was certainly no denying the vigour with which these two particular contenders for the leadership championed the middle classes in their speeches. It was partly a matter of shrewd political judgement. Polls showed that the Conservatives had lost two elections of 1974 because of the defection of a substantial number of voters who felt neglected and forgotten by Heath's Government. But much more it was a matter of deep personal conviction. Both politicians were unabashed believers in middle-class values.

Sir Keith Joseph had first developed the theme when he attacked Denis Healey's April 1974 budget for spelling 'the twilight of the middle class . . . [who] have virtues, not exclusively but pre-eminently, that any government needs to encourage – thrift, self-sacrifice, foresight, kindness'.[9] He expanded it in a series of speeches in the autumn of 1974 in which he passionately defended traditional middle-class values of public spiritedness, individual responsibility, initiative and self-discipline and fiercely attacked the left-wing progressives who had decried them. Although he clearly meant to avoid any narrow class bias, that was the impression given by his now notorious speech in Birmingham on 19 October when he seemed to imply that the breeding habits of those in social classes four and five were leading to national degeneration. The speech, which also paid tribute to Mrs Whitehouse and the moral fervour of Mr Gladstone, probably did more than anything else to destroy his chances in the contest for the Conservative leadership.

Margaret Thatcher, to whom Joseph pledged his support after he withdrew from the contest in November, was even more bold in her defence of middle-class values. In her contribution to a series in the *Daily Telegraph* on 'My Kind of Tory Party' in January 1975 she wrote:

> I cannot agree with those of my colleagues who attribute the loss of support to a 'middle-class' image. We lost because we did not appear to stand firmly for anything distinctive and positive. Sneering at 'middle-class values' is to insult the working class no less than the bourgeois. Do British workers have no deep feelings for freedom, for order, for the education of their children, for the right to work without disruption by political militants? . . . If 'middle-class values' include the encouragement of variety and individual choice, the provision of fair incentives and rewards for skill and hard work, the maintenance of effective barriers against the excessive power of the state and a belief in the wide distribution of individual private property, then they are certainly what I am trying to defend.[10]

Mrs Thatcher's own upbringing and background was quintessentially lower middle-class. Her father had started out as a grocer's boy and ended up owning his own shop. Her mother, the daughter of a railway worker, was a dressmaker. They were models of petit bourgeois respectability, in their daughter's words, 'both very neat and tidy, always well turned out'.[11] The family was brought up strictly. On Sunday no newspaper was allowed in the house, even sewing or knitting were frowned on, and three visits were regularly made to the Methodist Chapel. Margaret and her sister were forbidden to go to dances on Saturday evenings like other girls. Instead they were encouraged to read, to improve themselves and to talk politics with their father who was an active Liberal and became mayor of Grantham, the small Lincolnshire town where they lived.

For Margaret Thatcher, her parents personified the middle-class values of self-help, thrift, effort and voluntary good works. Her father did not press for payment of debts in his shop during difficult times, yet 'Though he had a Christian belief in the strong helping the weak, the better-off helping the poor, he believed the principle that should activate people was a wish to stand on their own two feet.'[12] Her mother shared that belief, although she was also a good neighbour who, when she did her twice weekly baking, always made something for the children to take round to someone who was poor or sick.

In her upbringing and her progress from the lower middle to the upper middle class via grammar school and Oxford, Margaret Thatcher was, in fact, remarkably similar both to Harold Wilson and Edward Heath. Yet she made far more of her background than either of them ever did. The lessons which she learned at home, that you should despise idleness and cultivate initiative and self-improvement, and at her father's shop, that you could only earn what you could produce and sell, remained firmly implanted in her mind and were constantly recalled in her speeches. When she talked economics, it was to the model of the Grantham household and the grocer's shop that she turned for inspiration and illustration.

The values of her upbringing inspired her political decisions. Almost her first act on becoming Secretary of State for Education in 1970 had been to revoke Labour's Circular 10/65 calling on local authorities to submit schemes for comprehensive reorganization. Many Conservatives were worried by this abandonment of a ten-year-old bi-partisan policy on education and by her fierce rearguard action to defend the remaining maintained grammar schools. She, however, was fired by her own memories of what Kesteven and Grantham Girls' School had done for her. There was also some concern in the party at the extent to which she courted the narrow middle-class pressure groups that had sprung up in the mid-1970s. For her, however, they were a natural constituency, fired by the same bourgeois values as her father. She chose to make her first public speech at her first party conference as leader at a reception of the National Federation of Self-Employed. Reminding her audience that she had been 'born into trade', she added, 'Next time you will know which party to support.'[13]

During the final stages of the Tory leadership contest Mrs Thatcher's opponents had made much of her middle classness. Ian Gilmour, a strong Heath supporter, told his constituents that the Conservatives should not 'retire behind a privet hedge', a cutting reference to her suburban housewife's image. Heath himself heavily emphasized the dangers of the party becoming exclusively middle-class and losing a broader view of the national interest. The majority of Conservative MPs were undeterred by these criticisms, however, and in February 1975 they elected Mrs Thatcher as leader.

For the next four years as leader of the opposition she continued to champion middle-class values. In speeches both in Britain and the United States she fiercely attacked the 'equality lobby' which she attributed to 'an undistinguished combination of envy and what might be termed "bourgeois guilt"'.[14] She suggested that the traditional voluntaryism and social responsibility of the middle classes should be harnessed to defeat the power of the trade unions and keep public services running in the event of industrial action. She also made a more direct appeal to middle-class self-interest promising that a government under her leadership would lower income tax, introduce more incentives and encourage the development of independent education and private medicine.

Mrs Thatcher also made an appeal to the working classes which was based on the assertion of essentially middle-class values. Her own experience underlined her conviction that it was open to anyone to climb up the social ladder and join the bourgeoisie. 'The charm of Britain,' she observed, 'has always been the ease with which one can move into the middle class.'[15] Like the Victorian Liberals, she assumed that it was the ambition of every working man to become a solid and independent middle-class citizen. She offered the vision of a society where everyone would practise the values and enjoy the lifestyle of the middle classes. The working classes would be encouraged to buy their council houses and so become owner-occupiers. Through profit-sharing schemes they would become company shareholders. Through the assisted places scheme their brightest children would be able to go to public schools. They would no longer feel the need to give their prime loyalty to collective class entities like trade unions nor to regard such things as private medical care as the prerogative of the well-to-do. They would, in fact, become middle-class in their attitudes and values.

The Conservative victory in the May 1979 general election looked like a clear gain for the middle classes. Quite apart from the direct benefits that they could expect from a Government so firmly committed to their well-being, there was the general psychological boost from the feeling that bourgeois guilt had finally been expunged from the body politic. As one senior manager put it, 'I think Mrs Thatcher will make the middle class respectable again.'[16]

On first sight, the results of the election seemed to confirm the idea that middle-class votes had put Mrs Thatcher in and that her victory marked a triumph for class politics. The election left the country more split than ever before between the predominantly bourgeois south and the proletarian north. The swing to the Conservatives was smaller the further north one went, with Scotland actually showing a swing to Labour. Those constituencies which came nearest to representing the classless social democracy of the 1960s and early 1970s, like the new towns of Hatfield and Welwyn Garden City, registered a higher swing to the Tories than others. The country did indeed seem to be polarizing into two distinct nations.

However, a closer examination of the voting shows that it was not the case that the middle classes rallied to

Mrs Thatcher. The swing to the Conservatives was actually highest among the skilled manual workers in social Class C2 who had seen their differentials seriously eroded during the years of pay restraint under both Labour and Conservative governments and who were also perhaps attracted by Mrs Thatcher's promise that they could become well-off, independent members of the property-owning class. More predictably, she also did well among the small businessmen and self-employed lower middle classes who had been so alienated by Edward Heath and whom she had wooed so assiduously. The upper middle classes, however, found her much less attractive. In Classes A and B there was a swing of 1.5 per cent to Labour. There may have been a slight element of snobbery in their rejection of the grocer's daughter. There was also a clear conflict of values between her petit bourgeois stress on enterprise and incentives and their wider and more liberal sentiments. It was significant that when she formed her Cabinet it was the more patrician members like William Whitelaw, Sir Ian Gilmour, Lord Carrington and Lord Soames who tended to be the 'wettest' and cast most doubt on the wisdom of her rather doctrinaire monetarist policy.

Has Mrs Thatcher's Government in fact operated in the interests of the middle classes and against those of the working classes? That is certainly the view of many commentators on the left. In June 1980 the magazine *New Society* carried an article by Professor Ralph Miliband on 'Class War Conservatism'. He argued that 'Taken together, the government's policies constitute the most formidable assault that has been mounted on organized labour, and the working class in general, since 1931.'[17]

It is certainly true that the working classes have so far suffered far more than the middle classes under Thatcherism. Unemployment has predominantly affected manual workers and cuts in public spending have hurt the least well-off. Admittedly the Government's economic policy of tight monetary restraint has also meant high interest rates which have hit industrialists, small businessmen and those with mortgages, but on the whole their sufferings have not been as great as those of many in the working classes.

It is also the case that the rhetoric and style of the

Government has been noticeably pro-middle and anti-working class. Gone are the traditional Conservative appeals to the 'one nation' theme and to the legacy of Disraeli and Lord Salisbury. Gone also is the post-war consensus over the intimate involvement of the TUC, the institutional expression of working-class collectivism, in the formulation of economic policy and the business of government. In Government just as much as in opposition, Mrs Thatcher and her ministers have continued to preach the bourgeois virtues of individual responsibility, self-help and voluntaryism.

In terms of its actual record as opposed to its rhetoric, however, the Thatcher Government has perhaps done less positively to help the middle classes than might have been expected. At first sight the first budget introduced by the new Chancellor, Sir Geoffrey Howe, for example, seemed to offer little to the poor but much to the better-off. The top rate of income tax was brought down from 83 to 60 per cent and the standard rate from 33 to 30 per cent. In fact, however, the independent Institute for Fiscal Studies calculated that, if rises in their mortgage payments because of the high interest rates introduced were also taken into account, the middle classes as a whole had lost proportionately more from the budget than the working classes. A similar analysis of the March 1981 budget found that it hit the better-off disproportionately hard. A senior manager earning £17,500 a year was left over £800 a year worse off, a loss of 5.9 per cent of his after-tax income, while a low-paid manual worker earning £78 a week lost £4 or 5.4 per cent of his net income. The overall effect of the 1981 budget was to take away most of the gains made by higher earners in the first Howe budget.

In other respects also, the Government has not acted as decisively in the interests of the middle classes and against those of the working classes as its pre-election rhetoric suggested it would. The 1980 Employment Act, for example, was extremely modest in the restrictions which it put on the power of trade unions. In failing to outlaw either the closed shop or secondary picketing it bitterly disappointed those like Mr John Gorst and the Freedom Association who had been in the van of middle-class protest against the labour legislation of the mid-1970s. The assisted places scheme which was designed to bolster the public school system was progressively watered down and measures positively to discriminate in favour of private medicine were similarly half-hearted. There has so far been comparatively little evidence of the swing of the pendulum from corporatism and bureaucracy to individual enterprise and incentives which Mrs Thatcher promised before her election and which endeared her to so many small businessmen and entrepreneurs.

Different groups in the middle classes have enjoyed varying fortunes under Mrs Thatcher's Government. Those working in the public sector have had to face the effects of tight cash limits and reductions in spending by both central and local government. There has been a general depression of earnings levels and a diminution of recruitment and promotion prospects. As a result morale is low, particularly in the civil service following the Government's decision in November 1980 to abandon the principle of pay comparability with the private sector. The subsequent offer of a 7 per cent pay increase provoked widespread strikes in the spring of 1981.

The position of those working in private business and industry is less clear-cut. The general economic recession has led to a sharp rise in executive unemployment. By November 1980 the Professional and Executive Register had one hundred thousand redundant managers on its books. However, executives in flourishing firms did well at the end of the 1970s, enjoying an average rise in their annual salaries of 19 per cent in the first full wage round under Mrs Thatcher's Government. The 1980 annual survey by Inbucon Management Consultants found that in the previous four years executives achieved a gain of 11 per cent in real terms in their earnings, and once again increased the gap between themselves and manual workers.

White-collar clerical workers in banking and insurance benefited from the substantial profits that their firms made as a result of high interest rates and the strong pound. Some entrepreneurs also did well out of these factors although their general effect on business and industry was adverse with a record number of bankruptcies being recorded in Mrs Thatcher's first full calendar year in office. Although the Government announced new incentives for entrepreneurial activity ranging from the creation of enterprise zones to the breaking up of the telecommunications and bus monopolies, it was unable to create an overall economic climate which favoured risk-taking and the setting up of new businesses. Although small employers and businessmen welcomed the repeal of Labour's Employment Protection Act, they disliked the high interest rates and the increase in the standard VAT rate to 15 per cent.

The professions have also enjoyed mixed fortunes. University lecturers, teachers and social workers have been adversely affected by public spending cuts and by a general atmosphere which is less favourable to the expansion of education and the Welfare State. Lawyers and doctors, on the other hand, have generally prospered. In October 1979 the long awaited report of the Royal Commission on Legal Services gave the entire legal profession a remarkably clean bill of health. It concluded that public criticism of high fees and restrictive practices were exaggerated and unjustified, and recommended that solicitors should retain their lucrative monopoly of conveyancing. A month later doctors received an equally significant boost to their morale with a pay rise of 26 per cent, the biggest in the history of the National Health Service. Consultants had earlier obtained a new contract of service which was more favourable than they had expected and allowed them to do more private work.

The advent of a Conservative Government wedded to the free market may well have created a climate in which the professions are inclined to be more entrepreneurial. At the end of 1979 the council of the Royal Institute of British Architects agreed to change its rules to remove the ethical ban on architects operating as a limited liability company and to allow them to advertise their services and become directors of property companies and building material manufacturers. It is an interesting departure from the traditional reticence and puritanism of the professions which could have implications for other groups.

Overall, although they have not benefited anything like as much as they would have liked or perhaps expected, the middle classes have perhaps not done too badly out of Thatcherism. A survey by the *Sunday Times* found that while the population as a whole was slightly worse off at the end of 1980 than it had been at the beginning of the year, those in the professions, middle and senior managers and company directors were all significantly better-off. White-collar workers were alone among middle-class groups in experiencing a fall in their standard of living in common with all those in working-class jobs. The Institute of Fiscal Studies found that even the hard-pressed and complaining civil servants had enjoyed a rise of 10 per cent in their standard of living during 1980 while skilled manual workers had suffered a fall of 6 per cent.

The brunt of the hardship brought about by the world-wide economic recession and exacerbated by the Government's tough adherence to monetarism has been borne by the working classes. To the left that is the result of deliberate Government policy with the weapon of unemployment being used to weaken the working-class and trade union movement. Whether that is the case or not, there can be no denying that so far many in the middle classes have escaped relatively lightly from the worst economic slump since the 1930s. It is not surprising that they entered the 1980s in better heart than they had been for some time. Well might they, for in numerous areas of life they remain the most privileged and powerful part of the community.

12

The Survival of the Species

More than a century after Karl Marx prophesied their disappearance, and thirty years after Angus Maude and Roy Lewis gloomily contemplated their decline and fall, the English middle classes are still alive and kicking. In some ways, indeed, they are even stronger now than they have ever been.

For a start, there are more of them. Taking the most basic occupational definition, the middle classes now form a larger proportion of the population than ever before and are continuing to grow. Table 5 shows that the proportion of economically active and retired males in the Registrar General's top two social classes has grown consistently over the last fifty years. The apparent drop in the percentage of those in Class II between 1921 and 1931 is accounted for by the downgrading of clerks to Class III in the 1931 census. It is safe to predict that the results of the 1981 census will show a continuation of this trend. Table 6, which gives a more detailed and up-to-date breakdown of the proportion of the total working population engaged in different types of jobs, shows that by 1978 46.3 per cent were in non-manual occupations and that by 1985 the proportion of non-manual workers is expected to be over 50 per cent. The fastest growing groups have been managerial, professional and clerical workers who have more than doubled as a proportion of the total working population in the last twenty-five years.

Other widely accepted indicators confirm this occupational evidence of an increasingly large middle class. The proportion of owner-occupied homes, for example, rose from 29.5 per cent in 1950 to 54.1 per cent by the end of 1978. Altogether, the number of households in owner occupation has gone up from 800,000 before the First World War to 10.5 million. As we have

TABLE 5

Economically active and retired males in England and Wales
(Percentages derived from the census)

Social class	1921	1931	1951	1961	1971
I	2·3	2·4	3·3	3·8	5·0
II	18·9	13·2	14·5	15·2	18·2
III	42·6	48·7	52·9	51·0	50·4
IV	22·0	18·2	16·1	20·8	18·0
V	14·1	17·5	13·1	9·2	8·4

already seen, the ownership of consumer goods once seen as conferring middle-class status, from washing machines to telephones, has steadily extended throughout the population. Car ownership, for example, has risen steadily from 2.3 million (about 11 per cent of the adult population) in 1950 to nearly 14 million (about 60 per cent) today.

The gradual spread of material benefits throughout the population has not made for a more classless or equal society, however. The middle classes have kept one jump ahead. As refrigerators became commonplace, they bought freezers. As car ownership spread into the working classes, they bought a second one, so that by 1977 roughly the same percentage of households had two cars as had one in 1950. Wide disparities still remain. In 1977 the Government's general household survey revealed that while nine out of ten households headed by a professional worker possessed a car, only a quarter of those headed by an unskilled worker had one.

Indeed economic differentials as a whole between the middle and working classes seem to have been maintained with remarkably little narrowing as the former have expanded and

TABLE 6

Occupational shares of total employment, 1961–1985 (Percentages)
SOURCE: Manpower Services Commission Manpower Review 1980.

Occupational category	1961	1971	1978 estimate	1985 projected	Change 1961–1985
A **Non-manual occupations**					
1 Managers and administrators	6·6	7·8	8·7	9·6	+3·0
2 Education professions	2·3	3·1	3·8	4·0	+1·7
3 Health professions	2·5	3·2	3·8	4·6	+2·1
4 Other professions	1·9	1·9	2·2	2·5	+0·6
5 Literary, artistic and sport	1·2	1·4	1·7	2·2	+1·0
6 Engineers and scientists	1·7	2·1	2·4	2·6	+0·9
7 Technicians and draughtsmen	1·8	2·1	2·4	2·7	+0·9
8 Clerical occupations	14·0	15·0	15·9	16·7	+2·7
9 Sales occupations	5·6	5·4	5·5	5·4	−0·2
All non-manual occupations	37·5	41·9	46·3	50·3	+12·8
B All manual occupations	62·5	58·1	53·7	49·7	−12·8

the latter contracted. A detailed study in 1960 found that since 1911 the gap in net earnings between higher professional and managerial groups and manual workers had remained virtually constant. Subsequent evidence suggests that the position is still broadly unchanged. The Royal Commission on the Distribution of Income and Wealth reported in the mid-1970s that there had only been a tiny shift in favour of the worse-off half of the population in the past twenty-five years.

There has admittedly been a narrowing of differentials in terms of actual pay. It has been calculated that since 1914 the salaries of those in the higher professions have risen by 26 per cent, whereas the wages of unskilled workers have risen by 54 per cent. The salary of a High Court judge (£32,000 in April 1980) is now five times the national average wage, whereas in 1938 it was thirty-five times as much, and in 1914 sixty-two times as much. However, this narrowing of differentials has been at least partly compensated for by the effects of fringe benefits, mortgage interest and life insurance relief and other tax allowances which act as a second welfare state for the middle classes.

For non-manual workers as a whole, fringe benefits, ranging from company cars through health insurance schemes to non-contributory pensions, add an average of 20 per cent to the value of their salaries. Manual workers on average only increase the value of their wages by 14 per cent through their fringe benefits. The better-off part of the population also do well out of the tax system. Between 1973 and 1978 income tax took 22 per cent of the income of the richest fifth of households in Britain, very little more than the national average of 19 per cent. However, 20 per cent of the income of the poorest fifth of households went in indirect taxes, compared to only 14 per cent of the income of the richest fifth.

Almost as striking as the economic inequalities which still persist between manual and non-manual workers are the widespread differences in their working conditions. The national study of poverty by Professor Townsend published in 1979 showed that the former in general worked longer and more awkward hours in less comfortable and pleasant surroundings, and received shorter holidays and fewer fringe benefits. For example, only 11 per cent of skilled manual workers (compared to 38 per cent of white-collar workers doing routine clerical jobs) worked for less than forty hours a week; only 26 per cent (72) were entitled to more than two weeks' holiday; 25 per cent (75) to at least one month's notice of dismissal; 34 per cent (54) to sickness payments from their employer; and 2 per cent (14) to personal use of a company car. 31 per cent of the manual workers (compared to only 8 per cent of the routine white-collar workers) had to endure poor working conditions. Similar comparisons between groups further apart on the social scale, like managers and unskilled workers, would, of course, show much greater disparities.

In view of the persistence of these inequalities, it is not surprising that the middle classes have remained consistently the healthiest part of the population. Death rates (i.e. the number of deaths each year for every one thousand people in a particular age group) among unskilled workers and their families have been around twice those for the professional classes ever since comparisons began in 1911. The perinatal mortality rate. (i.e. the number of babies per thousand who die before or within a week of birth) ranges from 16.3 in social Class I to 32.1 in Class V. Even the so-called diseases of affluence, like cancer and heart complaints, are more likely to be found among the working classes, partly because they are heavier smokers and drinkers. A survey of five hundred and forty electricians screened in 1980 found that they were considerably less healthy than a group of managers who on average were twelve years older. One third of the electricians had a moderate to high chance of developing heart disease in the near future, more than double the proportion among those of the same age in the managerial group.

The middle classes have not only remained better off, better treated at work, and healthier than the working classes. They have also, in a society which is allegedly becoming more classless, held their commanding positions in the major institutions of the country. As Table 7 shows, in several cases the proportion of those in positions of influence and power in the Establishment who were educated at public schools has actually increased over the last forty years.

TABLE 7

Percentage of those in positions of power educated at public schools
SOURCE: D. Boyd, *Élites and their Education* (1973)

Occupation	1939	1950	1960	1971
Civil servants (Under Secretaries and above)	84	59	65	62
Ambassadors	73	73	83	82·5
Judges (High Court judges and above)	80	85	82·5	80
Royal Navy (Rear Admirals and above)	21*	75	83·5	89
Army (Major Generals and above)	64	71	83	86
Royal Air Force (Air Vice-Marshals and above)	67	59	58	62·5
Church of England (Assistant bishops and above)	71	74·5	69	67
Directors of clearing banks	68	76	73	80

* Includes Dartmouth College.

[Research into the backgrounds of those at the head of British industry confirms a similar preponderance of public school educated men. A study of *Élites and Power in British Society* by two sociologists, Philip Stanworth and Anthony Giddens, published in 1974, found that 73 per cent of the directors of the largest industrial corporations and 80 per cent of the directors of financial concerns had been to public schools. The City in particular remains heavily public school dominated. Even if the old boy network is not quite as strong as it once was, it is still rare to find working-class accents on the floor of the Stock Exchange or in the boardrooms of merchant banks.]

The recent pattern of recruitment into élite positions in some of these institutions suggests that they will continue to have more than their fair share of public school products in commanding positions for a considerable time to come. At the end of the 1970s the Army was selecting about 55 per cent of its officers from public schools, the Navy around 28 per cent and the Royal Air Force 17 per cent. A survey of those ordained into the Church of England in 1973 found that 24 per cent had been educated at public schools, admittedly a smaller proportion than the 36.7 per cent found by a similar survey in 1962, but still very large compared to the 4 per cent in the population as a whole who had received such an education.[1]

Several other important English institutions have become more rather than less middle-class dominated since the last war. Parliament, as we have seen, has become progressively 'embourgeoised'. Mr Peter Walker recalls that when he entered the House of Commons in 1961, 'There were still a good many old-style knights of the shire on the Conservative benches, and on the Labour side a fair number of trade union leaders and real working men. Now we have a lot of people from broadly the same background who are very bright and are primarily concerned with moving amendments.'[2] Of the 635 MPs elected in the May 1979 General Election, 264 came from the professions (including 103 lawyers and 74 teachers and lecturers) and 219 from business (including 85 company directors and 87 managers and executives). Only 32 were manual workers. 68 per cent of the members of the present House of Commons are university graduates; 36 per cent were educated at public schools and a further 32 per cent at grammar schools.

The higher echelons of the Civil Service are another area where the middle classes have actually gained ground despite repeated attempts to create a more democratic entry system and to break the hold of the public school and Oxbridge-educated generalist. The proportion of direct entrants to the administrative class who came from the Registrar General's top two social classes increased sharply from 64 per cent in the early 1950s to 85 per cent in the early 1960s. It was partly to find ways of countering this trend that the Fulton Committee was set up in 1966. Finding that 73 per cent of direct entrants to the administrative class were Oxbridge graduates and 63 per cent from public schools, it recommended the introduction of a new system of administration trainees to attract a wider range of applicants and the promotion of more people up through the ranks from the executive grade.

In the event, the introduction of the administration trainee system has simply had the effect of further strengthening the middle-class hold on senior Civil Service posts. The intention of the post-Fulton reorganization was that 40 per cent of the new trainees would be recruited from the existing members of the executive class and 60 per cent by direct recruitment from outside. In fact by 1975 only 20 per cent were coming from the executive class and 80 per cent direct from the universities, more than half of them from public schools and Oxbridge. Moreover, a high proportion of those recruited internally were themselves from middle-class backgrounds.

The latest figures show an acceleration of this trend. The 1980 report of the Civil Service Commission revealed that 60 per cent of the previous year's successful external candidates for administration traineeship had Oxbridge degrees, and that half of them had been at public or direct grant schools. Upper-middle-class 'mandarins', educated in arts subjects at in-dependent schools and ancient universities, continue to reign supreme over the corridors of Whitehall. That may well be one of the main explanations for the paralysis which seems to have gripped British government. Greats men are supremely trained and equipped to write judiciously balanced white papers, sit on royal commissions, and produce elegant and non-committal briefs for ministers. They are not, however, encouraged by their background and education, as, for example, are French civil servants who have graduated from the *Grandes Écoles*, to take decisions and put practical action before debate and discussion.

A similar trend has taken place in higher education. The effect of all the measures taken to increase the opportunities of the working classes, from the 1944 Education Act to the expansion of new universities after the Robbins Report, has in fact been to increase the proportion of middle-class children going on to higher education. Research by Professor A. H. Halsey shows that the chance of a working-class boy going to university remained eleven times less than that of a middle-class boy throughout the period between the 1930s and the

1960s. The relative chances of working-class boys staying on at school until eighteen and going on to any form of higher education actually lessened during the same period. Those born into the bottom three social classes between 1913 and 1922 were five times less likely than those born into the top two to stay on at school until eighteen. Thirty years later they were six times less likely to stay on.

This trend has accelerated in the last few years. The destruction of grammar schools and direct grant schools has closed traditional avenues by which bright working-class boys obtained access to universities. Between 1976 and 1979 there was a steady increase in the proportion of candidates accepted by universities who came from the Registrar General's top two social classes. By 1979, children from those two classes, which made up a quarter of the population, were taking two thirds of new university places. Children of families in Class III, who made up half of the population, took 30 per cent of university places; those of partly-skilled workers (17.8 per cent of the population) took 5 per cent, and those from unskilled families (7.3 per cent of the population) took only one per cent.

At Oxford and Cambridge in particular the middle classes have kept and consolidated their hold. The separate examinations which both demand favour those schools with provision for a third-year sixth form. Admission figures for both universities over the past few years show a decline in the proportion of working-class boys gaining places, apparently matched by a rise in the proportion of middle-class girls. The composition of the student body at both universities remains predominantly upper middle class. The Cambridge admission figures for 1979, for example, showed that the children of professional and managerial workers took 70 per cent of all new places.

Even institutions dedicated to the promotion of working-class interests have become steadily more middle-class dominated. As has already been noted, the Labour Party, both at Parliamentary and local level, has become progressively more bourgeois. Its new leader, Michael Foot, comes from an upper-middle-class professional family, and is as much at home in the smart literary set of Hampstead as in his solidly working-class constituency of Ebbw Vale in South Wales.

The trade union movement is also being taken over by the middle classes. This is happening in two ways. First, as we have seen, white-collar workers are becoming unionized in large numbers. It has been estimated that by 1985 they will make up more than half of the total trade union membership in Britain. Already three of the biggest ten unions in the country are white-collar. Secondly, the full-time staff and the leaders of unions are increasingly being drawn from the ranks of the middle classes. The setting up and expansion of research, political and information departments has led to the recruitment of bright young graduates with left-wing sympathies. At the same time the growth of white-collar unions has led to the emergence of a new type of union leader who in background and lifestyle is closer to the manager he meets across the negotiating table than to some of the workers he represents. Geoffrey Drain, the general secretary of NALGO, is a graduate of London University and a former barrister whose annual salary in 1980 was £20,000. Alan Sapper, general secretary of the Association of Cinematographic, Television and Allied Technicians, was a professional scientist before he became a trade union official, while John Lyons, general secretary of the Engineers and Managers Association, is a Cambridge graduate and former manager in industry.

This take-over of both the Labour Party and the trade union movement illustrates one of the most conspicuous features about the English middle classes – their capacity to exploit and turn to their own use those institutions which were set up primarily to benefit the working classes. This talent is displayed particularly clearly in the fields of the state-provided health and education services. Socialists have traditionally argued that doing away with private medicine and education would automatically improve the quality of the public services because the middle classes would be forced to use them. In fact, the bourgeoisie are already using the National Health Service and state education system and because of their drive and their ability to 'play the system' have turned them to their own advantage. It is a reasonable assumption that no matter what new scheme is introduced to help the disadvantaged, be it cancer screening for women, special clinics for dyslexics or schemes to help the gifted child, the middle classes will be at the head of the queue.

The public library system, originally conceived to bring books within reach of poor working men and women, is now used extensively and even predominantly by the middle classes. They are also the main beneficiaries of public subsidies to the arts. The biggest subsidies go to opera, ballet and the theatre with virtually no public money going to support working-class cultural pursuits. While the bourgeoisie can enjoy heavily subsidised seats at the National Theatre or the Festival Hall, football or pop music fans have to pay the full commercial price for their tickets. As a result the average price for a pop concert is 30 per cent higher than for a classical concert. It is hardly surprising that when the Arts Council recently refused a grant to the new National Museum of Labour History to restore its collection of trade union banners on the grounds that they were 'not living art', Mr Terry McCarthy, the director, commented: 'When people hear of this and see money going to stately homes, the opera and the theatre, it just reinforces the view in sections of the Labour movement that the arts are a middle-class thing.'[3]

The history of the Workers Educational Association (WEA) provides a classic example of how the middle classes have taken over an institution set up directly and exclusively for the use of the working classes. The WEA was set up in 1903 by a group of trade unionists and co-operators who wanted to bring the standards and culture of the universities to ordinary working people. In his book *An Experiment in Democratic Education* (1914) R. H. Tawney, the first of a long and distinguished line of public school and Oxbridge-educated socialists who became WEA tutors, wrote: 'Our primary mission is to the educationally underprivileged majority who cease their full-time education at or about fifteen, and who need a humane education.' WEA classes still flourish today, but many of their students are retired bank managers and clergymen and middle-class housewives, worthy enough recipients of culture and enlightenment, but hardly the people that the founders of the WEA had in mind.

A more recent example of the same phenomenon is the Open University (OU). As originally conceived by Jennie Lee, the wife of the great socialist politician, Aneurin Bevan, and by Harold Wilson, who laid its foundations in the late 1960s, the OU was to be an institution which would give the socially and economically underprivileged the chance of the university education which they had never been able to enjoy. In the event, the vast majority of OU students have come from the middle classes, many indeed from the professions. The university authorities are so worried by the middle-class bias that applications are weighted, so that a lorry driver from Newcastle is given priority over a teacher from Hampshire. Even this reverse discrimination, however, has failed to turn the OU into what its founders intended it to be.

Another movement which in its original intention and its purpose could have brought immense benefit to working classes but which has, in fact, predominantly benefited the middle classes is women's liberation. As preached by its apparently radical disciples, 'women's lib' is all about taking working-class girls and wives away from the drudgery of their servile roles in the kitchen and the bedroom and opening new vistas of independence and creativity to them. In reality, however, it is largely middle-class women who have taken up interesting jobs and hobbies, because they could afford nannies and au pairs to look after their children and had the confidence to break out of their traditional roles and assert their individuality.

The working classes by contrast, have, if anything, actually suffered as a result of women's lib. There is evidence that middle-class women have gained jobs in shops and offices at the expense of working-class men. Male attitudes have remained more chauvinistic and traditional within the working classes with the result that women have had to take on two jobs rather than one, working in the factory by day and at home by night without the support and help that middle-class husbands are more inclined to give to their wives. As a result, far from being liberated, many have become more enslaved.

Culturally, politically and socially, the middle classes still dominate Britain and dictate standards and style to the rest of the population. Despite attempts to proletarianize them, the predominant accents on radio and television, particularly when authority is needed as with newsreaders and announcers, still tend to be impeccably upper middle class. The public like it that way. The most popular recent combination of newsreaders on ITN's *News At Ten,* was that of Reginald Bosanquet, late of Winchester and New College, Oxford, and Anna Ford, the grammar-school educated daughter of a Church of England vicar.

The same is true of political leaders. When Tony Benn expounds his faith in the working people and trade unions of Britain as agents for revolutionary socialist change it is in the unmistakable tones of Westminster School and Oxford. Admittedly Mrs Thatcher's voice raises some hackles for its plumminess but not as many as it would if she spoke in the style of Miss Janet Street-Porter. Being 'properly spoken' is still regarded by many in the working classes as a sign of gentility and authority, as many a con man and life insurance salesman has found to his advantage.

Notwithstanding their vicissitudes over the last thirty years, the middle classes have managed to maintain their status in the eyes of the population as a whole. Opinion polls consistently show that doctors, clergymen and lawyers are still among the most trusted and respected members of the community. The professions have in general managed to avoid government interference in their affairs and have been allowed to operate restrictive practices which might well provoke a national outcry if they were applied by any trade union.

The middle classes have also maintained their traditional role as opinion-formers and decision-takers. They dominate that broad group of intellectuals, campaigners, communicators and administrators who constitute the effective forum for discussion and decision-taking about major issues. Such national debate as there is about nuclear weapons, or the rights and wrongs of easier abortion, is almost exclusively confined to the bourgeoisie. Even in areas which predominantly concern the working classes, like child benefits or the impact of unemployment on society, it is the middle-class voice of the Child Poverty Action Group or the academic researcher which talks most loudly and clearly to both government and the public. The growth of audience participation programmes on radio and television has provided the articulate and confident middle classes with yet another platform for their views. It is rare to hear a working-class accent on *Any Questions* or its new television equivalent, *Question Time.*

There is perhaps no more striking illustration of the continuing strength of the English middle classes than that afforded by a comparison of the fate of their distinctive culture with that of the working classes. The vital working-class culture so sensitively described by Richard Hoggart in *The Uses of Literacy* has now all but disappeared. Its central features, the back-to-back houses with their communal closes, the streets with their corner shops and play areas for children, the rich oral tradition of folk phrases and club songs, the institutions of self-improvement and popular entertainment like the Sunday Schools, the reading rooms and the music halls, have been swept away by slum clearance and urban development, the coming of television and pop music and the growth of a new commercial mass-entertainment industry.

By contrast the distinctive culture of the middle classes has survived remarkably unscathed the ravages of the last thirty years. The villas and semis of suburbia have largely escaped developers and bulldozers. Ironically those few working-class dwellings which also escaped them have in many cases been bought up and gentrified by the bourgeoisie. Undisturbed and not uprooted into high-rise blocks of flats and new estates, middle-class communities have retained much more of their distinctive identity and their traditional culture. There are still many who lead lives remarkably similar to those that Angela Thirkell and John Betjeman wrote about in the 1940s, lives based around sales of work, evensong, tennis parties and drinks at the golf club. Of course the advent of 'pop' culture has not left them totally unscathed. The music coming through the loudspeakers at vicarage fetes or prep school sports day is now as likely to come from *Grease* as from Gilbert and Sullivan. But at least there is still a Church of England with one and a quarter million people going to its services every Sunday and a thriving independent sector educating more than half a million children, as well as a plethora of amateur operatic societies doing their damnedest to ensure that the Savoy Operas will never lose their place as the folk music of the middle classes.

Other of their distinctive institutions have also managed to remain remarkably unchanged and to flourish in an atmosphere which might appear uncongenial if not positively hostile. Many public schools are still pervaded by that curious mixture of godliness, good learning and games-playing that comes across so clearly in *Tom Brown's Schooldays*. A recent Sunday morning chapel service at a school in Kent had E. W. Swanton, the recently retired cricket correspondent of the *Daily Telegraph*, preaching on the theme of Christians as athletes. The second lesson, from Paul's letter to the Corinthians, called on men to 'run the race that ye may obtain (the prize)', and the hymns included 'Fight the Good Fight'.

It is, of course, partly because they have not entirely succumbed to modern whims and have retained many of their traditional values that the public schools are attractive to many parents. It is because they felt that those values were important that three-quarters of those parents in Bristol and Manchester with an income of £6000 or more who were interviewed in a survey carried out in 1976 on behalf of the Independent Schools Information Service said that they wanted to send their sons to independent schools. Boarding fees are now as high as £3500 in top public schools and parents make extraordinary sacrifices to afford them. One father recently moved his family into a smaller house and finally into a caravan to keep his three sons at a well-known school in the South East.

Admittedly, the public schools have had to broaden their intake in keeping with changing economic circumstances. Some professional people simply cannot afford the fees any longer and the sons of clergymen, doctors and others are increasingly going to state schools. Their places have been taken partly by a new influx of foreign pupils and of girls, and partly by an increasing proportion of boys from families without a public school tradition.

Many public school masters deplore this trend towards the nouveaux riches. I recall sitting a couple of years ago in the strangely spartan atmosphere of a masters' dining room which doubles as a gymnasium, and eating the uniquely public school combination of macaroni cheese and potatoes while a master told me: 'All our parents are interested in now is yachts. They don't have books in their houses any longer, only magazines.' Yet in taking the offspring of the vulgar up-and-coming bourgeoisie and of Arab oil magnates and turning them into gentlemen on a diet of Latin unseens, compulsory games and chapel, the public schools are once again performing the role for which so many of them were created a hundred years ago.

Like independent education, private medicine has boomed because some in the middle classes have been increasingly unhappy about the service provided by the state. It has also gained from widening its traditional catchment area. It is now no longer just the English upper middle classes who enjoy the benefits of jumping the queue for National Health Service beds. Private medical services in Britain are heavily used by foreigners and are even beginning to be used by the working classes. In 1979 the Electrical, Electronic, Telecommunication and Plumbing Union caused something of a stir in the trade union movement by negotiating a deal for private medical insurance for forty thousand of its members.

The demand from Arabs for places in independent schools and from trade unionists for private medical treatment shows how middle-class values and institutions are being kept going by the most unlikely supporters. Another unlikely source of support are the coloured immigrants from the Commonwealth who have come to Britain in the last thirty years. Those from the West Indies, although in their occupations, incomes and certain aspects of their lifestyle predominantly working-class, have at least kept alive one particular middle-class tradition. They have a higher level of church-going than the rest of the population, although they tend to belong to Pentecostalist and other fundamentalist sects rather than the established Church.

Many of the immigrants from Asia, and particularly from the Indian sub-continent, are much more obviously middle-class. They include shopkeepers and small businessmen who display far more noticeably than their English counterparts the traditional bourgeois values of hard work, self-help, thrift and independence. A recent survey of elderly immigrants found that they were much less inclined than native born English people to apply for state benefits and use state welfare services. Many shunned them for the same reasons as the pre-war middle classes, because of the social stigma involved in dependence on the state.

Two immigrants who were in the news in 1979 are perfect

exemplars of the values traditionally associated with the English middle classes. Mr Longanaden Chengalanee, who came over from Mauritius in 1962 to set up as a draper in Middlesex, achieved a lifelong ambition when he got his son into Eton. He had put down the boy's name when he was two and had subsequently worked long hours in his shop and gone without luxuries to save enough to meet the Eton fees.

Mr Mota Singh, who in 1979 became the first immigrant from the New Commonwealth to be made a High Court judge, shows an equally strong commitment to traditional English middle-class values. The son of a garage proprietor, he was born in Nairobi in 1930, and went to a public school in India where he was captain of the cricket team. He came to England in 1964 with his four brothers, who are respectively a solicitor, a chartered accountant, a public relations consultant and an articled clerk in a law firm. Mr Singh lives in Wimbledon and combines a passion for tennis and cricket with a strict adherence to the Sikh religion which, in his words, 'teaches the importance of discipline, hard work and the determination to succeed against all the odds. These are also British qualities. And if some of the British are overlooking these virtues, it is for the Sikh community to remind them.'[4]

The fact that certain bourgeois values appeal so strongly to coloured immigrants and that institutions like public schools and private medicine are receiving increasing support from equally unexpected sources shows both the continuing strength and the growing heterogeneity of English middle classness. Those two factors are also highlighted in the most comprehensive survey of social mobility in Britain, the results of which were published in 1980.

The Nuffield Social Mobility Survey, carried out by sociologists under the direction of A. H. Halsey, Professor of Social and Administrative Studies at Oxford University, and Dr John Goldthorpe, is based on data collected from interviews carried out in 1972 with more than ten thousand men aged between twenty and sixty-four. Its main finding is that while there has been considerable upward social mobility in Britain in the last sixty years, with more people reaching the top because of general economic progress and changes in the occupational structure, there has been no change at all in the relative chances of those born into different social classes of reaching the top.[5]

Goldthorpe found that the middle classes have grown and the working classes have shrunk during the present century. Although the 'service class', as he prefers to call those in managerial, professional and administrative occupations, still contains a preponderance of those who were born into it, there has also been a large injection of people from other classes. This widening of its recruiting base, he argues, has made the traditional middle class far less coherent and far more heterogeneous than it used to be. It is, in his words, 'a class of low classness'. The working class, by contrast, although smaller is more coherent and class-conscious. It contains very few people not born into it. As Goldthorpe says, 'People don't fall out of the middle classes like they used to. You can't fall out of a bureaucracy.'

This picture of an increasingly large and increasingly heterogeneous middle class helps to explain some of the phenomena which we have already noticed in previous chapters: the growing volatility in political behaviour, the tendency to division between traditional and radical, entrepreneurial and bureaucratic, publicly and privately employed, the failure to unite in defence of its own interests and forge a clear class consciousness, and the increasing militancy and adoption of patterns of behaviour previously associated with the working classes.

The overall message of the Nuffield Social Mobility Survey is clear enough, however. Dr Goldthorpe's findings on social mobility are confirmed by Professor Halsey's detailed work on educational opportunities. They show conclusively that despite nearly a century of legislation and planning to bring about equality the middle classes have consistently done better out of life than the working classes. Both men agree this message is a depressing one for all those who, like them, have believed that the Welfare State and the policies of social democracy would bring about a greater equality of chances and opportunities.

They are also both pessimistic about the chances of Britain moving any closer to equality in the 1980s. Because of the dominance of class, and the persistence of private schools,

Halsey is sceptical that comprehensive schools will be any more successful than the old tripartite system in producing a meritocratic system of education. Goldthorpe fears that economic recession will lessen further the chances of working-class children reaching the top and will make the service class look after its own offspring more jealously and protectively. 'Now that the economic conditions for the overall upward mobility that has taken place over the last fifty years are no longer there,' he says, 'the relative inequalities are likely to get worse.' The middle classes, as ever, look like keeping one jump ahead. Paradoxically, they may also be pioneering the way towards a simpler, more equal society in the future.

13

Towards the Future

If there is one lesson for the future which a study of the history of the English middle classes teaches, it is surely that any obituary of them is decidedly premature. The species may evolve but it will not disappear. Its resilience and capacity for survival are considerable, as the experiences of the last thirty years in particular have shown, and there seems no reason to doubt that at the dawning of the next millennium the British bourgeoisie will not only still be around, but also be bigger and probably better-off than they are today.

Admittedly, rather fewer of them are likely to be commuting to London on the 8.23. Many secretarial and clerical jobs are bound to disappear as the ubiquitous microchip is introduced into more and more office processes. A poster already prepared by ASTMS for display at railway stations warns that 'One chip equals a trainload of seven hundred commuters.'[1] New communications technology will also enable many managers and executives to work from home and forsake the daily trip to the office. Indeed, it could well be that in twenty years' time the middle-class ritual of daily commuting to work will largely have ceased.

That same technology revolution is likely to have an even more dramatic effect on the working classes. With the continuing decline of Britain's traditional manufacturing base and the growth of the service sector, there will almost certainly be relatively few manual workers left by the end of the century. Many of those now thought of as being in working-class occupations will either be unemployed or will have joined middle-class workers in the new service class. We are already beginning to witness the death of the traditional British proletariat. The process is most clearly evident in the malaise which has overtaken its own most distinctive creation, the Labour Party, which is gradually losing support and falling apart as its traditional working-class base is eroded.

Are we then beginning to see at last the fulfilment of the hopes and prophecies of the egalitarians and sociologists of the 1940s and 1950s – the creation of a classless, uniformly bourgeois society whose prevailing aspirations and opinions find their natural expression in the politics of middle-of-the-road gradualism and social democracy? The broad popularity of the new Social Democratic Party as evidenced in opinion polls might encourage such a view. Yet the findings of Dr Goldthorpe discussed in Chapter 8 indicate the fallacy of assuming that an increase in the affluence or job patterns of the working classes necessarily leads them to become 'embourgeoised' in other ways also.

Clearly the middle classes, as defined by occupation and probably by other criteria as well, are going to become a bigger and bigger proportion of the population as more people become employed in the service sector forsake their overalls and the factory floor and own their own homes. That has been the trend for the whole of this century, and there is every reason to suppose that it will accelerate in the next twenty years or so. Yet there are also good grounds for predicting that, far from leading to a more classless society, this could in fact increase social divisions by enhancing further the differences between the established and the new elements within the expanded middle class and greatly widening the gap between it and those left outside.

The existence and persistence of subtle social distinctions between the established upper middle classes and the parvenus have been a constant theme of the history of the British bourgeoisie. They provided the basis for Matthew Arnold's contempt for John Bright and his fellow Victorian manufacturers, for Professor Alan Ross's lists of U and non-U words, and for the observations of social commentators and critics like George Orwell and Bernard Shaw. There is every reason to suppose that they will continue into the twenty-first century. Of all groups in English society, the upper middle-class professional Establishment is perhaps most resistant to social change. Their jobs as doctors, lawyers and senior civil servants are less susceptible than most to the microchip revolution. Their distinctive institutions, such as the Church of England, the public schools, and now, after a recent shaky period, *The Times*, seem assured of a relatively healthy, if not in all cases a prosperous future. The comprehensive-school-educated, *Daily Mail*-reading operators of word processing machines, who will increasingly swell the ranks of the new service class, are likely to remain as cut off as ever from their charmed circle.

The gap between the expanding middle class and the shrinking working class is also likely to widen in a period of economic recession. Admittedly, some people in professional and managerial jobs may well find life considerably tougher in the next decade or so. Already many of those working in the public sector are finding their relative standard of living falling and their career prospects contracting as a result of economies in public expenditure. It has been widely predicted that around three thousand university teachers will be made redundant between 1981 and 1984. There will also inevitably be more redundancies among executives and managers in private industry and more bankruptcies among entrepreneurs as the present economic recession continues. In the professions, over-production of qualified entrants for whom there are no permanent jobs available seems likely to be a growing problem. At the end of 1980, for example, there were two hundred vacancies on the Law Society's jobs register, but over two thousand qualified solicitors seeking employment, a further nine thousand serving articles, and six thousand students intending to join the profession.

Compared to the prospects for many in the working classes in the 1980s and beyond, however, the outlook for professional, managerial and even white-collar clerical workers is still fairly good. The continuance of economic recession and of de-industrialization in Britain will lead to the loss of far more manual than non-manual jobs. Unemployment, and particularly long-term unemployment, is likely to continue to remain predominantly a working-class experience. In a contracting economy the middle classes will tend to become more exclusive and recruit fewer members from below. Admittedly some of them may drop down the social scale. Already a small but growing number of university graduates are going into skilled and semi-skilled manual jobs as electricians, plumbers and carpenters. Even this trend, however, is likely to prove more damaging to the traditional working classes as it will cream off some of their more attractive jobs.

In overall living standards and lifestyle, the gap between the middle and working classes seems almost certain to grow wider in the next decade. While the former remain relatively affluent and continue their move into private health care for themselves and private education for their children, the latter will mostly depend on increasingly hard-pressed public welfare services. This development of two nations is likely to be exacerbated by the continuation of social trends that are already apparent. Even such a basic and universal activity as shopping, for example, is becoming more class-based with one part of the population increasingly using the delicatessens, health food shops and craft shops which are proliferating in the 'nicer' parts of our towns and cities, and another the discount stores and cut-price warehouses which are springing up in equal profusion in the poorer parts.

Given this likelihood of greater social inequalities, is the stage set for fiercer class conflict in Britain in the last two decades of the twentieth century? Will the working classes become an alienated and underprivileged minority like the blacks and in their frustration and resentment turn on the growing bourgeoisie? Already in its opposition to Thatcherism the Labour Party is resurrecting the rhetoric of class warfare and promising that when it next comes to power it will mount a frontal assault on public schools, private medicine, the House of Lords and other manifestations of the upper middle-class Establishment.

Apart from this sabre-rattling in the Walworth Road, however, there is very little evidence of growing popular antagonism towards the middle classes. Despite the very high level of unemployment, and the increasing polarization in British society between the haves and have-nots, surprisingly few people seem to feel strongly about class differences. Only 5 per cent of those questioned in a national opinion poll carried out for *The Times* in June 1980 thought that class distinction and snobbery were the factor most to blame for Britain's present problems, and only 12 per cent rated lack of equal opportunity as a serious problem at all. One leading political commentator suggested that politicians should draw the lesson from the poll that the class war was over and that there were not many votes to be won by advocating the abolition of public schools or the steep increase of higher rates of taxation.[2]

Certainly there is a good deal of envy in modern British society. However, it is found as much within as between the different classes. There is probably more concern among skilled workers with the preservation of their differentials compared to the unskilled than with the earnings of those in white-collar jobs. Comparisons with and resentment of middle-class earnings do not seem to be the major factors behind high wage claims by blue-collar trade unions. Other loyalties and hostilities over-ride those of class, as a comment made by a working man to the journalist Jeremy Seabrook in 1978 makes all too clear:

> When the barricades go up, it won't be the middle class on one side and the working class on the other; it will be white on one side and black on the other with just a few race traitors on their side.[3]

Assuming that they are going to continue to grow and to remain immune from the threat of serious attack from below, how will the middle classes develop and what will be the effect on society as a whole of their increasingly dominant position within it? Historically, the middle classes have been made up of three broad groups, each with its own distinctive ethic and influence. The professional upper middle class has stood for liberal values of independence, tolerance and disinterested public service. Small businessmen and entrepreneurs have championed a robust individualism and upheld the principles of thrift, self-help and competition. Those in managerial and clerical jobs, the biggest group within the middle classes, have been more content to swim with the contemporary tide. In the twentieth century that has led them to espouse the outlook and values of corporatism, collectivism and instrumentalism.

It is safe to predict that these three very different and often contradictory currents of English middle classness will continue to flow strongly into the next century. As the middle classes have grown in size so they have become more heterogeneous and it becomes increasingly difficult to talk of a single bourgeois ethic. It will rather be through the separate development of these three very different strains that the middle classes will make their mark on society.

Of the three groups, those who have adopted the traditional working-class values of collectivism and instrumentalism are perhaps the most dominant, and certainly the most noticeable, in our own day. The growth of what might be termed trade union attitudes among middle-class groups of workers has been a marked feature of the last few years. An article in the *British Medical Journal* in 1979 urged doctors to emulate the tactics of non-professional unions in the Health Service to fight Government spending cuts. The revised handbook of medical ethics issued in the same year by the British Medical Association contained the statement, unthinkable ten years earlier, that it was not always unethical for a professional man to withdraw his services.

Similar attitudes were displayed by some of the independent television producers and directors who went on strike for three months in the autumn of 1979 and *The Times* journalists who staged a week-long strike in August 1980. During both these disputes, well-paid, middle-class people behaved as if they were poor, down-trodden workers. A manifestly self-interested action to get more money was elevated into a high moral crusade, and any recourse to militancy or to anti-management attitudes was welcomed as a sign of virility and of proper trade union behaviour. Several of the social workers who went on strike for up to a year in 1979 found it an exhilarating and even morally uplifting experience for similar reasons.[4]

Perhaps the most striking assumption by a middle-class group of attitudes and behaviour once associated only with working-class trade unionists has been in the traditionally docile and deferential ranks of the civil service. The history of one of the leading civil service unions, the Civil and Public Services Association, was published in May 1980 with the triumphant title *From Humble Petition to Militant Action.* When, six months later, a *Times* leader writer ventured to remind civil servants of their traditionally high responsibilities and devotion to duty, and to suggest that it would be deplorable if these were 'blown away by the breath of unionized grievance', he was immediately taken to task by the

Secretary General of the Council of Civil Service Unions for living 'in the dear, dead days of long ago when Civil Service militancy did not exist'.[5] Just how dead those days were was shown by the events of the spring and early summer of 1981 when a concerted campaign of industrial action by civil servants in pursuit of a pay claim inflicted considerable harm on the workings of Government.

It is, indeed, quite possible that those in white-collar jobs will be the most militant and disruptive of all workers in the 1980s and 1990s. They will increasingly come to dominate the trade union movement. As the strength and morale of the traditional manual working classes is sapped by the progressive de-industrialization of Britain, those in middle-class clerical and managerial occupations seem most likely to exercise their industrial muscle. Computer operators and power station engineers have as much ability as the miners or railwaymen to 'hold the country to ransom', and they may well prove increasingly determined to use it.

But if one element among the middle classes is likely to push Britain further down the road of material self-interest and militant bloody-mindedness, what of those other elements represented by the small businessmen and the professions? The whole direction of British society in the last thirty years may have been away from entrepreneurship and individualism towards corporatism and collectivism, but the values of independence, risk and competition are not dead. There are still plenty of people willing to venture their capital and embark on an enterprise entirely on their own account.

Among the professions traditions of disinterested service and responsibility still survive. Trade unionism may be creeping into the Church of England, but when clergymen were offered a pay rise of 18 per cent in 1979 (to give ordinary parish clergy a minimum annual income of £3300), many refused to take the full amount and argued that it was wrong to take more than was being urged on low-paid workers in the public sector. When in November 1979 a strike by engineers at Charing Cross Hospital threatened the delivery of vital fuel supplies, doctors and nurses mounted their own counter-picket to make sure the supplies got through.

The action by the Charing Cross doctors and nurses

provoked conflicting reactions in the letters column of *The Times*. Some correspondents saw it as a wholly admirable exercise of standing up to trade union bully boys and entirely in accordance with traditional professional ethics. Others regarded it as a piece of foolish hypocrisy, given that doctors themselves had earlier been on strike and needed to stand side by side with trade unionists to fight cuts in the Health Service and secure a better deal for all who worked within it.[6]

Those two points of view exemplify a very real division of opinion among the middle classes about how far they should go in opposing trade union militancy and strike action. On one side there is a feeling that the tradition of voluntary action could and should be harnessed to break the disruptive power of the unions when it is clearly harming people. This view, which naturally commends itself to many small businessmen and some in the professions, was powerfully expressed by Mrs Thatcher in a speech shortly before she became Prime Minister:

> We have a great national tradition of voluntary service. There are enough people in this country resolved to keep it going and determined not to yield to bullying – enough to stave off this kind of national disaster if it ever threatened. At such a time, it would be the duty of Government to harness this spirited reserve to the service of our people.[7]

On the other side there is a feeling that the middle classes have wholly lost the boy-scoutish enthusiasm they displayed in the General Strike of 1926 and have no desire to be part of a holy war against working-class militancy. That view, which is held by many on the left and by the leaders of the white-collar unions, has been cogently expressed by Clive Jenkins:

> It is now unthinkable that there could ever be a mass intervention from volunteers from the middle classes in a national dispute. The truth is that many white-collar workers in both sectors have begun to despise their lives of genteel poverty and have discovered that the world has more to offer them. In doing this they also have had to discover the bargaining power latent in their collective strength.[8]

Which of those two points of view more nearly captures the mood of the English middle classes as they enter the last two decades of the twentieth century? Are the old entrepreneurial and professional embers of self-help and voluntary action, fanned by Thatcherism, about to burst alight and consume the power of the trade unions, or have the cold waters of instrumentalism and collectivism dowsed those traditional ideals of the middle classes?

The reality lies somewhere between the two extremes. The middle classes still have a strong commitment to voluntary action. They will rally to a call for help, but they will do so, as they always have done, because someone is suffering and a job needs to be done rather than out of any ideological or political zeal. It seems highly unlikely that there will be a set-piece class battle in the next twenty years with the middle classes enthusiastically being recruited to overthrow the power of the trade unions. The will for such a fight is just not there, except perhaps in the minds of a small Poujadist minority. For one thing, too many of the middle classes are now themselves members of trade unions. More important, their overall mood is one of compromise and conciliation rather than conflict. That could prove to be one of the most important influences that they bring to bear on society as a whole.

Aristotle believed that those states with a large middle class would have the best and most stable government, avoiding the partiality that came if either the very rich or the very poor were dominant. There are good grounds for thinking that the growing dominance of the middle-class vote in modern Britain will make for less adversarial politics and more middle-of-the-road government. In February 1974 that vote failed to back Edward Heath in his stand against the might of union power as represented by the miners and went to a large extent to the Liberals instead. In October 1974 many in the middle classes voted for a similarly moderate line. In May 1979 they swung against Mrs Thatcher because they were worried about the stridency and the missionary zeal with which she embarked on her crusade against organized labour. At the same time, more people in the higher professional and managerial occupations voted for the Liberals than for Labour. In the last three elections the middle-class vote has been consistently delivered in favour of moderation, conciliation and co-operation rather than conflict.

On the basis of this recent experience, an increasingly

middle-class electorate in the 1980s and 1990s seems likely to favour the Liberals and the new Social Democratic Party. The emergence of the new party, indeed, may well be a reflection of changes in society which are leading to the decline of the old class-based pattern of voting and the growth of a hetero-geneous middle stratum. Its founders, the so-called 'Gang of Four' of Roy Jenkins, Shirley Williams, David Owen and William Rodgers, although recognizably bourgeois in their own backgrounds and outlook, are at the same time more classless than the leading figures in either the Labour or Conservative parties. Their guiding political principles – support for a mixed economy, a strong commitment to Britain's continued membership of the Common Market, concern for the Third World, and a belief in the importance of decentralized, local community initiatives – are those which opinion polls have shown to have most appeal with middle-class voters and least with the traditional working classes. It is not surprising that support for the Social Democrats seems to be strongest in the south of England and weakest in the north and in Scotland where Labour seems likely to hold on as the party of the under-privileged working-class minority.

If one element in the English middle classes appears likely to steer the country as a whole in a more militant, money-grabbing direction in the future, and another much bigger element to point it towards moderation, there is a third group which may influence it in yet another direction. Clive Jenkins may be right in saying that the middle classes will not intervene in their thousands in the event of a major strike by trade unions. But he may be wrong in saying that they have 'begun to despise their lives of genteel poverty'. There is growing evidence that, in fact, the reverse may be the case. Those in the professions and elsewhere who have represented the noblest ideals of English middle classness have always tended to put a higher premium on cultural, intellectual and spiritual develop-ment than on the mere accumulation of wealth and material possessions. Many of them are now acquiescing calmly and quietly in the lowering of their living standards.

Mrs Thatcher wants to reverse this trend. She is gambling on Britain being saved by the traditional enterprise, ambition and competitive drive of the commercial middle classes channelled into productive and wealth-creating industry. She is appealing to the old materialistic and money-getting bourgeois values. It may well be, however, that this appeal will fall on deaf ears because more and more of the middle classes are now prepared to trade money for leisure and to accept a lower standard of living than their counterparts abroad, or even some of their own working-class countrymen. Britain may yet be saved by middle-class values, but they will be very different from those extolled by the Prime Minister.

Samuel Brittain and other economists have argued that what has become known as the British disease is caused by the excessive expectations of the population which cannot be fulfilled. A small but increasing number of middle-class people, particularly among the young, are now beginning to abandon those expectations for more limited ones which are more realistic in an age of scarce and expensive energy and raw materials. They may well be the harbingers of a new post-industrial society, based on high technology and low consumption, a society whose early foundations are already so strong in Britain that one distinguished observer from abroad, Mr Bernard Nossiter of the *Washington Post*, has described the country as offering 'a future that works'.[9]

In a poll carried out for *The Times* in June 1980, 60 per cent of middle-class respondents (compared to only 43 per cent of working-class respondents) said that they would not work longer hours for more money. 61.5 per cent (50.5) said that they had no ambition to be rich, and 30.5 per cent (18) said that they had no ambition to earn more than their present earnings. British executives, professionals and entrepreneurs are on the whole much less willing than their European and American counterparts to let their work invade their home and family lives. Outside office hours, they distance themselves from their work as much as possible, often preferring to garden, to do jobs around the house or to play games rather than to catch up on developments in their field of study to gain further qualifications.

The movement towards a less ambitious and competitive lifestyle is most obvious among young people. It is true that the pendulum has swung from the period in the late 1960s and early 1970s when middle-class youth largely shunned careers in conventional bourgeois areas such as banking, industry and business. There are now more graduates queuing up to become merchant bankers, accountants and solicitors, and fewer wanting to go to further study or become social workers. But there is still a strong attraction towards careers like medicine, teaching and even craft work, which offer rewards in terms of their intrinsic and social value rather than in straight financial terms and towards a lifestyle that is more relaxed and more simple than that of their parents. The era of dropping out of public school or university to smoke pot and weave baskets in a commune in rural Wales may have passed, but the spirit which searches for a simpler and more natural life is still there, and the prediction which Anthony Sampson offered readers of *Newsweek* magazine in 1976 remains valid:

> Viewed from Britain's southeastern counties, the bastion of the middle classes, it is possible to imagine this country relaxing quite contentedly into a pre-industrial life-style, with more and more young people taking to pottery, folkweave, growing vegetables and drinking old ale in pubs. The British middle classes appear to be noticeably less demanding and extravagant in their pursuit of pleasure than their equivalents abroad, without the same fervent desire for safaris in Africa or fashionable ski resorts that mark the Germans or the French.[10]

As yet, of course, it is only a minority within the middle classes who are moving in this direction. In many ways, however, it is a natural extension of their historic role and identity. At its best and most distinctive, English middle classness has been a matter of standing for and living out certain values: the Christian gentility of Chaucer's 'parfit gentil Knyght', the innocent humour and humanity of Samuel Pepys, the Quaker sobriety and earnestness of John Bright, the active compassion and commitment to the service of others of Alec Dickson. There is a certain quiet and dignified simplicity in those lives which accords well with the demands of a less ostentatious and high-consuming society.

In a future where there seems bound to be more leisure time for everyone this group within the middle classes displays another value which will become increasingly relevant to the rest of society. As well as appreciating that leisure is worth more than the money gained by extra work, they have also traditionally seen their leisure time as a creative and active part of their lives, to be filled by cultural and voluntary activities as much as by more passive forms of recreation. A society in which the middle classes are increasingly dominant ought to be one which will not just cope with but also positively benefit from the decline of work and the growth of leisure.

In opting for a simpler existence and putting the quality of life above material wealth, the children of professional and business families might seem to be abandoning the traditions of their class. Yet, as we have seen, the English middle classes have never really had their hearts in the business of making money. The retreat by the sons of the Victorian mill-owners and manufacturers into country estates and gentrification; the reluctance of public school pupils and Oxbridge graduates to go into industry; the fact that vicars are rated above sales managers in the social scale; all these are manifestations of a feeling which lies at the heart of middle classness, that there are more important things in life than work and making money.

The professional and entrepreneurial middle classes have always been among the most innovative and dynamic elements in British society, pointing the way towards new economic and social paths later trodden by others. There is every reason to think that they will continue to fulfil this role in the future. Indeed, their newly emerging lifestyle and philosophy, based as it is on their traditional values, may offer the only way of curing the British disease and of coming to terms with the world as it is likely to be in the twenty-first century.

NOTES

Introduction

1. On the strength of the middle classes in Eastern Europe see W. Conner, *Socialism, Politics and Equality* (Columbia, 1979).
2. G. Orwell, *The Lion and the Unicorn*, (1941), p. 67.
3. Referred to in the letters column, *Daily Telegraph*, 7 December 1978.
4. *Guardian*, 22 January 1980; *Observer*, 24 August 1980.
5. R. Lewis and A. Maude, *The English Middle Classes* (London, 1949), p. 9.
6. P. Hutber, *The Decline and Fall of the Middle Class and How It Can Fight Back* (London, 1976), p. x.

Chapter 2: Who are the Middle Classes?

1. Lewis & Maude, *op. cit.*, p. 13.
2. *The Times*, 11 January 1975.
3. D. Butler and D. Stokes, *Political Change in Britain* (2nd edn., London, 1974), p. 477.
4. I. Reid, *Social Class Differences in Britain*, (1977) p. 26.
5. Lewis and Maude, *op. cit.*, p. 109; *The Times*, 5 January 1975.
6. *Economist*, 24 January 1948.
7. G. Orwell, 'The English People' in *Collected Essays, Journalism and Letters*, III (London, 1968), p. 20.
8. Lewis and Maude, *op. cit.*, p. 102. In his research for *The Affluent Worker* John Goldthorpe found that the car workers of Luton rated wealth as the main determinant of social class.
9. *Guardian*, 21 November 1980.
10. *Guardian*, 24 February 1979.
11. Data from R. Webber, *Parliamentary Constituencies: A Socio-Economic Classification*. OPCS Occasional Paper 13 (London, 1978).
12. M. Young and P. Willmott, *Family and Kinship in East London* (London, 1957); M. Young and P. Wilmott, *Family and Class In A London Suburb* (1960).

13.　P. Nuttgens, 'Doing More for the "Doers" in Society', *Times Higher Education Supplement*, 1 February 1980.

Chapter 3: What is Middle Classness?

1.　G. Orwell, 'The English People', p. 5.
2.　*Midweek*, BBC Radio 4, 27 September 1979.
3.　G. Turner, 'The Middle Class At Bay' (Part Two), *Sunday Telegraph*, 31 July 1977.
4.　*Ibid.*
5.　Quoted in A. Marwick, *Class, Image and Reality* (London, 1980), p. 165.
6.　*Sunday Times Reporter*, February 1979.
7.　*Guardian*, 24 September 1979.
8.　I. Reid, *op. cit.*, p. 207.
9.　Alan Clark writing in the *Guardian*, 2 May 1979.
10.　*Guardian*, 18 August 1980.
11.　*Public School*, BBC 2, 17 January 1980.
12.　*The Times*, 11 January 1975.
13.　K. Roberts and others, *The Fragmentary Class Structure* (London, 1977).
14.　*The Times*, 11 January 1975.
15.　*Private Schools*. A Labour Party Discussion Document (London, 1980), p. 8.
16.　See, for example, John Goldthorpe's studies in Luton discussed below on pp. 129–30.
17.　M. Drabble, *The Ice Age* (paperback edn., 1978), p. 20.
18.　R. Butt, 'A Testing Time for the Tories', *Sunday Times*, 15 February 1979.
19.　Figures from the Wolfenden report on the future of voluntary organizations (London, 1977).

Chapter 4: The Rise of the Middle Classes

1.　Aristotle, *The Politics*, Book IV, ix, 8.
2.　Quoted in R. H. Tawney, *Religion and the Rise of Capitalism* (paperback edn., London, 1964), p. 266.
3.　J. Ferne, *The Blazon of Gentrie* (1884).
4.　R. H. Tawney, *op. cit.*, p. 120.
5.　*Ibid.*, p. 202.
6.　See C. B. Macpherson, *The Political Theory of Possessive Individualism* (Oxford, 1962).
7.　Quoted in F. C. Palm, *The Middle Classes Then and Now* (New York, 1936), p. 102.
8.　On the general development of class consciousness at this time

see A. Briggs, 'The Language of Class in Early Nineteenth Century England' in A. Briggs and J. Saville (eds.), *Essays in Labour History* (1967).

9. *Ibid.*, p. 57.
10. Quoted in I. Bradley, *The Call to Seriousness* (London, 1976), p. 51.
11. *Ibid.*, pp. 153–4.
12. *Westminster Review*, vol. I, no. 1 (January 1824), pp. 68–9.
13. W. J. Reader, *Professional Men* (London, 1966), p. 79. I have made considerable use of this book in this chapter.
14. D. C. Somervell, *English Thought in the Nineteenth Century* (London, 1929), p. 80; J. S. Mill, 'The State of Society in America', *London Review*, January 1836.
15. Quoted in A. Briggs, *op. cit.*, pp. 56–7.
16. Quoted in Lewis and Maude, *op. cit.*, p. 55.
17. W. F. Monypenny & G. E. Buckle, *The Life of Benjamin Disraeli*, II (London 1910), pp. 82–3.
18. J. Morley, *The Life of Richard Cobden* (London 1896), I, p. 249.
19. M. P. Kelly, *White-Collar Proletariat* (London, 1980), p. 79.
20. H. B. Thomson, *The Choice of a Profession* (London, 1857), p. 5.
21. A. Briggs, *op. cit.*, p. 61.
22. J. Morley *op. cit.*, I, p. 392; quoted in I. Bradley, *The Optimists* (London, 1980), p. 52.

Chapter 5: The Victorian Heyday

1. M. Arnold, *Culture and Anarchy*, ed. J. Dover Wilson (paperback edn., Cambridge, 1971), p. 63; W. Bagehot, *Collected Works* (London, 1915), III, p. 371; Palmerston quoted by Lewis and Maude, *op. cit.*, p. 49.
2. *Edinburgh Review*, October 1840, p. 41; Lewis and Maude, p. 56.
3. J. A. Banks, *Prosperity and Parenthood: A Study of Family Planning among the Victorian Middle Classes* (London, 1954).
4. R. D. Baxter, *The Taxation of the UK* (London, 1869), pp. 105–6.
5. Quoted in W. L. Burn, *The Age of Equipoise* (paperback edn., London, 1968), p. 271.
6. I. Bradley, *The Call to Seriousness*, p. 180.
7. Quoted in H. McLeod, *Class and Religion in the late Victorian City* (London, 1974), p.152. I have made considerable use of this fascinating book in this chapter.
8. Quoted in J. R. de S. Honey, *Tom Brown's Universe* (London,

1977), p. 67. This is another book which I have found very useful.

9. *Ibid.*, p. 33.
10. M. Arnold, *Friendship's Garland* (popular edn., London, 1903), pp. 136–7.
11. J. Morley, *Studies in Conduct* (London, 1867), p.267; T. Carlyle, 'The Gospel of Mammonism' in *Past and Present* (London, 1843); W. Morris, *Art & Socialism* (1884).
12. M. Arnold, *Culture and Anarchy*, p. 101.
13. J. Morley, *op. cit.*, p. 271.
14. M. Arnold, *Friendship's Garland*, p. 137.
15. F. K. Prochaska, *Women and Philanthropy in Nineteenth Century England* (Oxford, 1980).
16. G. W. E. Russell, *Portraits of the Seventies* (London, 1916), p. 177.
17. N. McCord, *The Anti-Corn Law League* (London, 1958), pp. 57–8.
18. M. Arnold, *Friendship's Garland*, p. 152; M. Arnold, *A French Eton.*

Chapter 6: The Middle Classes Lose Confidence

1. W. Morris, *Socialism, its Growth and Outcome* (London, 1893); quoted in F. C. Palm, *The Middle Classes Then and Now*, p. 4.
2. W. S. Churchill, *Lord Randolph Churchill* (1906), I, p. 268.
3. R. Price, 'Society, Status and Jingoism' in G. Crossick (ed.), *The Lower Middle Class in Britain 1870–1914* (London, 1977), p. 102.
4. W. Morris, *Works*, XXIII (London, 1915), p. 184.
5. R. Church, *Over the Bridge* (London, 1955), p. 51.
6. G. Crossick, *op. cit.*, p. 24.
7. *Nonconformist*, 17 December 1879.
8. B. Webb, *Our Partnership* (London, 1948), pp. 162–3.
9. *Manchester Guardian*, 17 October 1900; *Fortnightly Review*, new series, XV (March 1874), p. 305.
10. Lewis and Maude, *op. cit.*, p. 107.
11. G. Crossick, *op. cit.*, p. 29.
12. Lewis and Maude, *op. cit.*, p. 75.
13. *Ibid.*, p. 75.
14. G. Crossick, *op. cit.*, p. 26.

Chapter 7: The Middle Classes Start Feeling Guilty

1. Lewis and Maude, *op. cit.*, p. 65.
2. Herbert Stead, founder of Browning Hall. I owe this reference

to Dr James Dickie with whom I have discussed the settlement movement.

3. P. Clarke, *Liberals & Social Democrats* (Cambridge, 1978), p. 46. Clarke's is a superb study of this group.
4. Quoted G. Crossick, *The Lower Middle Class in Britain, 1870–1914*, p. 41.
5. *Brighton & Hove Herald*, 2 October 1920. I owe these references to Miss Michelle Gabbidon who delivered a paper on 'The Language of Candidates in Brighton Municipal Elections, 1892–1923' at History Workshop 14, Brighton, November 1980.
6. *Daily Telegraph*, 12 March 1926; *Morning Post*, 1 June 1926. Both quoted in K. Roberts and others, *The Fragmentary Class Structure*, p. 21.
7. *The Times*, 10 January 1930.
8. *The Times*, 13 November 1919.
9. Lewis and Maude, *op. cit.*, p. 89.
10. *Economist*, 28 July 1945; K. Roberts, *op. cit.*, p. 30.
11. J. Bonham, *The Middle Class Vote* (London, 1954).
12. Lewis and Maude, *op. cit.*, p. 87.
13. *The Times*, 29 May 1947.
14. Lewis and Maude, *op. cit.*, p. 95.
15. *New Statesman*, 8 May 1948.
16. R. Blake, *The Conservative Party from Peel to Churchill* (paperback edn., London, 1972), p. 264.
17. G. Orwell, 'The English People', p. 23.
18. R. R. Stokes, MP for Ipswich quoted in K. Roberts, *op. cit.*, p. 30.

Chapter 8: Towards a Classless Society

1. F. Johnson, 'Privilege and the Prole', *Daily Telegraph*, 2 June 1977.
2. C. Booker, *The Neophiliacs* (paperback edn., London, 1970), p. 122.
3. G. Orwell, 'The English People', p. 20.
4. E. Heffer, *The Class Struggle in Parliament* (London, 1973), p. 52.
5. Lewis and Maude, *op. cit.*, p. 75.
6. *Ibid.*, p. 127.
7. *Looking Ahead.* NALGO Correspondence Institute Prospectus (London, 1979), p. 26.
8. R. Lewis, 'How the Middle Classes are slowly being taken over', *The Times*, 17 February 1975.

9. *Observer*, 2 April 1978.
10. C. Jenkins and B. Sherman, *White-Collar Unionism: The Rebellious Salariat* (London, 1979), p. 10.

Chapter 9: The Radical Middle Class

1. C. Booker, *The Neophiliacs*, p. 123. This book, on which I have relied heavily, gives an illuminating and entertaining account of the activities of the New Oxford Group.
2. C. Pritchard and R. Taylor, *The Protest Makers* (Oxford, 1980); F. Parkin, *Middle Class Radicalism* (Manchester, 1968).
3. F. Parkin, *op. cit.*, pp. 40–1.
4. G. Orwell, 'The English People', p. 5.
5. Research by I. Gordon and P. Whiteley published in *Political Studies*, Vol XXVII, No. 1, p. 103. See also on this theme B. Hindess, *The Decline of Working Class Politics* (1971).
6. M. Kogan, *The Politics of Education* (Harmondsworth, 1971).

Chapter 10: To the Barricades

1. Published in the *Guardian*, 6 January 1976.
2. E. Heffer, *The Class Struggle in Parliament*, p. 280; *New Statesman*, 4 January 1974; *The Times*, 14 August 1974.
3. Peter Walker speaking in Droitwich, reported in *The Times*, 4 November 1974; N. Scott, *A Primrose Path?* (Bow Group Pamphlet, 1975) reported in *The Times*, 1 August 1975.
4. *The Times*, 25 February 1976.
5. P. Hutber, 'A Bolder Bourgeoisie', *Telegraph Sunday Magazine*, 21 November 1976.
6. *The Times*, 13 January 1975.
7. Quoted in T. May, 'Middle Class Unionism' in R. King and N. Nugent (eds.), *Respectable Rebels* (London, 1979), p. 119.
8. *The Times*, 16 March 1977.
9. *Times Higher Education Supplement*, 11 February 1977.
10. J. Raynor, *The Middle Class* (2nd edn., London, 1970), p.44.
11. *The Times*, 15 January 1975.
12. The Middle Class Volunteer Reserve Publication 2, 26 September 1974.
13. Quoted in J. McHugh, 'The Self-Employed and the Small Independent Entrepreneur', in R. King and N. Nugent, *op. cit.*, p. 56.

14. *Sunday Times*, 10 November 1974.
15. Quoted in N. Nugent, 'The National Association for Freedom' in R. King and N. Nugent, *op. cit.*, pp. 96–7.
16. *Newsweek*, 1 November 1976, p. 14.

Chapter 11: The Turning of the Tide

1. *The Times*, 1 April 1975.
2. *The Times*, 24 January 1975.
3. *Daily Telegraph*, 10 November 1976.
4. S. Haseler, *The Death of British Democracy* (London, 1976), pp. 75–76.
5. *The Times*, 9 November 1974.
6. *Telegraph Sunday Magazine*, 21 November 1976; P. Johnson, *Enemies of Society* (London, 1977), p. 261; *The Times*, 13 January 1975; *Observer*,
7. M. Drabble, *The Ice Age*, pp. 252–3.
8. *The Times*, 30 January 1975.
9. *The Times*, 1 April 1974.
10. *Daily Telegraph*, 30 January 1975.
11. Interview with Kenneth Harris, *Observer*, 5 October 1975.
12. *Ibid.*
13. *The Times*, 25 October 1975.
14. *Margaret Thatcher in North America* (London, 1975), p. 5.
15. Profile by Laurence Marks, *Observer*, 6 May 1979.
16. G. Turner, 'The Middle Class At Bay' (Part Two), *Sunday Telegraph*, 31 July 1977.
17. *New Society*, 19 June 1980, p. 280.

Chapter 12: The Survival of the Species

1. *Guardian*, 16 January 1980; R. Towler & A. P. M. Coxon, *The Fate of the Anglican Clergy* (London, 1979), p. 213.
2. Interview with the author, October 1978.
3. *Guardian*, 28 August 1979.
4. *Sunday Telegraph*, 14 October 1979.
5. The research is published in J. H. Goldthorpe, *Social Mobility & Class Structure in Modern Britain* (Oxford, 1980) and A. H. Halsey, A. F. Heath and J. M. Ridge, *Origins and Destinations: Family, Class and Education in Modern Britain* (Oxford, 1980). The comments quoted at the end of the chapter were made in interviews with the author for an article published in *The Times* on 9 January 1980.

Chapter 13: Towards the Future

1. *Guardian*, 18 September 1979.
2. G. Smith, 'Politicians take note: the class war is over', *The Times*, 27 June 1980. The polls appeared in the paper on 23 and 26 June.
3. J. Seabrook, *What Went Wrong?* (London, 1978), p. 93.
4. See M. Brodgen and M. Wright, 'Reflections on the Social Work Strike', *New Society*, 4 October 1979.
5. *The Times*, 1 November 1980, 5 November 1980.
6. See, in particular, the letters in *The Times*, 6 December 1979.
7. *Guardian*, 12 February 1979.
8. C. Jenkins and B. Sherman, *White-Collar Unionism*, p. 139.
9. B. Nossiter, *Britain: A Future That Works* (London, 1978).
10. *Newsweek*, 1 November 1976, p. 16.

INDEX